The United Nations University is an organ of the United Nations established by the General Assembly in 1972 to be an international community of scholars engaged in research, advanced training, and the dissemination of knowledge related to the pressing global problems of human survival, development, and welfare. Its activities focus mainly on the areas of peace and governance, environment and sustainable development, and science and technology in relation to human welfare. The University operates through a worldwide network of research and postgraduate training centres, with its planning and coordinating headquarters in Tokyo.

The United Nations University Press, the publishing division of the UNU, publishes scholarly and policy-oriented books and periodicals in areas related to the University's research.

The oceanic circle: Governing the seas as a global resource

Elisabeth Mann Borgese

 United Nations
University Press

TOKYO · NEW YORK · PARIS

United Nations University Press
The United Nations University, 53-70, Jingumae 5-chome, Shibuya-ku, Tokyo, 150-8925, Japan
Tel: (03) 3599-2811   Fax: (03) 3406-7345
E-mail: sales@hq.unu.edu
http://www.unu.edu

United Nations University Office in North America
2 United Nations Plaza, Room DC2-1462-70, New York, NY 10017, USA
Tel: (212) 963-6387   Fax: (212) 371-9454
E-mail: unuona@igc.apc.org

United Nations University Press is the publishing division of the United Nations University.

Cover design by Joyce C. Weston

Photograph by Sally Widerstrom

Printed in the United States of America

UNUP-1013
ISBN 92-808-1013-8 (cloth)

UNUP-1028
ISBN 92-808-1028-6 (paper)

Library of Congress Cataloging-in-Publication Data

Borgese, Elisabeth Mann.
  The oceanic circle / Elisabeth Mann Borgese.
   p.   cm.
  Includes bibliographical references and index.
  ISBN 9280810138
  ISBN 9280810286 (pbk.)
  1. Oceans – Social aspects.   2. International Ocean Institute.
  3. Club of Rome.   I. Title.
  GC11.2.B67   1998
  333.91'64–ddc21   98-40090
                                                        CIP

This book is dedicated to Krishan Saigal, as a token of gratitude for all he has taught me.

Contents

Foreword

The Club of Rome, an institution concerned with the world *problématique* which regards itself as a catalyst of change and a centre of innovation, sets forth initiatives for solutions in the studies and debates it conducts, in a context of complete intellectual independence.

The ensuing report to the Club of Rome on the oceans provides opportunities for in-depth debate and discussion. Our colleague in the Club of Rome, Elisabeth Mann Borgese, has brought to this text the best of her life-long studies and immense world-wide experience in activities at the very highest level on and about the oceans, which she has compiled in this report with all the devotion and enthusiasm of which she is capable. We realize that some of the ideas contained herein for submission to public and professional opinion are likely to be controversial.

The pointed comments made by Ruud Lubbers, distinguished member of the Club of Rome Executive Committee, in his substantive introduction stress the importance and complexity of the issues discussed by Elisabeth Mann Borgese. In keeping with her previous work experience, views and vision, at the end of this report, the author puts forward a number of specific operational proposals for solving the problems before us. It is, however, the view of the Club of Rome Executive Committee members that no single solution embodies ultimate or absolute answers, but rather that a suite of alternative solutions must be envisaged.

It is in this spirit, then, that the Club of Rome Executive Committee accepts this eloquent text as a new report to the Club of Rome.

Rather, however, than taking a stand on the operational proposals made, which may number among the many possible, it issues an invitation for a world-wide discussion on the subject, to begin at once. There is a definitive need to heighten a global public awareness along these lines and spur our collective imagination, which is at least as important today as the available knowledge base.

Ricardo Diez-Hochleitner (President), July 8, 1998

For the Club of Rome Executive Committee

Belisario Betancur (Vice-president); Bertrand Schneider (Secretary General); Ruth Barnela Engo-Tjega; Umberto Colombo; Orhan Güvenen; Yotaro Kobayashi; Eberhard von Koerber; Ruud Lubbers; Manfred Max-Neef; Samuel Nana-Sinkam; and Felix Unger.

Preface

In this book before you two paths come together. Thirty years ago Arvid Pardo, the Ambassador of Malta to the United Nations, delivered his historical speech defining the oceans as "the Common Heritage of Mankind." Only a few years later the International Ocean Institute was founded and the first conference under the heading of "Pacem in Maribus" took place. Both institutions developed impressively (and acted as a sort of paranymphs giving birth to the law of the seas); and in both Elisabeth Mann Borgese, the author of this book, played the crucial role. She devoted her life to the oceans. This is the first path.

Thirty years ago a few eminent persons came together in Rome sharing their concerns about "Limits to Growth." This became the Club of Rome. The Club of Rome was very much about environment, but in fact its mission became broader. What governance is needed to safeguard the development of economy and technology all over the globe in such a way that quality of life is preserved and improved: how to achieve "the man in the center"? Elisabeth Mann Borgese became one of the most active members of the Club of Rome sharing insights and contributing to concepts of governance. Her moral concerns about how to give shape and substance to a more and more interdependent world, and how to take profit of different cultures and civilizations, matured more and more. This is the second path.

These two paths (how to relate to the oceans and how to develop a global system of good governance) come together in this book "The Oceanic Circle." In that way they culminate together in a climax in this year 1998. 1998 has been declared by the United Nations as the

Year of the Ocean. It is therefore the excellent moment to give special attention to the role of the oceans. Historically the oceans were – next to a limited function in terms of a resource for fishing (as near to the coast as possible) – in the first place seen as large, dark and dangerous waters which had to be bridged to reach other countries, territories, terrestrial areas. Today we have learned to realize the richness of the oceans; not only in terms of fish, but also in their biodiversity and as a buffer to balance our climate. Today it is about valuing the oceans in their richnesses.

At the very same time we have started to realize the threats to the oceans. Because of technology, economy and the contemporary prevalence of the market system there is an acceleration of production and consumption and beyond that an increased migration to coastal areas, mega-cities near the oceans, and exploitation in terms of offshore and tourism; all leading to an increased interface of mankind and the oceans.

It started with fish. However, the time of abundance is already over for decades. Therefore one was compelled to start to think in terms of sustainable use of the oceans. But we have learned that the problem of sustainable use is much more general and global. The increased interface of mankind and the oceans fuels the need for a new way of thinking and new goverance.

A few months ago the Independent World Commission on the Oceans published its report "The Oceans, Our Future." Elisabeth Mann Borgese played a significant role in establishing the Independent World Commission on the Oceans and in its work.

This book "The Oceanic Circle" is a much more comprehensive study and builds further on "The Oceans, Our Future." It is symbolic that Elisabeth Mann Borgese baptizes her book "The Oceanic Circle" citing Mahatma Ghandi giving credit to wisdom beyond the western Enlightenment. "Life ... will be an oceanic circle whose center will be the individual."

In this year 1998 we write six years after the conference in Rio de Janeiro on environment and development. This conference was a result of "Our Common Future" and the concept of sustainable development as formulated in the eighties. UNCED produced a treaty on biodiversity and a convention on climate change. The agenda for the 21st century was set, although still in a primitive form. To the oceans especially chapter 17 was devoted. Rio was also another step to the conceptualization of new principles to realize sustainable development; to realize harmony in a more and more interdependent world, safeguarding solidarity and a future for generations to come.

One of these principles is the precautionary principle: take care applying new technologies; abstain as long as there are uncertainties. This new golden rule is a complement to the positive attitude towards technology as formulated in "Our Common Future." Indeed, technology is at the very same time a solution for many environmental problems and threats, as well as it can be a threat in itself.

The words "economy" and "ecology" both have their roots in the Greek word "oikos," meaning "our common home."

In the economy one applies the factor interest, respectively one discounts. This is about a system to make rational choices there where resources are scarce. This selection criterium is also rational because it is based on the experience that one applying efficient systems of technology, economy, and management can achieve increases in productivity. The increasing productivity is the "mirror" of the interest-rate. This concept is based on the experience about further potential managerial and technological progress. Totally in line with all this economists "discount" the future. Doing so, "values" in the future are for them less relevant than values today.

Ecologists start from a different perspective. They consider the future to be as important as the present. They are skeptical about improvements in technology unless they are proven. In this sense ecologists have a totally different perspective from economists. They invoke the precautial principle to avoid decisions that society may later have cause to regret. Before Rio the conventional wisdom was that internalizing external effects into prices would be the answer to tensions between economy and ecology. Now we know that this is needed, but not enough. A good symbiosis between economy (promoting creativity) and ecology (based on awe for nature and caution for the future) has to be developed further. "The Oceanic Circle" is also about this symbiosis.

Another new principle of Rio is about the value of cultural diversity. Creativity, people rooted in their culture and the dialogue of cultures are considered to have positive value. In order to be successful with sustainable development eradication of poverty is needed; and to empower people we need community sustainability and respect for culture.

Elisabeth Mann Borgese proves able in this book to go one step further. She goes beyond respect for indigenous cultures; she tries to incorporate values and visions from different cultures. Doing so she practices just the opposite of Huntington's "Clash of Civilizations." "The Oceanic Circle" is a fascinating book, because it makes clear that concern for the oceans has become more and more a concern about mankind; about global solidarity and solidarity with generations to come. It is about how to realize "the man in the center."

The Club of Rome time and again draws attention to the need to be holistic. That need is a consequence of the need to bridge scientific disciplines, beyond the specialization Enlightenment has generated.

And next to that there is the need for inclusive thinking. That is the capacity of integrating the missions of different societal institutions. Holistic is about overcoming specialization. Inclusive is about overcoming specific interests.

Elisabeth Mann Borgese uses the opportunity to link Giarini's book devoted to the significance of non-monetized values to explain that there is a need for a new "general theory of work": general in the sense that "money values" are not the sole aspect of work and human activity. The general theory of work has to include also non-paid work as relevant. The relevance of non-paid "work" has to increase by realizing that after the stages of under-development, newly industralizing countries and maturing economies respectively, there has to be a new stage in which not the maximalization of the GNP per citizen, but the optimalization (striking a balance between paid and non-paid work) has to be "the agenda" for mankind living in dignity. This notion is important to overcome extreme economization of life.

The political history and economy of the oceans are important to study, from Hugo Grotius with his successful plea for "Oceans to be free, not under control of any political power," to Arvid Pardo with his plea for the oceans as our common heritage, to the law on the sea with its Exclusive Economic Zones extending in fact enormously the territorial responsibility of nation states; all the way until we start to realize that nation states have to assist each other in order to cope with the problems of coastal management and with the peaceful and sustainable uses of the ocean. The agenda of peace and the agenda for development prove once again to be very related to each other.

But beyond the need for international solidarity and intergovernmental efforts to cope with the ocean, it becomes clear that nation states alone cannot achieve sustainable development and quality of life. In fact we need new governance. This new governance does not require only new forms of governmental cooperation and institutions; it asks as well for an increased role for civil society. The civil society, and more in particular the non-governmental organizations, have begun a long march to go for quality of life, by action on their own and by putting pressure not only on governments but also on transnational companies.

A new governance culture is emerging in which the judges come to verdicts, not only based on paper-law, but also on soft-law; and in which companies have started to internalize societal values in their mission statements and their codes of conduct. The wish to be sustainable invites us to implement global ethics. A new symbiosis between governments, business and civil society is emerging. But there is still a long way to go to counterbalance the one-sided economization of life.

Elisabeth Mann Borgese writes in an intriguing way about sovereignity. She is right. It proved to be "hubris" for many countries and therefore we need now nation states to work together, especially regionally. And sustainable development of the oceans is only an example of this new global need. Next to this need for cooperation between nation-states and in international agencies, there is this emerging civil society, emerging all over the globe: citizens, non-governmental organizations, cultures and religions, working together realizing a global dialogue and the global sovereignty of peoples. The new information and communication technology gives enormous possibilities to connect people and to empower people. Therefore the world is not any longer only a total of the nation-states; it is also about participatory democracy globally, and global sovereignty of peoples.

The history of mankind as global history of the globally interrelated mankind has only begun. "The Oceanic Circle" will raise awareness about the oceans ... our future. This challenge will clarify at the same time the developing concept of goverance in an era of globalization with the man in the center.

Ruud Lubbers

Acknowledgements

This work is largely based on the work of the International Ocean Institute and the Club of Rome. In many ways it is a continuation of the work of the Independent World Commission on the Ocean, spelling out some of the recommendations that could only be hinted at in the report of the commission. It attempts to reflect the needs and aspirations of poor people and countries.

Special thanks are due to Ian McAllister for his invaluable help, especially in the sections dealing with economics, to Max Börlin and Scott Coffen-Smout, who assisted with research on indicators and the economic value of the ocean, and to Orio Giarini and Ruud Lubbers, who reviewed the manuscript and made valuable suggestions which have been incorporated in the text.

In this structure, composed of innumerable villages,
there will be ever-widening, never ascending circles.
Life will not be a pyramid
with the apex sustained by the bottom.
But it will be an oceanic circle
whose centre will be the individual,
always ready to perish for the village,
the latter ready to perish for the circle of villages,
till at last the whole becomes one life
composed of individuals,
never aggressive in their arrogance,
but ever humble,
sharing the majesty of the oceanic circle
of which they are integral units.
Therefore, the outermost circumference will not yield power
to crush the inner circle
but will give strength to all within
and will derive its own strength from it.

Mohandas K. Gandhi, *India of My Dreams*, R.K. Prabhu, ed.,
Bombay, 1947

Prologue

Some of you readers may be familiar with a new type of illustrated book that appeared in art and children's bookstores a few years ago, giving you the idea of 3D illusions.

The page before you, flat and glossy, shows a computer-designed abstract pattern. You are instructed to bring it very close to your eyes and stare at it, your mind relaxed, until the contours blur and become unfocused. You then are to remove the picture very slowly and steadily to a comfortable reading distance, and, lo and behold, your eyes refocus, but somehow differently. The flat surface breaks; a deep space opens up behind it; trees, animals, mountains, waves clearly detach themselves from the background, as three-dimensionally plastic as a hologram. You see something you had no idea of before. A new dimension has been added to your perspective.

The introductory text advises you that you have to be "open-minded" to have the benefit of this experience. People with fixed ideas, often older people, are unable to change perspective in this manner.

I myself found it difficult to learn, but now I really enjoy the blurring, the unfocusing, the getting lost of the old perspective, the sudden emergence of the new and deep perspective, the emergence of a different universe on that page.

We want to take you through that process in this book. We want to blur your wonted perspective and open up a deep new one. The figures are there, detaching themselves like holograms from the multi-layered background – if you can only see them; a new world: the world of the ocean; the majesty of the oceanic circle.

3

The old perspective focused your eyes on the *land*, the continents, as the real thing where human existence was rooted, where history, where evolution took place; where nature was being "conquered" by "civilization" and nature and culture interacted. The continents were "separated," "isolated" – their "security" protected by oceans, of which only the top layer was experienced and exploited for *land-life*. Fishing and navigating are activities that go back to prehistoric days; but what was under the ocean surface was myth and mystery.

Now try to unfocus, in space and in time. Feel the pulse of life: expansion and return. Expansion and return. Unearthly life forms sustained by chemosynthesis, moving up from the darkness of the deep seabed to the surface where the sunlight grows stronger as the primeval vapours dissipate. Photosynthesis taking over from chemosynthesis as the motor of life. Life moving upward, moving outward, *from the ocean*. It was the ocean's flora that generated the atmosphere which you have been breathing ever since some of the ocean fauna converted from gill-breathing to lung-breathing and began to crawl from the sea to the land where green plants had preceded them to continue the work of the ocean flora to generate breathable air. They multiplied and diversified. They grew wings to swim in the air; they erected themselves on their lower extremities to reach up with their arms to pray and to build.

They began to return to the ocean: mammals and birds, whales, dolphins, and seals; penguins and diving ducks. It is amazing to see the birds flying in the deep waters, beating their wings, with outstretched necks and feet, to catch their fish; to see how dolphins and seals reconverted to oceanic shape.

And we humans followed suit. Like lemmings we hurried from the inlands and highlands back to the coast, falling over each other, crowding each other, devastating the coast scape like a plague of locusts, and venturing out into the ocean, farther and farther out, deeper and deeper down.

Now refocus. Do you see the surface breaking, and the new dimension emerging?

If, before, you saw the sea and the sea-floor as a continuation of the land, you now see the land as a continuation of the sea. Some people, for instance, the people of the Pacific, do in fact see it that way. The ocean is the real thing, covering almost three-quarters of the surface of our blue planet; the continents are islands floating on the world ocean; the ocean links and unites the continents, rather than separating and isolating them. The world ocean is our common heritage.

The importance of the world ocean as a potential supplier of goods (food, fibre, genetic resources, metals, minerals), services (trade routes, tourism), energy, and as a repository of national, regional, and global security cannot be overstated. Above all, however, the world ocean is an essential part of the biosphere; it is a crucial factor in the carbon cycle and a determinant of the planet's climate.

The ocean's contribution of "ecosystem services" is very much larger than that of terra firma.

Coral reefs and mangrove swamps, for instance, serve as "disturbance regulators." Where you have them, the power of tsunamis is broken, and coastal populations and property are safe behind their protective shield. They also serve as habitat/refugia, breeding grounds, and nutrient cyclers. Leaving apart the colossal quantity of unknowns, it appears that by far the largest portion of the total global flow value of the planet's ecosystem services is contributed by the "water system," consisting, by more than 90 per cent, of the world ocean.

While the ocean covers over 70 per cent of the planet's surface area,[1] it accounts for 99 per cent of the volume that is known to sustain life – most of which is still unknown, and "the more we know the more we know how little we know." While we are rightly concerned with the anthropogenic decline in biodiversity, scientists are continually discovering new concentrations of diversity. In recent years scientists, exploring the ocean's middle depths beyond the reach of sunlight, have discovered a host of new species composing productive ecosystems thus far unknown to us but already whetting the appetites of industrial, high-tech fishing companies. The deep sea bottom, of which little more than 1.5 per cent has been explored, harbours thousands, perhaps millions, of species of small invertebrate animals, besides the unearthly creatures – crustaceans, molluscs and giant worms – inhabiting the volcanic sea-floor spreading centres. In an area of about 21 square metres on the ocean floor, off the Atlantic coast of the United States at a depth of between 1,500 and 2,500 metres, scientists sampled and found 90,672 individual organisms representing 798 species – of which as many as 460 were unknown until then.[2]

What we do know, however, is that the ocean is a medium different from the earth: so different, in fact, that it forces us to think differently. The medium itself, where everything flows and everything is interconnected, forces us to "unfocus," to shed our old concepts and paradigms, to "refocus" on a new paradigm. Fundamental concepts, evolved over the millennia on land, like sovereignty, geographic boundaries, or ownership, simply will not work in the ocean medium where new political, legal, and economic concepts are emerging. Eventually they will act on the social, economic, and political order of the next century.

Problématique – solutique

The Club of Rome is well prepared to play a role in formulating and propagating a better understanding of the majesty of the oceanic circle. The Club was founded, in the late 1960s, on the concept of interdependence of all the great issues of our time and their interaction in what the founder, Aurelio Peccei, called the *problématique*. We had experienced this *problématique par excellence* in the oceans ... Fish, currents, waves and winds respect no "boundaries" contrived by human minds. The law of the land cannot swim. Every major marine activity impacts on every other one. Fishing and aquaculture; offshore oil, gas, mineral and metal exploration and production; tourism and water sports; shipping and navigation; coastal engineering and development; military and peaceful uses of the seas and oceans – all impact on one another. Sometimes this impact is positive; sometimes it is negative. It is simply not possible, in any meaningful way, to deal with these activities separately. They constitute the *problématique* of the oceans. Ambassador Arvid Pardo of Malta, the father of the new Law of the Sea, clearly recognized this in his historic address to the First Committee of the United Nations General Assembly on 1 November 1967 ... It has been enshrined in the Preamble of the United Nations Convention on the Law of the Sea, 1982:

... the problems of ocean space are closely interrelated and need to be considered as a whole ...

Such interdependence of issues and problems demands *interdisciplinary approaches* if solutions are to be forged. Each interrelated issue and problem will call for different insights, disciplines and expertise. Integrated, not sectoral, solutions must be sought – called, in the language of the Club of Rome, "*solutique*." In the case of the oceans, we began to construct models in the 1960s, then to negotiate, adopt, ratify, and implement what Ambassador Tommy Koh of Singapore, the President of the Third United Nations Conference on the Law of the Sea (UNCLOS), called "a Constitution for the Ocean," embracing, in one *solutique,* all major uses of the seas and oceans. We all knew it would have to be part of, and model for, a constitution for the world in the next century.

The essence to be distilled from the *problématique* is that peace and security are inseparable from economic justice and environmental security. This must imply a reshaping of North-South relations on the basis of international social justice, as well as profound changes in industrial production taxing and distribution systems in the North.

The first ocean input into the work of the Club of Rome was a chapter in the volume *Reshaping the International Order (RIO): A Report to the Club of Rome,* compiled under the direction of Nobel laureate Jan Tinbergen. The chapter "The New International Economic Order and the Law of the Sea," written by Arvid Pardo and myself, tried to indicate how the emerging Law of the Sea Convention could reinforce the goals of the developing countries in a new international economic order (NIEO). Strangely enough, that was new thinking as late as 1974.[3]

We identified eight major issues on which UNCLOS and NIEO could reinforce each other.

– First, the nascent Convention was to be founded on the concept of the sovereign equality of all states, whether developed or developing (LOS Convention Preamble).

– Second, and probably most important of all, there was the concept of the "Common Heritage of Mankind," which potentially changed the relationship between poor and rich countries as it replaced the humiliating "donor-recipient" relationship with one among equal partners – all of whom had a right to share in the resources that had been declared to be the Common Heritage of Mankind. The Common Heritage concept comprises an *economic development* dimension, an *environmental protection* dimension, a *peace-building dimension*, and an *ethical dimension.*

– Third, the establishment of the *Exclusive Economic Zone,* bestowing sovereign rights over all resources and economic uses in a 200-mile zone to the coastal state, reinforced the NIEO principle of sovereignty over natural resources reaffirmed in a number of UN resolutions and declarations. What was happening to the concept of "sovereignty" in general, in an increasingly interdependent world, is another question to which we shall return.

– Fourth, the Convention reinforced the principle of regional organisation, South-South cooperation and self-reliance. Articles 122 and 123 are fundamental for the UNEP-initiated Regional Seas

7

Programme; Articles 276 and 277 mandate the establishment of regional centres for technology cooperation, development and transfer; capacity-building at national, regional, and global levels is stressed throughout the Convention.

- Fifth, the Convention reinforced the principle of equitable participation of developing countries in financial decision-making, in particular, through the establishment of the International Sea-bed Authority and its decision-making organs. This, however, was later reversed by the so-called "Implementation Agreement."
- Sixth, the Convention promotes technology cooperation and sharing, for deep sea-bed mining technologies in particular (in Part XI of the Convention) and for all other marine technologies in general (in Part XIV of the Convention), particularly through the establishment of regional centres for the advancement of marine science and technology (Articles 276 and 277).
- Seventh, the Convention protected the interests of developing countries in international sea-borne trade through the requirement of a "genuine link" between shipowners and the country of registration of a ship, thus harmonizing the efforts of UNCLOS with those of UNCTAD to protect the interests of developing countries in shipping and sea-borne trade against "flags of convenience."
- Eighth, the Convention protects the interests of land-locked states, among them the poorest countries, again reinforcing the efforts of UNCTAD and the advocates of NIEO.

Thanks to a grant from the Government of the Netherlands, the chapter was subsequently expanded into a full-length monograph.[4] In 1976 the Club of Rome and the International Ocean Institute jointly held their annual conference in Algiers, to discuss the implications of the Tinbergen report, including the study on the Law of the Sea. For about a decade, support for, and advancement of, the Law of the Sea Convention was then included in every manifestation of developing countries, whether the G77 or the Group of Non-Aligned States, or UNCTAD or regional groups. As the ratification process dragged on in the late 1980s and early 1990s, other burning issues – the debt crisis, hunger, civil unrest, and regional wars – took the limelight. Interest in the Law of the Sea Convention began to dim. Pressure from the United States and some of its allies, plus the march of time, did the rest. As the generation of decision makers and civil servants involved in the making of the Convention and aware of its signal importance was replaced by a new one quite unaware of it, the Convention was lost sight of. Developing countries stood idly and indifferently by as the industrial states began to dismantle Part XI of the Convention, which, with all its flaws and defects, was the only existing institutional embodiment of the concept of the Common Heritage of Mankind.

History moved on. The evolution of ocean affairs and the activities of the Club of Rome have now to be viewed in a broader context. In 1987, the Report of the World Commission on Environment and Development[5] advanced the concept of *sustainable development* front-stage, to be further developed and articulated in conventions and programmes of action at the great Earth Summit of the United Nations Conference on Environment and Development (UNCED) in Rio de Janeiro in 1992.[6] Like the Common Heritage of Mankind concept, sustainable development was to encompass economic development, including the eradication of poverty, and the conservation of the environment including biodiversity and the conservation of the planet's climate. That neither economic development, nor the protection of the environment, could be attained without peace went without saying. But that it went without saying constitutes one of the fundamental weaknesses of the Rio undertaking. Institutional arrangements for the enhancement of security, whether at national, regional, or global levels, were simply not addressed. That was left to another forum, that of the Secretary-General of the United Nations who developed it in his *Agenda for Peace*.[7]

The *Agenda for Peace* is a re-examination of the concepts of "security" and "threats to security," which today do not originate so much from inter-state military aggression as from intra-state civil strife driven by economic inequity, abuse by so-called representatives of states of most basic human rights and freedoms, environmental distress, and cultural elements, including religious, linguistic and ethnic disaggregation. "Comprehensive security," just like the concept of the Common Heritage of Mankind, thus comprises economic, environmental, and ethical dimensions. That these issues are still dealt with by different fora, largely ignoring one another, makes a mockery of the commonly professed recognition that comprehensive, broadly interdisciplinary and trans-sectoral approaches and institutions are needed.

In 1995, the International Ocean Institute studied the interactions between the *Agenda for Peace* process and the UNCLOS/UNCED process and the potential contributions of the Law of the Sea to the implementation of the *Agenda for Peace*.[8] The study emphasized the importance of regional cooperation and organization in the sustainable management of ocean space and resources, as well as in the enhancement of regional security. It showed that the trends towards the establishment of zones of peace and nuclear-free zones, on the one hand, and towards the establishment of regional seas programmes for the management of the peaceful uses of the seas and oceans, on the other, are *converging* towards the common goal of comprehensive or human security. The study proposed regional mechanisms for the implementation of policies integrating development, environment, and security concerns.

The Club of Rome, meanwhile, was making important contributions to the promotion and further analysis of the implications of "sustainable development" in post-industrial societies.

In the present context, two contributions appear of particular relevance. The first is the work of Orio Giarini[9] arguing the inadequacy of "mainstream economics" in coping with the issues inherent in "sustainable development" in a post-industrial economy and the need for new approaches to transcend the temporal and cultural mindsets of both "socialism" and "capitalism," each rooted in the first wave of the industrial revolution of eighteenth- and nineteenth-century Europe.

The second major contribution was the Club's emphasis on governance, focused on the institutional implications and requirements of "sustainable development" in the twenty-first century.

Giarini's work was not originally ocean-oriented, but it seemed to me that it contained the seeds for an "Economics of the Common Heritage," a concept that I have elaborated in my first Report to the Club of Rome.[10]

Giarini's concept of "dowry and patrimony"[11] comprises the total stock of man-made goods and services, quantifiable in monetary terms or not, within the scope of the "market" or outside, as well as natural assets, including environmental resources. It is that aggregate and dynamic stock that is the real "granary" or "store house" of wealth and welfare, present and future. The mere annual flows of GNP ignore large components of the economy (everything that takes place *outside* the market) and, yet more serious, the exhaustion of resources and destruction of cultures and the human spirit. So inadequate a measure of "progress" is GNP that the production of "bads" (e.g., pollution) is counted as the generation of "goods": a misleading measure indeed, yet one by which governments are wont to measure their accomplishments.

The "service economy," Giarini suggests, as it has been evolving in the industrialized states, offers new approaches to the conservation and augmentation of the real wealth and welfare of nations or the global stock of dowry and patrimony. While high technology, through miniaturization and dematerialization, automation, just-in-time production, etc., is reducing the demand for "raw materials," thus decreasing at least one kind of pressure on the environment, the relation between "production" and "service" in the post-industrial world has changed dramatically. Services, including research and development, management, advertising, distribution, training and retraining, maintenance, repair and recycling, or final disposal, are now accountable for some 60 per cent of the entire economic processes of the industrialized countries.

When such numbers are used, one should not lose sight of distortions and inequities that impact on the market pricing system. Thus, for example, the lack of "market power" of most developing nations means that the industrialized world is accessing raw materials and, indeed increasingly, manufactured products at prices dictated by the market clout of the major multinationals – nor is there any end in sight. In short, the GNP weightings of industrial nations incorporate "bargain basement" price structures imposed on the third world (and often abetted by their very own élites, with their Swiss bank accounts and ostentatious lifestyles).

In some sense, the "real value" of a product extends beyond its mere exchange value. "Exchange value" implies "ownership." I exchange what I own for what you own. "Purchasing power" is built upon the ownership of some form of marketable rights – be they linked to land or labour or capital (including knowledge). "Utilization value," on the other hand, de-emphasizes the concept of "ownership." It is not based on an exchange transaction between producer and consumer but on a cooperative relationship between "prosumers," both parties contributing to the production as well as the utilization process, no matter whether the product is bought and owned or leased and not owned.

The significance of Giarini's thinking is that he does not reject "ownership," but extends its narrow Roman-Law interpretation (*ius utendi et abutendi*) to include *user rights* within a *trusteeship* concept with broadened ethical implications. Ownership as trusteeship, with responsibilities towards humankind as well as to nature, is a concept familiar to early Judaeo-Christianity as well as to many non-European cultures and religions. Giarini does not reject Western values, but hinges them into a larger system that is no longer dominated by Western thought of past centuries. And this is of course what we must

11

attempt to do when we deal with the oceans, which are our common heritage and link us all.

Ocean economics can only rely on the market to a limited extent. The greater part of ocean economics is based on a non-property and non-sovereignty reality. Ocean economics must incorporate the economics of resources which are the common heritage of mankind and must be managed but cannot be appropriated. The cultural, ethical as well as institutional implications of this need much further study. The oceans have not only a resource value which can be quantified in monetary terms; they have much more important values of a different kind, very difficult or impossible to quantify. The oceans are part of our life support system and ocean economics will have to recognize the vast preponderance of the non-quantifiable components of the system.

Uncertainty and vulnerability are major factors in contemporary economics as a whole. In ocean economics they are of overwhelming importance. Human ignorance of ocean processes, combined with human negligence (e.g., human error in tanker accidents) and human deviousness (e.g., maritime fraud), on the one hand, and, on the other, the "gigantism" of the greater part of the marine industries (oil rigs, tankers, each of hundreds of millions, or even billions of dollars' value) and the enormity of the damage, quantifiable and nonquantifiable, that they can cause, puts unbearable stress on the insurance business and forces it to think anew. As Giarini puts it, insurance economics may be playing the pioneering role in the contemporary phase of the industrial revolution that textile economics played during the first phase of this revolution.[12]

Giarini's work has the potential of making a significant contribution to the development of "ocean economics" as part of, and model for, an economic theory for a post-industrial and post-European culture. At the same time he and his colleagues might have much to gain using the oceans – as we did in the field of law – as their great laboratory for the development of their theory, considering that the problems that they have identified "on land" are magnified "at sea" and thus can be examined as under a giant microscope.

Giarini's latest work[13] stresses the dignity of work and the right to work as an integral part of the new economics, but disaggregates this right into various phases: a ground phase of part-time employment during working age, when governments must guarantee to everyone a decent minimum standard of living (housing, food, education, and medical care). On top of this, everyone should have the opportunity to develop his/her own initiative and entrepreneurship to enhance his/her standard of living. Unpaid service to the community (e.g., caring for the old, the sick, the children; disaster relief; etc.) would complete the working cycle. Lifelong education is an integral part of lifelong work.

This model of human work comes close to the Ghandian model which similarly postulates guaranteed employment for everybody and a guaranteed minimum standard of living. On top of this individuals are to develop their own capacities and earn more, not to accumulate personal wealth but to increase communal well-being. Unpaid service to the community would constitute a large portion of the work cycle.

Giarini's model transcends the market system as well as the centrally planned system. As a matter of fact, it transcends "economics" as such, as a specialized science, and reintegrates it into its pristine context comprising the social sciences, philosophy, and ethics. Considering the environmental aspects of economics, furthermore, it must comprise the natural sciences as well.

This new economics calls for more government intervention or governance, not less, as is the current Western fashion. At the same time, it calls for more freedom of initiative and greater decentralization than is to be encountered in a centrally planned economy.

The Club of Rome's work on governance[14] is extremely relevant to the evolution of law and institutions for sustainable ocean development and management.

Dror emphasizes the ethical aspects of governance, which should be inculcated through education, in particular, the education of leaders. Lifelong education, as an integral part of the work cycle, education through "universities without walls," education utilizing the most advanced forms of educational "technology," evidently should extend to potential leaders and the leadership of today, and it must convey a sense for the "new thinking," including civic responsibility towards the community and towards nature, the awareness of uncertainty and non-linearity, and the need for adaptation to change. King, Diez-Hochleitner, Federico Mayor, Giarini, Dror, Schneider, and others all agree on the crucial importance of the "development of human resources" as a basis of governance for sustainable development.

Dror's comments on the "outdated doctrines of state supremacy," his understanding of the increasing importance of activities at the subnational level (local communities, cities, subregions, NGOs) and of "political culture" in continental governance, his consideration of "global and continental governance at one end of the spectrum, and local and grass-roots governance at the other," reflect "the majesty of the oceanic circle." The governance design attempted in the present volume could be considered as a practical application of the principles he proposed. The question of how to redesign the governance of mega-cities and their relations with other layers and forms of governance is crucial to the design of institutional arrangements for integrated coastal management, since most of the megacities are in fact in coastal areas. Their integration into coastal management has been given little or no attention by the ocean management literature.

These are just some examples to indicate the convergence of concerns and concepts, *problématique* and *solutique*, between the Club of Rome's more general work on governance and the more specific quest for effective ocean governance.

This convergence is equally clear between "The First Global Revolution" and what has been called "The Blue Revolution."

King's and Schneider's appraisal of the importance of technology "transfer," or, rather, technology cooperation or codevelopment, and their suggestion for the establishment of networks of institutions of excellence in this sector; their conception of the limits of the market economy; the importance they attach to the non-governmental organizations and their efforts, especially at the village level: all this complements and harmonizes with the work undertaken by the International Ocean Institute and reflected in this book.

Schneider's *Barefoot Revolution* elaborates on the achievements of the NGOs at the village level: an extremely informative and inspiring report. Schneider's chart of activities to be undertaken to enhance participation and empowerment of villagers in the management and improvement of their living standards is extremely useful and quite generally applicable.

It is, however, surprising, that Schneider, as many others before and after him, concentrates exclusively on rural, agricultural villages. Coastal and fishing villages are not even mentioned, and yet it is urgent that their decay be halted and their livelihood upgraded. This is essential if the sprawling of coastal megacities, lumping together over 60 per cent of the earth's population, and the further degradation of coastal areas and coastal seas is to be halted.[15]

While the organizational principles are similar for rural and coastal villages, the environmentally and culturally as well as economically sustainable technologies that must be developed within the coastal communities will be different. Water and effluent treatment; mariculture and aquaculture technologies; small-scale wave energy production, e.g., for the refrigeration of fish; the planting of crops to desalinate saline soils, or of edible halophiles; the introduction of new employment generating industries, such as pharmaceuticals and cosmetics from ocean flora and fauna; the establishment of protected sea areas for the recuperation of depleted stocks of fish, seabirds and sea mammals and the management of ecotourism in protected areas; participation in the monitoring of water quality and data management: micro-electronics, information technology, bio-engineering technologies[16] and alternative energy technologies; together with the organization and management and development of human resources, will be the key to empowerment of coastal and fishing villages and their active participation in integrated coastal and ocean management.

The International Ocean Institute, in cooperation with numerous local NGOs, has recently embarked on a project fusing "the barefoot revolution" and "the blue revolution" to include coastal and fishing villages as a step towards the implementation of the principles on ocean and coastal management that we believe in.

Meanwhile, the Brundtland Report and the Rio Conference went further in recommending rather precise guidelines for an institutional framework of governance for sustainable development. These are entirely compatible with those developed by the Club of Rome. They reflect the majesty of the oceanic circle.

They can be summed up under four headings: this institutional framework in a borderless world must be
– comprehensive,
– consistent,
– trans-sectoral or multidisciplinary, and
– participational, bottom-up rather than top-down.

"Comprehensive" means that it must reach from the local level of the community through the levels of provincial and national governance to regional and global levels of international organization. This, in response to the fact that, as the Brundtland Report puts it, the "boundaries" between levels of governance – local, national, regional, global – have become "transparent": in the oceans, obviously, even more so than on land.

"Consistent" means that regulation and decision-making processes and mechanisms at all levels of governance must be compatible. The importance of this principle was highlighted in the discussions on

15

straddling fish stocks and highly migratory fish stocks in areas under national jurisdiction and in the high seas, but it is equally important for all other aspects of sustainable management.

"Trans-sectoral" or "multidisciplinary" means activities in the environment cannot be considered separately sector by sector, but must be seen in their interaction, which may be positive or negative. The recognition that "the problems of ocean space are closely interrelated and must be considered as a whole," enshrined in the Preamble to the United Nations Convention on the Law of the Sea, has institutional implications of some magnitude. For, if these problems must be so considered, there must be fora or institutions or decision-making mechanisms or processes capable of doing it, whether at the local, the national, the regional or the global level.

"Participational" means that regulation must not be imposed by central or federal governments, then to be ignored or flouted by local communities whose livelihoods may be impaired by such regulations, but that these communities must be involved in the making of regulation and in management. Thus the notion of "co-management" is gaining ground in countries as far apart, culturally, as Canada and India.

"Sustainable development," of course, is a broad and often ambiguously used term. Its best definition perhaps is given by Brundtland, not in *Our Common Future*, but in an address (the Sir Peter Scott lecture) she delivered in Bristol on 8 October 1986:

There are many dimensions to sustainability. First, it requires the elimination of poverty and deprivation. Second, it requires the conservation and enhancement of the resource base which alone can ensure that the elimination of poverty is permanent. Third, it requires a broadening of the concept of development so that it covers not only economic growth but also social and cultural development. Fourth, and most important, it requires the unification of economics and ecology in decision-making at all levels.

This fourth dimension obviously determines the new required forms of governance.

More recently Ignacy Sachs discerned five dimensions of eco-development:
- social sustainability, i.e., greater equity in asset and income distribution;
- economic sustainability, meaning that economic efficiency needs to be evaluated in macro-social terms;
- ecological sustainability, i.e., expanding the carrying capacity of

ecosystems, reducing consumption of fossil fuels and waste, increasing self-restraining and developing technologies which produce low waste and are resource-efficient;
- spacial sustainability, which means attaining a balance between rural and urban areas, reducing congestion and concentration in metropolitan areas, eliminating ecosystem destruction, and promoting modern regenerative agriculture and decentralized industrialization;
- cultural sustainability, i.e., having ecodevelopment in cultural continuity.

These recognitions are indeed useful. In practical terms, however, little progress has been made at the institutional level – perhaps because the scope is simply too broad.

In the more concrete setting of *ocean and coastal management* considerably more progress has been achieved in many countries, both developed and developing. Community-based councils or commissions or round tables, including what is now generally called all "stake-holders," i.e. all those whose livelihood depends on the management of ocean and coastal spaces and resources: municipal government as well as "civil society," the scientific community, fishers' associations, shipping companies, offshore oil companies, coastal developers, tourist organizations, coastal engineers, port and harbour masters, non-governmental organizations, etc.

At the national level, inter-ministerial councils, including all ministries and departments responsible in one way or another for marine activities, under the chairmanship of one lead department (e.g., the Navy, or Fisheries, or the Environment) or of the Prime Minister, are making their appearance in state after state.

Coordination between local (municipal) and national arrangements is to be secured through "co-management" as mentioned above. Beyond the limits of national jurisdiction, comprehensive governance at the regional level is needed, and beginnings, at least, are already on course. The recent revisions of the Barcelona Convention, broadening its scope from "environment" to "environment and development" concerns and establishing the first regional Commission for Sustainable Development,[17] is a landmark on that long and difficult road.

At the global level, the role of the General Assembly in the making of a global oceans policy harmonizing regional, national, and local components, is under discussion. The integration of the policies of the UN Specialized Agencies and Programmes (FAO for fisheries, IMO

17

for shipping; UNEP for environment; IOC and UNESCO for marine sciences, UNIDO for marine technologies; UNDP for coastal development, ISBA for sea-bed mining) is to be pursued by subcommittee of the Administrative Committee for Coordination (ACC), with its Secretariat at IOC/UNESCO. Both developments are still somewhat inchoate, but must be a part of the current efforts to restructure the United Nations system.

In my last book[18] I have tried to analyse these trends and build a dynamic comprehensive interactive model of ocean governance on them. It is the purpose of this volume to refine and enrich this model through interaction with the ongoing work of the Club of Rome and the International Ocean Institute. As life originated in the ocean and the ocean, to which we are returning, forces us to rethink terrestrial concepts and change perspectives, the contribution of *ocean governance* to the making of a world order for the next century should be inspired by the majesty of the oceanic circle.

Synopsis

This book is organized in six chapters. Chapter 1 stresses the importance of the oceans within the global life support system. This importance, often neglected, cannot be overrated. Without the pretence of offering a lesson in oceanography, the chapter traces the development of marine sciences and technology from the animal kingdom through the "primitive era" to some examples in our own era. This will set the physical parameters for the book. It will deal with the threats to the health of the oceans and the biosphere in a somewhat wider context than is generally assumed. "The more we know the more we know how little we know." Science and technology, though fundamentally important, are not enough to stem the race toward ecocatastrophe. The magnitude of uncertainty will be emphasized. Carbon cycles, water cycles, and mineral cycles symbolize the majesty of the oceanic circle.

Chapter 2 will attempt to fathom the cultural dimension of ocean space, for the way we deal with the oceans, or nature in general, is largely determined by our cultural background. If we take humankind as a part of nature, we get one result; if human activities and nature are two separate subsystems, we get a different picture. The chapter will give a succinct overview of the role of the oceans in the historic and cultural evolution of humankind, as expressed *inter alia* through literature, the arts, music. It will also deal with the oceans and warfare. The linkages between cultural, economic, and naval developments will be highlighted.

Chapter 3 is organized in four sections. The first section describes the wealth of the ocean in three parts; first: the current "market value" of ocean-related goods and services, which can be expressed in dollars and cents. This part is far larger than had been estimated in the past. By far the biggest factors are sea-borne trade, which accounts for over 90 per cent of all international trade, and the explosive growth of ocean-related tourism, including cruise ship traffic. Most recent developments in the underwater fibre optics cable industry have added another amazingly large factor. The second part gives some indication of the market value of some of the new ocean industries likely to come to fruition in the next century; and thirdly, we will look at the value of the ocean as part of our life support system.

Considering the overwhelming importance of the non-quantifiable, not-monetarizable part of the wealth of the ocean; considering also that there is widespread dissatisfaction today with the notion of GNP or GDP as indicators of wealth and welfare, the second section of this chapter explores what might be appropriate indicators for assessing the real wealth of the oceans. There is a vast literature on social and environmental indicators today, but this literature focuses on the terrestrial economy. The oceans have been sadly and inexplicably neglected. The third section deals with the ethical or spiritual dimension of the emerging economics of sustainable development – in the oceans as a case study – which, however would be applicable more generally. The fourth section, finally, will try to deduce some fundamental principles and practical guidelines from the previous sections.

Chapter 4 will confront "land perspectives" with "ocean perspectives." A medium quite different from the earth, the oceans force us to think differently. Just as one cannot apply the laws of gravity in outer space, many "terrestrial" concepts simply will not work in the ocean medium. These concepts include property in the Roman Law sense, sovereignty in the sense of the "Westphalian era," and "territorial boundaries," which neither fish nor pollution will respect. The chapter will focus on the concept of the Common Heritage of Mankind, with its economic, environment, and disarmament dimensions and its relations to "sustainable development" and "comprehensive security." It will start with an analysis of the United Nations Convention on the Law of the Sea, with only cursory attention to legal and perhaps transitory details, while emphasizing the truly innovative concepts and principles of this "Constitution for the Ocean," which are "systems-transforming" and have provided the foundation for the whole process emanating from the United Nations Conference on Environment and Development (Rio de Janeiro, 1992). All this will be seen in the broader perspective of the restructuring of the United Nations system.

Chapter 5 will try to capture the emerging shapes of ocean governance. Based on all the foregoing, this chapter will develop a "normative vision" of ocean governance and management, cognizant of the "transparency" of the "boundaries" both horizontal (as between disciplines, departments, ministries, specialized agencies and programmes) and vertical (as between levels of governance: local, national, regional, and global), and committed to the principles of sustainable development, common and comprehensive security, equity, common heritage, and participation. The chapter will examine the regimes established by the various post-UNCED Conventions, agreements and action programmes (climate, biodiversity, high-seas fisheries, small islands, coastal management, land-based sources of pollution) as they interact in the oceans, and will try to find ways in which they could be used so as to reinforce rather than duplicate one another.

Chapter 6, finally, will examine perspectives on the "blue planet" as a whole. The UNCLOS/UNCED process, triggered by the dramatic changes that have taken place during the first three-quarters of this century, is itself a powerful agent of change. This final chapter will widen the horizon. The ocean will be considered as a great laboratory for the making of a genuinely new international/national political, legal, and social order. The lessons to be learned from 30 years of work with the oceans will be examined and their potential contribution to the "*solutique*" of the fundamental issues facing us as we enter the new millennium (insecurity, poverty, inequity, human and environmental ruin) will be elucidated. We may never reach the majesty of the oceanic circle, but the way is the goal.

Notes

1. *Biodiversity in the Seas.*
2. Graham, p.7.
3. I remember that at that time, one of the great leaders both within NIEO and UNCLOS, who shall remain unnamed, told me the two had nothing in common and that, in Law of the Sea matters, a country like Mexico had more in common with Norway than with Bolivia.
4. Borgese and Pardo, 1975, 1976.
5. *Our Common Future*, 1987.

6. The Rio Conference adopted a Declaration of Principles; a Framework Convention on Climate Change; a Convention on the Conservation of Biodiversity; an Action Programme, *Agenda 21*, Desertification; Forests. It mandated the calling of a number of follow-up conferences (on the protection of straddling stocks and highly migratory stocks in the high seas; on integrated coastal management; on Small Island Developing States, and established an intergovernmental body for the elaboration of a convention to control desertification. All this work has proceeded on schedule. Chapter 17 of *Agenda 21*, the most substantive of all the chapters, is devoted to sustainable development of the seas and oceans. All other UNCED documents – including even those on forests and desertification, have important linkages to sustainable ocean development. UNCED performed a vital function in elucidating that the problems of ocean space are closely interrelated not only among themselves but also with those of terra firma, the atmosphere and outer space.

7. Report by the Secretary-General to the United Nations General Assembly, 1994; *Addendum*, 1995.

8. *Oceans and Peace: the Potential Contributions of Ocean Governance to the Implementation of the Agenda for Peace*. The Proceedings of Pacem in Maribus XXIII, Costa Rica, 1995, with a preface by Federico Mayor. Paris: UNESCO, 1997.

9. *Dialogue on Wealth and Welfare, The Limits of Certainty*.

10. *The Future of the Oceans*, 1986.

11. The World Bank recently reassessed the wealth of nations in terms of produced assets, natural capital and human capital (*Monitoring Environment Progress*, 1995). Only 16 per cent of this wealth consists of produced assets, both in developed and developing countries, according to the Bank. Natural capital constitutes 17 per cent in developed, 32 per cent in developing countries. A footnote suggests that this figure is probably underestimated. Human capital, or human resources, contribute by far the largest part: 67 per cent in developed countries, 52 per cent in developing countries.

12. Giarini and Liedtke, 1997.

13. *Ibid*.

14. Dror, 1995; King and Schneider, 1991; Schneider, 1988; Rosensohn and Schneider, 1993, among others.

15. Already Karl Marx recognized that the problems of sprawling megacities and decaying villages had to be dealt with together. With amazing foresight, he recommended the "combination of agriculture with manufacturing industries; gradual abolition of the distinction between town and country, by a more equable [*sic*] distribution of the population over the country." *The Communist Manifesto*, Penguin Books, 1967, 1968, and 1969, p.105.

16. Rosensohn and Schneider stress the importance of co-development of biotechnology, and the difficulties in obtaining it. "The new biotechnology applications are increasingly proprietary, owned primarily by private sector corporations in industrial countries. The benefits of this technology are generally not accessible to most developing countries, due to institutional, political and infrastructural constraints and a lack of investment." Thus the spectacular advances in genetic engineering "tend to increase rather than diminish the gap between the haves and the have-nots."

17. It is remarkable that NGOs are represented in the Mediterranean Commission on Sustainable Development *on an equal footing* with governments, proper linkages are established between regional and municipal decision-making, and the "sectoral approach" characterizing the earlier phase of the Regional Seas Programme has been transcended.

18. *Ocean Governance and the United Nations*, 1996.

1

Ocean perspectives: physical

Our ignorance of the ocean is profound, and although we have learned much during the last hundred years, our knowledge of ocean processes and life in the oceans will remain forever incomplete.

Animal science and technology

In many ways the creatures inhabiting the oceans and coasts are by millions of years ahead of us. They know the currents and the trade winds and the temperatures and use them for their global navigations. Sea-turtles, eels, tunas, or whales – they know their routes and schedules more securely than our modern ocean liners. Right whales, it has recently been discovered, can sail. They stand on their heads with their large tails out of the water like a sail. They use their dorsal fins as a keel and their flippers as rudder, so they can tack – a technique it took humankind thousands of years to acquire! Migrating birds, as was recently discovered, have tiny magnets built into their brains, which, like compasses, aid their steering. And every sophisticated tool we have invented to exploit the living resources of the sea, the animals had invented long before us.

Fishes fish: with nets, with rod and line, with spears and harpoons, with sophisticated chemicals, and sonar for locating their catch. The *larvacean,* a small planktonic herbivorous creature, low on the food chain and on the scale of evolution, ancient in time, has invented the first fishing net. It builds itself a spacious gelatinous house in which it places a system of large nets made of strong, fine threads. The house has three gates. Two of them serve as water inlet and outlet, maintaining a gentle flow of water through the nets. The third is an emergency exit. When the nets become clogged or otherwise malfunction, the larvacean slips out through the third door and builds itself a new house, with a new system of nets.

The oldest line fisher is the anglerfish. Rod and line, called the *illicium*, protrude from just above the mouth. The illicium may be four times as long as the animal itself, and is equipped with a light at the end which is used as a bait. Some fisherfolk, much later, found out that a light, or a brightly coloured object, makes a good bait.

Horrid are the poisons injected with a thousand needles by the sea anemone into a carelessly passing fish. They paralyse, and without further struggle the fish is drawn into the anemone's mouth and swallowed whole. Corals and many jellyfish are also equipped with these stinging cells, which are called *nematocysts*. They have a long hair which is normally coiled inside them. When the cell is disturbed, the barbed hair pops out.

Swordfish and narwhal are well equipped spear fishers. They move rapidly through a school of fish, large or small, slashing vigorously left and right. Then they turn around and, at a more leisurely pace, make a meal of those their spears have wounded.

Besides his keen vision and an extremely refined olfactory sense enabling him to detect a substance in dilutions down to one part in several million, the shark has a "sixth sense" to rely on for locating his prey. This is the so-called lateralis system – common, in more or less developed form, to all fish – which is vibration sensitive and enables the shark to locate such disturbances as a ship sinking miles away. He can also use it actively to echo-locate objects by the time relations of reflected vibrations he emits himself.

The sperm whale possesses highly developed long-range hunting sonar enabling him to precision-target squid or fish in the ocean depths from a distance of several miles.

Luminescence, or the production of light without waste heat; aero- (or hydro) dynamics, the reduction of drag to attain speed with relatively reduced energy; these are other examples where "animal science" (or accumulated wisdom) and "animal technology" were way ahead of human achievements. The London *Daily Telegraph* (14 January 1989) carried an article under the headline "Shark Technology Found to Reduce Drag on Aircraft." It turned out that the skin of sharks is covered with microscopic parallel grooves called "riblets," which are aligned in the direction they swim and reduce their drag and noise. Now the British Institute for Maritime Technology hopes to apply "riblet technology" to aeroplanes, submarines, turbine blades and propellers on a commercial scale. Actually there is a new science, "biotics," which studies the achievements of animal technology and its applicability to human technology – a "transfer of technology," so to speak, from the animal kingdom to the realm of humanity.

"Primitive" science and technology

Among humans, "primitive" sailors, preceding the Christian area and during the first millennium A.D., the Chinese and Indians, Egyptians and Phoenicians, the Greeks and the Vikings must be credited with quite a bit of knowledge. A fourth-century text describes the skills of a famous Indian pilot named Suparaga:

He knew the course of the stars and could always readily orient himself. He also had a deep knowledge of the value of signs, whether regular, accidental, or abnormal, of good and bad weather. He distinguished the regions of the ocean by the fish, by the colour of the water, by the nature of the bottom, by the birds, the mountains and other indications.[1]

Primitive sailors foresaw a storm before it had come, and a tempest before it struck. They took soundings, gathered sea-bottom samples, marked the prevailing winds and currents, recorded depths, anchorages, landmarks, and tides.

The Phoenicians may have circumnavigated the continent of Africa over 2,500 years ago. They travelled to Malta, Sicily, Sardinia, and Spain. They passed the straits of Gibraltar and may even have reached Britain, establishing trading stations all along the way.

The Roman merchantman dominated the Mediterranean for five centuries, from Britain to the Black Sea. The Romans sailed around India, traded with Malaya, Sumatra, and Java, and reached the borders of China. The Roman grain ships were enormous, the "tankers" of antiquity, 180 feet long and with a capacity of 1,300 tons of cargo. "What a tremendous vessel it was," Lucian wrote of one of the sailing ships, carrying grain from the Nile valley and gold from the Nubian mountains to Rome, "the crew was like an army!"

The Vikings came down from the fjords and settled Iceland and Normandy, visited London, Hamburg, Paris, Lisbon, and Pisa, circumnavigated the North Cape and discovered Spitzbergen. They sailed the Black Sea and the Caspian. They passed the Dardanelles and arrived at Byzantium. They discovered America around 1000, sailing from Iceland to Greenland and then down the eastern seacoast as far as Cape Cod or even further.

The magnetic compass was used widely on Chinese ships in about 1000 A.D., quite possibly as early as 850, with its first beginnings reaching back as early as the first century B.C. The earliest description of a floating compass dates from the middle of the eleventh century. It was a thick leaf of magnetized iron with upturned edges, cut into the shape of a fish. From China, the compass spread to the Indian Ocean and was taken over by the Arabs, who transmitted it to the Mediterranean where it was first used in the twelfth century. "Dead reckoning" ("dead" being a mutilation of "deduced") for direction finding, maps, hourglass to measure time and speed; astrolabe, sextant or crossbar to measure the altitude of the stars; and trigonometry to calculate wind- or current-induced deviations from the established course, came into use about the same time.

The Chinese made maps about 800. The first sea chart in Europe is the Carta Pisana, dating at about A.D. 1275. The principle of the rectangular grid on which to plot the map goes back as far as the third century.

Archeological finds in the Mediterranean indicate that there may have been astronomical computers in antiquity. Aristotle was an early expert in marine biology and in the chemistry of seawater, but he knew nothing about the basins containing these things. The ocean was still thought to be ringing the earth, which was flat.

Not much was added, during the next couple of millennia, in the Western world. During the ages of exploration, in the fifteenth and sixteenth centuries, the oceans, or at least their surface, began to take on more realistic contours. Henry the Navigator, Infante of Portugal (1394–1460) founded the first interdisciplinary, international oceanographic institution near Sagres, where he gathered mathematicians, astronomers, chart makers, captains, and chroniclers from Portugal and Spain, Venice, Genoa, and the Arab countries. They worked on chart design, they improved compasses, astrolabes and quadrants, they compiled astronomical tables. They laid the foundations for the great voyages of exploration. Christopher Columbus was a student of Sagres. Sagres gave the world whole generations of great seafarers, from Gil Eanes, who rounded Cape Bohador in 1433, to Vasco da Gama, who landed in Calicut on the west coast of India in 1498.

The birth of modern oceanography

But the real beginning of modern oceanography is of very recent date, just a little over a century ago. Edward Forbes, a British biologist who studied marine animals and died in 1854, and Matthew Fontaine Maury, a US naval officer who studied currents, tides and wind systems and died in 1873, are considered by some as the fathers of oceanography, biological and physical. But the real impetus to modern oceanography came from the famous global cruise of HMS *Challenger* (1872–1876). It took the scientists of the *Challenger* – or the "philosophers," as they were called by the navy crew – 10 years after the end of their voyage to complete the 50 thick volumes presenting the results of this first major oceanographic cruise. The report discussed with full detail of text and illustrations the currents, temperatures, depths and constituents of the oceans, the topography of the bottom, the geology and biology of its covering and the animal life of the abyssal waters. That they could do this with the rudimentary technology at their disposal at the time seems almost miraculous. That which is achieved now with power winches, piston corers, and remote-controlled "boomerangs," they accomplished with hand-driven winches, lead lines, and baskets. In the mid-Pacific, they lifted manganese nodules from a depth of 5,000 metres, analysed their composition, configured their density and distribution, and made wild and wonderful guesses about their origin. Their computers they carried in their heads. Their navigational aids consisted of a compass, a chronometer (clock), and a quadrant; the pictures of the ocean's flora and fauna, produced today by deep-towed television and photo cameras, they etched with pencil and watercolour. One wonders whether human ingenuity is at its best producing high technology or obtaining the most complex and imposing results by the simplest means.

Since that time, oceanography has grown, expanded, and diversified at an astonishing rate. The development of acoustic, seismic, and optical sensors, magnetology, radioactive fossil dating, remote sensing, deep-sea drilling technology, the construction of deep-sea submersibles as well as satellite technology, microelectronics and computerized data processing, have made it possible to monitor large ocean areas in real time and to penetrate the ocean depths, right down to the ocean floor and its subsoil, through strata upon strata of sediments and basaltic rock, to the molten core of the planet earth.

The creative combination of *in situ* measurements, computer modelling and remote sensing will determine the future development of oceanography.[2]

Using computer modelling technology developed at the Massachusetts Institute of Technology, combined with satellite measurements of sea-surface undulations with subsurface acoustic measurements of how sound travels through bodies of water, a team of MIT scientists has recently come up with a description of the circulation in the Western Mediterranean which may enhance our understanding of the ocean's impact on climate.[3] In cooperation with scientists from Germany and Australia, the team is planning to apply the same methodology, on a larger scale, to the Pacific Ocean, where processes are operating which appear to be slowing, or even regulating, global warming trends. According to scientists of Columbia University's Lamont-Doherty Observatory, a naturally occurring air-ocean circulation system in the tropical Pacific has sped up the redistribution of heat to regions where it dissipates more easily.[4] The Pacific's cooling effect may explain why global temperatures in this century have risen only half as much as models predicted.

The new technologies have enabled us to reconstruct the evolution and transformation of ocean basins, to document with empirical data the theory of tectonic plates and continental drift, which has literally revolutionized our understanding of the history of the earth, including the ways in which plants and animals have evolved and been distributed over the oceans and continents. Plate tectonics, in a way, reveals to us that creation has not been a once-and-for-all happening but that it is an ongoing process regenerating and recycling the earth and its resources over eons, manifesting the many dimensions of the majesty of the oceanic circle. It is an awesome spectacle: in space and in time.

The oceanic circle

Ocean space is traversed by a system of currents, driven by the temperature differences between equator and poles, by winds, and by the rotation of the earth which deflects their course (Coriolis force). Compared to the earth's rivers, the quantity of water transported by these currents through ocean space is imposing. Measured in "sverdrups," that is, millions of tons of water per second, all the rivers on earth combined carry about one sverdrup, while the Gulf Stream in the Western Atlantic and the Kuroshio off Japan each carry more than 70 sverdrups. The volume of water that flows in the Gulf Stream is about 100 times that of all rivers on earth combined.

> All the rivers run into the sea; yet the sea is not full;
> unto the place whence the rivers come, thither they return again.[5]

Clouds dump about 450,000 cubic kilometres of fresh water into the ocean every year; rivers carry another 50,000. Fresh water returns to the atmosphere through evaporation: about 510,000 cubic kilometres a year, equivalent, approximately, to a water column of 1.41m.

A slow constant drift of sun-warmed surface water moves towards the cold polar regions; a counter current of cold bottom water, from the poles towards the equator; rising up again in the tropical zone as the surface water moves away. In the North Pacific and North Atlantic the wind piles the waters up in huge mounds in the middle of the oceans. Driven by the Coriolis force, the waters flow around these mounds in great gyres.

Oceans and continents

Ocean space encloses mountain chains that dwarf anything we know from our terrestrial experience. The Alps measure 680 miles in length and 80 to 140 miles in width. The highest peak, Mont Blanc, rises 15,781 feet from a ground elevation of 3,400 feet. But the mountain chain traversing the world ocean, called the Mid-Ocean ridge system, measures 40,000 miles in length, and it averages 1,250 miles in width. The peaks rise 15,000 feet from the ocean floor. The deep trenches, most of which are in the Pacific, are the deepest depressions on the planet. The Marianas Trench, curving for 1,250 miles along the Mariana Islands, reaches a depth of 36,198 feet. It is like another planet, twice as large as earth. Its texture and shape are different. It is made of sheer volcanic basalt, and there are no such mountains on earth.

The ridge's rugged crest is about 125 miles wide and lies at some points only about 10,000 feet below sea level. Right through the middle of the entire ridge system runs a valley, 8 miles wide at its narrowest, 130 miles at its widest. The Grand Canyon, 1 mile deep, 4 to 18 miles wide, and 280 miles long, is puny in comparison.

The valley is a giant crater spewing masses of lava welling up from the earth's mantle. As the lava is chilled by the water it forms strange pillows which adorn the ridge crest, amongst sea pens, fans, sponges and gorgonians. Flowing down the ridges, the lava creates new ocean floor, forcing the continents apart – roughly speaking, during a human lifetime, the length of a human body. Something like 2.5 sq. km of new ocean floor is generated every year, century after century, millennium after millennium, billion after billion of years.

Ocean floor is devoured by the deep trenches. Where more floor is devoured than is created by the ridge system, oceans shrink. The Atlantic Ocean is expanding; the Pacific is shrinking. The Mediterranean will close as Africa and Europe will join – sometime in the future.

Thus oceans are born, and oceans die. The life of an ocean is approximately 300–400 million years, and the planet is made over, inside out and outside in. Only the continents, which are too light to be sucked into the trenches, keep floating outside on their tectonic plates, like bits of foam, merging, separating, transforming, gyrating, changing climes, flora, and fauna.

The kryosphere

Meanwhile, over the eons, glaciers expanded and receded; sea levels fell and rose; salinity increased and decreased. During periods of the Pleistocene, when glacial ice was almost gone, the sea level was 100 feet above what it is now. Another such rise would not only make the Maldives disappear and cover the coastal plains of Bangladesh, it would also flood large areas of Northern Europe, inundate the valleys of the Mississippi, the Amazon, the Nile, the Euphrates, the Indus, and the Ganges, and submerge the flood plains of China.

Water, it appears, was one of the original chemical compounds of the nascent earth. According to some theories it continues to well up, and in another few billion years, it might cover the whole earth.[6] Conceivably, it might freeze again, and the earth might look like the moon Europa.

Under the earth's polar ice, highly diversified communities of algae, unicellular animals and various small crustaceans, so-called "epontic communities," have been discovered. Underwater video cameras revealed that the ice underside was teeming with krill, feeding on algae that grow in and under the ice in deep dark winters. Could there be epontic communities under the ice of the moon Europa's ocean?

Air, water and ice interact in the polar regions. The dimensions of the polar ice masses, again, are imposing. 80 per cent of the earth's fresh water is frozen, constituting the planet's kryosphere. About

5,000 icebergs are generated annually on the west coast of Greenland alone. The Labrador current carries about 7,500 southward annually. An equal number of icebergs are generated annually in the south polar region, to drift northward. The largest observed thus far was 350 km in length, 90 km in width – with 250 m of its height under water, it had a total mass of 8,000 cubic km!

As the ice cracks, large amounts of heat and moisture pass from the water, at a temperature of −1°C, to the atmosphere, at a temperature of −20°C. Up to 1,000 watts per square metre can flow from the cooling-down water into the atmosphere. As the seawater freezes, the salinity and density of the adjacent water rise. The process contributes to a large extent to vertical circulation. Thus the Weddell and Greenland seas are the two breathing holes of the world ocean. It is here that surface water passes into the deep bottom layers, taking along oxygen and trace elements. We are just beginning to understand the role of the polar seas as a sink for carbon dioxide and other greenhouse gases.[7]

We are also just beginning to understand the role of these enormous movements – north-south, east-west, and vertical – for the distribution of pollutants and the interaction between ocean floor, water column, and atmosphere.

The carbon cycle

Through photosynthesis by microscopic plants in the surface layer of the ocean, carbon dioxide is drawn from the atmosphere and oxygen is released. Marine plants produce annually 36 billion tons of oxygen, equal to 70 per cent of oxygen in the atmosphere. The ocean absorbs carbon dioxide from the atmosphere. Although we do not know how much, we do know that there is over 60 times more carbon dioxide in the ocean than in the atmosphere. The exchange of oxygen and carbon dioxide (and other gases) has a profound effect on the earth's climate.

How much of this carbon dioxide comes from the sea-floor and how much is absorbed from the atmosphere is not yet very clear. What has become clear from continuous measurements over the past decades is that there is a great deal of oscillation between summer and winter. The oscillation is highest in the far north and very small in the oceanic regions of the southern hemisphere. In summer, plant photosynthesis exceeds biological respiration from plants, animals and bacteria, and carbon dioxide is taken out of the air. In winter, just the reverse occurs, and atmospheric carbon dioxide rises. The amplitude of this seasonal oscillation is increasing, probably indicating that forests and other biota are growing because of the fertilizing effect of increased atmospheric carbon dioxide![8] This, in turn, would lead to the absorption of more carbon dioxide and mitigate the greenhouse effect.

Methane is another "greenhouse gas." Although there is a lot less in the atmosphere than there is carbon dioxide, each molecule has a much larger heating effect. It is estimated that methane accounts for perhaps 25 per cent of the total greenhouse heating effect after a few decades. A better understanding of the methane cycle would be needed for an intelligent response to the greenhouse effect.

Science reports[9] a dramatic event that must have taken place about 55 million years ago, when suddenly there was a sharp rise in temperature and a significant shift in the carbon cycle, evidenced by isotope signals in foraminifera and in mammal teeth. There was much death of foraminifera on the ocean floor, contrasting with the appearance of a legion of new species on land, from rodents to primates.

According to scholars of the University of Michigan and their model of the global carbon cycle, the explanation of this revolutionary event appears to have been a gradual warming of the ocean that triggered a 10,000-year-long burst of methane from the sea floor. The effect, as retrodicted by the model and confirmed by the rock record, faded away during the next 200,000 years. The Michigan scientists assume that there may have been other such bursts during the billions of years of earth-and-ocean evolution.

Reef history

Biodiversity waxed and waned. Today we are deeply concerned about its waning: the disappearance of tropical forests, the bleaching and dying of coral reefs, the two richest reservoirs of biodiversity.

The history of the coral reef – the oldest ecocommunity on our planet – is worth recalling.[10] The oldest reefs are the simplest, built by algae alone. They go back to Precambrian times and can be found in rock formations in all parts of the world. Called stromatolites, these blue-green algae were closely related to those still surviving today. Over millions of years, individual colonies grew upward for tens of feet. In the early Cambrian, 600 million years ago, the first animals associated themselves with the reef. Cuplike stony beasts called archaeocyathids emerged like low trees from the meadows of algae. Bottom-feeding trilobites crawled around in between.

This form of community life did not last long, however. By the end of the Middle Cambrian, about 540 million years ago, the archaeocyathids were wiped out by some ecocatastrophe. There were no reefs for about 60 million years. But what are 60 million years? Bigger and better reef communities made their appearance in mid-Ordovician times, about 480 million years ago.

Stromatolites still formed the basis, but coralline red algae and also the first sponges, shaped like encrusted plates or hemispheres or shrubs, joined the community. And the first real corals emerged. Near the end of the Devonian period, just over 350 million years ago, worldwide climate changes decimated life in the oceans. In the coral reefs, only the stromatolites survived for the next 13 million years.

The Carboniferous age, followed by the Permian, brought the reign of the bryozoans and brachiopods over the reef community. Chambered sphinctozoan sponges and sea lilies began to play an increasingly important role.

All this was wiped out by a new, even worse, ecocatastrophe at the end of the Paleozoic, about 230 million years ago, and there were no more reef-building communities for another 10 million years. Then, in the mild climes of what is now the Mediterranean, a new reef community emerged. In mid-Triassic times the scleractinians, the progenitors of the more than 20 families of corals living today, made their first appearance in Germany, the southern Alps, Corsica, and Sicily. Sponges, sea urchins, molluscs joined in and flourished. But about 100 million years ago a revolution took place. Its protagonists were the rudists, a group of bivalves with cylindrical and conical shells that built upward as though in imitation of coral-building patterns. Starting from nowhere, the rudists cemented their power over the next 60 million years. They dwarfed the corals and repressed their building. Then, some 65 to 60 million years ago, they disappeared as suddenly as they had come.

This, again, was a period of great dying in the oceans. Nearly one-third of the animal families that flourished in the late Cretaceous period no longer existed at the beginning of the Cenozoic. Many corals, molluscs, clams, and sponges went down with the rudists at that time. Temperature changes, the drying up of shallow seas, or the emergence of harsh, seasonal continental climates may account for it, together with factors still unknown.

From their cosmopolitan ubiquity of earlier ages, reef-building communities were now more restricted, essentially to areas between 35 degrees latitude north and 32 south. The richest developments now are in the western Pacific, the Indian Ocean and the Caribbean. The most stupendous creation is the Great Barrier Reef off Australia.

The modern reef community consists of algae, corals, sea fans, sponges, sea anemones, tunicates, barnacles, molluscs, and the like, and a great variety of fish. Butterfly- and anglerfish, damsel- and squirrelfish, parrot fish, triggerfish, wrasse, grouper and grunt, pipefish, snake eels, and scorpion fish: all find food, shelter, and oxygen in the reef's caverns and branches – an exuberance of colours and shapes that is matchless in nature.

Population eruptions of starfish in recent years threatened the Great Barrier Reef of Australia and other reef regions in the Pacific. The phenomenal increase in starfish was thought by some to be due to human influences. Others ascribed it to natural causes.

Eutrophication is killing the reef's myriad forms of life off Oahu, Hawaii; in the Caribbean they are affected by oil and rising water temperatures. The corals die. The tiny polyps that make up these vast colonies cease to extend their tentacles to filter food from the waters' microscopic life, and the green algae living on the surface of their bodies die. Fungi take their place, or else more robust algae cover and suffocate the corals. The scene becomes dark and dull. The fish move away and die, and erosion takes its course.

Recent studies, however, are a little less gloomy.[11] Bleaching, it now appears, is the result of the departure, by death or otherwise, of certain algae, called zooxanthellae, which cover the coral in a symbiotic relationship. But the bleached and apparently dead coral reef appears to carry a reserve of zooxanthellae somewhere deep inside, which eventually recover the reef and make it revive. It also seems that reefs can adapt to a variety of algae, and that the whole system is far more complex and resilient than had been supposed. Corals can now be "farmed" – like fish and pearls – and reefs can be reseeded with farmed coral.

Man the measure?

This is not to excuse human ill-treatment of nature. What we are inflicting on the oceans, from land, through the atmosphere, from ships and platforms is an abomination, nothing less. But looking at the present crisis in the deep perspective of time and space makes one wonder. Are we as big as we think we are? Humans may be the rudest of rudists, but they too will disappear. Are our concerns perhaps partly inspired by anthropocentric megalomania combined with an obsession with original sin – so typical for the Western human?

Statements like the following appear somewhat overbearing in this broader context:

The other point that I want to make about the shift into the information age, and to tie this into the problem of conservation, has to do with the *reclassification of nature* [emphasis added] in an information age, is that Nature itself, the concept of Nature which has been a relatively stable concept as the concept of species, are now destabilized concepts. Nature has, in an age of genetic engineering, Nature has virtually no meaning whatsoever as a stable concept. Species becomes a very fluid concept as well. Now you can make what you want to of that as a social value.[12]

Nature in this symposium was viewed as *human-made*. It is we who decide how much of it we want, and that much we conserve. What is our real place in the awesomeness of the world ocean and its transformations through the eons of time?

A humbler attitude towards nature, somewhat belittling our power and our impact, should not be construed as a licence to pollute. The load of lethal and nature-altering matter we are generating is simply inadmissible. Most certainly we must change our ways; we must change our attitudes. For even if we are much less important than we think we are – even if our impact on climate change and biodiversity were minimal in space and time – it is clear by now to any one who wants to see that we are killing ourselves by mishandling our environment, of which the ocean is the most vulnerable component.

Our food, our water, the air we breathe, are poisoned. Plagues, presumed dead, are resurrecting. New diseases, allergies, immune deficiencies, cancers, respiratory troubles are attacking our children and the aged, our domestic animals, even our pets. Birth rates are declining in many parts of the world while, in others, new plagues, like AIDS, are depopulating villages and regions. Uprooted by the mismanagement of terrestrial and marine environment, growing masses of environmental refugees are jeopardizing social stability and human security.

The majority of humankind, as is well known, lives near the coasts, and by poisoning the ocean we are poisoning ourselves. We must save the seas to save ourselves. The sheer instinct of self-preservation, common to all living beings, should impel us to change our ways. Self-preservation, however, requires other-preservation.

> All beings tremble before danger, all fear death. When a man considers this, he does not kill or cause to kill.[13]

Our attitude towards nature must change; our ethics must change. No matter what our impact on the biodiversity of the future may be, somewhere deep down we know, we have another instinct, imbedded perhaps more deeply in other cultures than in our Western culture, which tells us that it is not permissible to maim and kill our fellow creatures, whether for the sake of profit or out of negligence. At the sight of every oil-drenched bird and cancer-deformed fish that the ocean washes onto our beach, we may feel that little sting that tells us what we do to these creatures we are doing to ourselves and our children. We hear the voice urging us

> To see your Self in all creatures and all creatures in your Self.[14]

We get the message:

> To best serve one's parents one must learn to practice kindness toward all animate life ...[15]

The Africans have an adage, recently quoted by the Secretary-General of the United Nations,[16] which says:

> The world is not ours – it is given to us in trust for future generations.

And this is, basically, what all Asian and native American cultures are teaching. As history is burying the remnants of colonialism and post-colonialism with the concomitant Eurocentrism, these non-European world views are coming to the fore, mingling with the emerging Western "ecological world view."

This shift, with all its implications, is of fundamental importance if we are serious about doing things differently.

Ocean pollution

A few decades ago scientists were sure they knew the amount of anthropogenic pollutants entering the oceans each year, and they could predict their impact on water quality, flora, and fauna. Today's scientists are considerably more cautious.[17]

– It has recently become clear that many chemical measurements in the sea made more than 10 years ago are dubious, making it difficult to establish time trends where changes in concentration develop over a longer time scale. The inaccuracy of past data has become apparent as new analytical techniques and quality-control procedures have been developed, and recent measurements of ambient concentrations are lower than those previously reported.

- Anthropogenic pollution is difficult to assess against an uncertain background of natural pollution. Interactions between sea floor, water column, atmosphere, land and rivers are of unfathomable complexity.

- Over 40,000 km of actively divergent plate boundaries lie beneath the world oceans. Not only are the active areas a continuous major source of heat, but intermittent ejection of molten magmatic and hydrothermal fluids produce massive underwater clouds of sulphur and metallic compounds at high temperature. Few quantitative data are available on these natural inputs, but their magnitude implies that they are significant on a global basis. The proportions of natural and anthropogenic pollutants in the total mass are difficult to ascertain.

- The same uncertainties arise with regard to the proportions of natural and anthropogenic inputs from rivers. Monitoring is done on a limited scale: only for a small number of river systems and a few contaminants. In dealing with nutrients, for example, a variety of river systems have been studied and the results extrapolated to provide an estimate of the total global gross river input, giving figures for the natural fluxes of dissolved nitrogen, phosphorus, and silicon and for the fluxes of suspended nitrogen and phosphorus. Human inputs have also been estimated. Although there are large discrepancies between the various estimates, it can be said that the anthropogenic flux of dissolved nutrients is at least comparable to, and in some areas significantly greater than, the natural flux.

- Atmospheric inputs are difficult to estimate. Interpretation of data is complicated because chemical composition varies with differences in vertical distribution, duration, intensity and droplet size of the precipitation. Techniques are not at present available to make direct measurements of the relevant gas fluxes across the air-sea interface. Furthermore, some chemicals entering the ocean from the atmosphere can be reinjected into the atmosphere via bursting bubbles or gas exchange. Unless this recycled material can be taken into account, the calculated deposition may be anomalously high. Existing databases are inadequate.

- A most serious problem arises from synthetic organic compounds.

New chemicals (500–1,000) are introduced to the market every year, and known chemicals are turned to new purposes. Their environmental fate and consequences are seldom known. Thus, concentrations of bound chlorine in fish fat range from 30–200 ppm in most samples, of which 5–10 ppm are attributable to known contaminants such as DDT, PCBs, dioxins, and chlorophenols. *The rest (up to 95 per cent) is unaccounted for.*

– With regard to radioactive material entering the ocean via dumping and atmospheric tests of nuclear weapons – but not including the manufacture and operation of military nuclear equipment as well as the operation of nuclear-powered ships, where no information is available – it is remarkable that anthropogenic pollution, according to the Group of Experts on Scientific Aspects of Marine Pollution (GESAMP) estimate, constitutes no more than 1 per cent of the total coming from natural sources (volcanic activities on the sea floor).

With all these uncertainties and caveats, it is not surprising that GESAMP abstains from offering a chart globally quantifying anthropogenic pollution of the ocean as against the background of pollution from natural sources. Here, nevertheless, an attempt has been made to summarize the most pertinent GESAMP data in table 1.1, which, however, remains incomplete, fragmentary, and impressionistic.

Instrumentation for marine environmental monitoring[18]

Instrumentation systems are utilized for
1. Collection
2. Measurement
3. Data handling
    (a) in situ
    (b) from shipboard or ocean platform
    (c) in land laboratory
    (d) from planes or satellites (remote sensing)

Navigation and position
(1) Radio direction finder
(2) Loran-A and Loran-C systems
(3) Global Positioning System

Instrumentation for physical oceanography
(1) Echo sounder
(2) Pressure sensor

Table 1.1 **Ocean pollutants**

Pollutant	Source		Quantity	Concentration			Trend
	Natural	Man-made		water	sediment	org.	
Dredged material			215 million tonnes t/y				
Industrial wastes		x	17 million t, 1982				Decreasing
			6 million t, 1984				
Sewage sludge		x	15 million t/yr 1980–1985				Gradually decreasing
Liquid organo-halogen compounds		x	100,000 t/yr, 1980–1988[1]				Phased out
Lost fishing gear		x	150,000 in 1975, much more today				Increasing
Plastic containers		x	450,000 tonnes, 1985				
Sediment	x	x	135,000 mt/yr				
Oil dumped from ships		x	3.1 billion t, 1979				Decreasing
Pesticides and PCBs		x	2.8 billion t, 1985				Decreasing
			data lacking for most parts of the world				
Radioactive material, dumped		x	60 pbq				
Weapons tests	x	x	200,000 pbq 1954–1962				
Radioactive material	x	x	200,000,000 pbq				
Mercury	x	x		0.37–7.0 Ng/l	0.01–0.6 ppm	0.1 ppb	
Selenium		x		0.1–0.2 μg/l	0.15 ppm	var.	
Lead	x	x		25–150 ng/l	10–100 ppm	1–16 ppm	
Arsenic	x	x		1.4–42 μg/l	20–300 ppm	var.	
Cadmium	x	x		0.2–200 ng/l	0.5 ppm	2 ppb	

(3) Reversing thermometer
(4) Thermometer with sampling bottle
(5) Bathythermograph set
(6) Salimeter
(7) Mark III-CTD Profiling System
(8) Neil Brown Instrument System
(9) Current meter
      Current velocity: rotor
      Current direction: compass
      Current temperature: semiconductor
      Current conductivity: electrodes
      Current depth: pressure cell
(10) Acoustic Doppler Current Profile
(11) Wave gauge
(12) Tide gauge, with or without well
(13) Acoustic tide gauge recorder

Instrumentation for meteorology
(1) Ship-borne meteorological instruments
(2) Aanderaa automatic all weather station with wind vane and anemometer
(3) Pressure cell
(4) Air temperature metre
(5) Rainfall metre
(6) Thermoradiometer
(7) Sea level gauge

Instrumentation for ocean chemistry
(1) Dissolved oxygen metre
(2) Acidometer – Ph meter
(3) Dissolved oxygen, Ph, and temperature system

Instrumentation for marine biology
(1) Fluorometer
(2) Seawater sampler
(3) Plankton net and trawl

Instrumentation for marine geology and geophysics
(1) Echo sounder
(2) Sea floor mapping system (side scan sonar)
(3) Deposit sampler

(4) Sub-bottom profiling system
(5) Deep sea survey camera and TV
(6) Digital seismic recording system
(7) Seabeam

Monitoring: who pays?

We must learn to better understand ocean processes, even though we are aware that we never will fully understand them.

Advances in marine scientific research have already given rise to a great number and variety of national, regional and global monitoring programmes and projects, such as UNEP's "Mussel Watch," IOC's Ocean Circulation Experiment, or the European Union's Ocean Modelling Study analysing the variability and effects of the summer monsoon. Another project, sponsored by the USA, France, Japan and Australia, concerns deep currents beneath the Pacific, studied by means of 60 underwater buoys.

The most comprehensive of these programmes is the Global Ocean Observation System (GOOS) launched in the wake of the United Nations Conference on Environment and Development (UNCED). It is carried out in cooperation between the Intergovernmental Oceanographic Commission of UNESCO (IOC), the United Nations Environment Programme (UNEP), and the World Meteorological Organization (WMO). The cost, including the cost of creating, in every coastal state, a national oceanographic service, is estimated at US$4 billion a year. The programme is generously supported by the insurance industry. During the past decade the industry had to cover enormous costs from natural disasters, many of which were linked to global warming which, in their own words, "threatens to bankrupt the whole industry."[19] GOOS is expected to enable insurance companies to predict reliably the path and intensity of major storms several months in advance, thus enhancing disaster planning through early warning systems.

About 80 to 90 per cent of all material dumped at sea results from dredging. Between 1980 and 1985 the reports provided to the Secretariat of the London Dumping Convention record an average of 215 million tonnes of dredged material dumped anually, which represents some 20–22 per cent of all dredged material, the rest being disposed of elsewhere.

Marine transportation, including tanker operations, other shipping activities and accidental spills from ships, accounts for an estimated

46 per cent of the total input of oil to the sea. World oil consumption has decreased from 3.1 billion tonnes in 1979 to 2.8 billion tonnes in 1985, but since 1986 the trend in consumption has again been upward. The decade 1976–1986 saw a dramatic drop of 25 per cent in the amount of oil moved by sea, 431 million tonnes less in 1986 than in 1977. Another notable trend has been the steady increase in the transport of finished products (mostly non-persistent) in contrast to crude oil. In 1977 the transport of finished products represented 15 per cent of total exports but the figure had increased to 25 per cent by the following year, and crude oil exports were 33 per cent less. The number of oil spillages has declined steadily in the last decade, from an annual average of 670 events in the first five years, to 173 in the last five. For major accidents with over 5,000 barrels (725 tonnes) spilled the corresponding averages are 20 and 7 events. Lloyd's Register of Shipping shows that the number of serious casualties in tankers over 6,000 gross registered tonnes averages 2.5 per 100 ships in the period 1977–1981, but only 1.8 in the period 1982–1986.

If the insurance industry is to be the principal gainer from improved monitoring services and a better understanding of ocean processes, the shipping industry is next in line. Energy, trade, finance,

Table 1.2 **Global economic losses from weather-related national disasters 1980–1996 (US$m)**

Year	Overall losses	Insured losses
1980	1.5	0.1
1981	7.8	0.4
1982	2.1	1.0
1983	6.2	2.9
1984	2.3	1.0
1985	5.0	2.0
1986	6.7	0.2
1987	9.6	4.3
1988	3.2	0.8
1989	9.7	4.5
1990	15.0	10.0
1991	27.0	8.0
1992	36.0	22.5
1993	22.5	5.5
1994	22.5	1.8
1995	38.5	9.0
1996 (prel.)	60.0	9.0

Source: Münchner Rückversicherungsgesellschaft & Worldwatch Inst., Washington, D.C.

agriculture, construction, and tourism are equally involved. They should all contribute their fair share to the global monitoring effort. Their voluntary participation should develop into "customary law," eventually to be incorporated into conventional law in the form of an ocean development tax. To this we shall return in chapter 3.

Science and ocean governance

The ocean sciences, or science in general, cannot be considered in isolation. They are part of the whole system.

We will indeed need a new legal framework, if science is to flourish: not for the benefit of the rich countries alone, but on the basis of equity and sharing and the full participation of the developing countries. The basis for such a development has already been laid down in the 1982 United Nations Convention on the Law of the Sea.

We will need an economic system that de-emphasizes short-term individual interests and competition and reinforces long-term social values and cooperation. The forerunners of these new theories are already at work.

We will need a decision-making and management system capable of synthesizing short-term and long-term individual and social interests and aspirations and of implementing the plans and programmes chosen on the basis of the new economic/ecological and socio-political thinking. Such systems are in the making.

We need new and different technologies, less wasteful of natural and human resources. The sharing of such technologies and their joint development will depend on the legal and institutional framework we are to produce and must harmonize with the cultures in which they are to be embedded.

Culture, law, institutions, technologies, all feed back on each other; all are part of each other:

As a net is made up by a series of knots, so everything in this world is connected by a series of knots. If anyone thinks that the mesh of a net is an independent, isolated thing, he is mistaken.[20]

Which takes us back to *problématique* and *solutique,* and the majesty of the oceanic circle.

Notes

1. Needham, with the collaboration of Ling and Lu Gwei-Djen, 1965, 1971.
2. Gotthilf Hempel, 1992.

3. *Sea Technology,* April 1997.
4. *Science,* 14 February 1997.
5. Ecclesiastes 1:7.
6. Miller, 1996.
7. See Hempel, 1992.
8. Revelle, 1992.
9. Kerr, 1997.
10. I summarized this history (after O.A. Jones and R. Endean, eds., *Biology and Geology of Coral Reefs*, Vol. 1, 1973), in *The Drama of the Oceans* (1975) but it is worth retelling in the present context.
11. *Science* 279, "Coral Reefs Dominate Integrative Biology Meeting," 6 February 1998.
12. Buchanan, 1994.
13. The *Dhammapada, v. 129.*
14. Sri Aurobindo Birth Centenary Library, vol. XII, Pondicherry: Aurobindo Ashram, 1971.
15. The Teachings of Buddha.
16. Kofi Annan, Press Conference, 1 May 1997.
17. The following paragraphs are condensed from IMO/FAO/UNESCO/GESAMP, 1990.
18. After Xu Yukun, International Cooperation Department, State Oceanic Administration of China: syllabus for IOI training programme.
19. "Insurers acknowledge that if global warming becomes reality, consequent claims might threaten to bankrupt their whole industry." Panos Institute, 1997.
20. The Teachings of Buddha.

2

Ocean perspectives: cultural

Life began in the oceans.[1] The world ocean was, as Marston Bates put it, a sort of "thin organic soup in which almost anything might happen."[2] In this mixture of dissolving minerals, large molecular compounds of carbon combined and recombined for millions of years, finally making cells. Many more millions of years went by before the cells, passing through various phases of evolution, had "learned" photosynthesis, that is, the direct use of sunlight to produce high-energy phosphates. By that time the monocellular beings had developed the pigment chlorophyll, which made possible the trapping of light. Thus the cell began to use sunlight to synthesize glucose, releasing molecular oxygen as a by-product which entered the atmosphere. About 3,000 million years ago, the amount of oxygen thus released was sufficient to make cell respiration possible. Living matter in the oceans made its own environment as it made itself. Pre-Palaeozoic plankton – especially the blue-green algae that are still with us today – filled the atmosphere with enough oxygen to make possible the evolution of the metazoan some 600 million years ago.

From the ocean, life expanded into estuaries, rivers and lakes, where the true finfish evolved, many of whom eventually returned to the sea: the first wave of re-migrants, to be followed by others. Reptiles too returned, as did birds, their proud wings shrivelling into flippers, their legs (clumsy on land) turned into agile rudders. Even the mammals returned, whale, dolphin, seal and otter, and readapted to fishlike forms and habits. And humans may be next.

According to some, the land-based existence of Homo sapiens may be of brief duration, episodic. According to at least one respected scientist, Sir Alister Hardy, man's upright position, his body-hairlessness, the subcutaneous layer of fat he is prone to accumulate – all point to the possibility that his early evolution was bound, not to tree-dwelling, but to swimming in the balmy waters of tropical seas.[3]

More recent experiments, made by immersing tiny babies into deep water where they swim spontaneously and fearlessly, their eyes open without pain, emerging to breathe like dolphins or seals, would tend to confirm Sir Alister's thesis. Quite possibly, then, men could swim before they could walk upright.

The blissful gurgling, smiling, and kicking of a newborn baby, enveloped for the first time by the body-warm waters of the bathtub, manifests voluptuous creature comfort, as though it were a return to the maternal womb, a micro-ocean, the salinity of its fluid resembling that of primeval waters. Every micro-ocean re-stages the drama of the origin of life in the gestation of each embryo, from one-cell protozoan through all the phases of gill-breather and amphibian, to mammalian evolution, to man's birth – the expulsion from the micro-ocean to dry land.

And every human, in turn, is a good bit of planet ocean: 71 per cent of his substance consists of salty water, just as 71 per cent of the earth is covered by the oceans.

We do not know how, but humankind, before the dawn of history, knew that all life began in the oceans and enshrined this knowledge in uncounted myths and legends the world over, unconnected – establishing, as it were, a first intellectual bond uniting the entire species.

Genesis recounts that "In the beginning, the Spirit of God moved upon the face of the waters." *Fiat lux* (Let there be light!) was His first command of creation. Next He divided the waters which were under the firmament from those which were above it; and God said, "Let the waters under the heaven be gathered together unto one place, and let dry land appear; and it was so. And God called the dry land Earth, and the gathering together of the waters called he Sea." Genesis also reports that God first made the fishes in the sea and the birds in the air and the beasts on land, and, last of all, he made man. How did the ancients *know*?

A Swiss scholar, F. Morven, has collected the legends from the sea in a beautiful volume of that same title.[4] Morven reminds us that, in virtually all the mythologies of the world, water is given primacy over the other elements. It was the first thing, after which came all others.

The Manova Sastra tells the story of the creation in the same order as the Bible: the world was obscure and confused, as if in a deep sleep. God, existing by virtue of His own powers, manifested Himself in five elements and scattered the darkness. By wielding His power, He produced first of all the waters, imparted movement to them by means of fire and created an egg, as brilliant as the sun, from which Brahma, father of all reasoning beings, emerged.

The ancient Indian scriptures referred to the sea as "Ratnakar" where all jewels are to be found. The ancient Puranic story refers to the *Sagara Manthan*, a process whereby the ocean is churned to yield all its gems and riches, including Lakshmi, the goddess of wealth. And after the wealth is exhausted, comes the poison which threatens to destroy the world and which nobody except Shiva could consume and that only by retaining it in the throat.[5]

The Puranic story, like all ancient parables, hints at the coming together of the intellectual, mental (*daivic*), and materialistic (*asuric*) forces if riches are to be gathered from the oceans; and like Shiva, the nectar can only be protected by consuming (destroying) the poison if the world is to be saved from being destroyed or polluted: and this has to be through detachment, decrease of wants and voluntary restraint on consumption.[6]

According to the Greeks and Aztecs, even the gods were "born of water." Morven then surveys a wealth of myths of creation, from Peru and Mexico, North America, India, and the land of the Kalmuck, Hindu lore and Muslim wisdom, Scandinavian sagas and Slavic traditions – one more beautiful than the next; a wreath of poetic, creative dreams.

Water, Morven summarizes, contained the seeds of everything. In most traditions and cosmogonies, the earth was covered by waves, awaiting the creative agent which was to make the earth rise above them.

The oceans are not only life-giving; they also take life. They are as destructive as they are creative, and that divine wrath at man's sinfulness brought on torrential rains and tidal floods that engulfed the earth was known to the people of Israel as to those of Peru, Babylon, Japan, and India. The authors of the Bible even knew that, before the Flood, the continents were all in one piece; there were no islands, and it was the Flood that separated the continents – the earliest version of continental drift!

Sea monsters and sirens, serpents and evil spirits have been thought to lurk in the oceans and on the sea-bed; they lured sailors to perdition. Hindu mythology has woven the creative and destructive aspects of the ocean into one pattern of endless, cyclic recurrence.

"Oh King of Gods," Brahma said to Vishnu,

> I have seen it all perish, again and again, at the end of every cycle. At that time, every single atom dissolved into the primaeval water of eternity, whence originally all life arose. Everything then goes back to the fathomless, wild infinity of the ocean which is covered with utter darkness and is empty of every sign of animate being.[7]

Could it be this ambivalence between good and evil that makes the ocean so "human," the mirror of our souls?

> La mer est ton miroir!
> Tu contemples ton âme
> dans le déroulement infini de sa lame
> et ton esprit n'est pas un gouffre moins amer
>
> The sea is thy mirror!
> Thou contemplateth thy soul
> in the infinite extent of its swell,
> And thy spirit is no less bitter an abyss

Baudelaire says this, in one of the most inspired poems of *Les fleurs du mal*.

The sea, like a mother, provided nourishment to infant humanity which possibly fished before it hunted. The inventiveness of primitive humankind in fish-catching has amazed many an anthropologist. We are familiar today with the same basic equipment, as Robert C. Miller points out in his beautiful book, *The Sea*: "Hand lines with baited hooks, fish traps of various kinds, and nets adapted to different types of fishing such as shore seining or fishing from boats, seem to be at least as old as recorded history."[8]

The earliest cave dwellers in the Mediterranean region in Mesolithic times had become fishermen by the seventh millennium B.C. Large numbers of fishbones were found in their caves. Three thousand years before our own time, as I noted in *Drama of the Oceans,*

fishing had developed into a highly organized craft. Miniatures discovered in Minoan houses destroyed in an earthquake about 1500 B.C. show boats full of tackle, rods and hooks, and divers plunging into the sea with their bags, one of them carrying what looks like a large sponge.

Homo erectus, the only human species living in Southeast Asia 800,000 years ago, was a seafarer, capable of piloting a vessel over at least 600 km of deep fast-moving waters, from Java to the Indonesian

48

island of Flores. Recent excavations of stone tools found on Flores between layers of volcanic rock appear to prove it.[9]

And since the stone age, fisheries have constituted the basis of the economies of coastal communities. Fishing encouraged ship-building and enhanced the spirit of science and exploration, international trade and naval power. The power and influence of the Hanseatic League, the mediaeval federation of North European cities that made a still perceptible cultural impact on Hamburg, Lübeck, Bremen, Riga, Tallin, and Krakau, was based on its herring fishery. When the herring fishery collapsed in the fifteenth century, so too did the power of the League, which shifted to the Low Lands, where Sephardic Jews coming to Antwerp and Amsterdam after 1492, as well as Protestants, gave it new strength in the sixteenth century. It was as though seapower followed the migrations of fish. For three centuries (until the eighteenth century) Holland was the strongest maritime power, its economy based largely on its herring fishery. England, Scotland, and Norway followed.

"He who rules the sea, rules the land," has been a conventional wisdom. The Venetians at the peak of their power formulated it, *"Chi xe paron del mar xe paron de la tera"* (He who is master of the sea is master of the land), and the same idea was known to the Danish kings, *"Herre over Vandet, er og Herre over Landet."*[10]

Many a proud nation's fate was sealed by the outcome of naval battles. Suffice it to mention the Battle of Salamis (480 B.C.), most skillfully planned by Themistocles, which stemmed the tide of Persian expansion in Europe. The battle is splendidly described in *The Persians* by Aeschylus, who himself had been a mariner in the Athenian navy at Salamis. Actium and Lepanto are other familiar names in the long series of naval conflicts that tilted the balance of power in favour of Rome and Christendom respectively. Queen Elizabeth I of England and King Philip II of Spain fought at sea, and Spain went down with its Armada in 1588; Napoleon was undone at Trafalgar (1805); and the Tsars' empire succumbed to ascendant Japan in the naval battle of Tsushima Strait (1905).

A brief departure from the universally accepted notion that "Neptune's trident is the sceptre of the world" came with the theory of geopolitics, between the two world wars. Borrowed by the German Karl Haushofer from the British Harold Mackinder, this held that he who rules Eastern Europe, commands the heart of the earth – the Heartland – and he who rules the Heartland rules the earth. "Land power wields the seas, not conversely."[11]

Short-lived, geopolitics went down with the Third Reich, and after the Second World War, the strategic importance of the oceans and of naval power – now in the form of missile-carrying submarines – has been stressed more emphatically than at any time before. Techno-logical developments (high-flying spy planes and satellites) have made the dry earth unsafe as a repository for a second- or for that matter a first-strike force. The balance of terror today rests hidden in the opaque waters of the deep sea. Escalating submarine power in an insane race for supremacy, some superpowers of today or tomorrow may end by destroying themselves, the rest of humanity and life in the oceans as well – closing, perhaps, one of those cycles at the end of which every single atom dissolves in the primaeval waters of eternity, when everything returns to the fathomless, wild infinity of the oceans, in utter darkness, bereft of life.

The end of the Cold War has given rise to a "New Geopolitics" – endorsed by scholars as well as admirals, in Canada, in India, in Japan and other places,[12] ocean-centred, but ascribing new roles and missions to navies: not war-fighting but peace-building, not com-petitive, but cooperative, in the service of monitoring and surveil-lance, law enforcement, research and rescue, disaster relief, and humanitarian assistance.

The ocean, that mighty body of water that both separated and united human beings, has been a "Great Educator" which made peoples great. Seafaring populations have provided history's most remarkable merchants and explorers. Seafaring people have cherished freedom, too. They felt as free as the oceans. Republics are the creation of maritime peoples; tyranny was born inland.

Hegel has a prophetic page in his *Philosophie des Rechts* on the role of the seas in industrial societies, which he compares with the role of the earth in agricultural societies. He was aware of the culture-forming, educative influence of the ocean and invited us to compare the maritime nations, in their industriousness and enlightenment, with those nations whom destiny had denied navigation and who, "like the Egyptians and the Indians, sank into stupor and the most horrid and shameful superstitions."

Hegel's knowledge of the geography and culture of Egypt and India obviously was not what it should have been, but his emphasis on the teaching and culture-creating aspects of the oceans is undoubtedly correct. "The sea made man's soul, and the waves give him intelligence," a Finnish proverb has it. Throughout recorded history, the oceans and man's relationship to the oceans have inspired architects, painters, musicians, and writers. The whole arsenal of a people's crafts and sciences, or art and lifestyle, of world view and collective purpose goes into the building of a ship. A ship epitomizes man's attitude toward other men and toward nature.

Ships have been a favourite subject of paintings and miniatures almost as long as there has been painting, from the Egypt of the Pharaohs to the present time. Seascapes, though not too frequent in classical painting, show wave crests stylized into almost tapestry-like patterns (*The Birth of Venus,* by Botticelli) or dwell on the chiaroscuro of billowing mountains and vales merging with, and reflecting, an equally photodynamic cloudscape, as in Tintoretto's magnificent *Christ at the Sea of Galilee.*

But it is with the Romantics and post-Romantics, Impressionists, Fauves, and Expressionists, and their new and intense relationship with nature – with Monet, Cézanne, Gauguin, Van Gogh, Turner, Watteau, the Germans, the Dutch, to mention only a few, and Hokusai in Japan – that the ocean becomes an inexhaustible model for the painter, a looking-glass for his soul as it mirrors the firmament and stars. Turner painted *The Snowstorm* after living through a tempest at sea, off the coast of England. "I got sailors to lash me to the mast to observe it," Turner recorded, bringing to mind Odysseus tied to the mast in order to listen to the song of the Sirens. "I was lashed for hours," Turner continued, "and I did not expect to escape, but I felt bound to record it if I did." The result, Edward Lockspeiser writes, "was the greatest of his seascapes ... which, said Turner, 'no one has any business to like ... I did not paint it to be understood. I wished to show what such a scene was like'."[13]

Hokusai's famous print, the *Hollow of the Wave at Kanagawa* – which, incidentally, was the picture chosen by Debussy for the cover of the orchestral score of *La Mer* – was eloquently described by Edmond de Goncourt, in a study published in 1896:

The design for the Wave is a sort of deified version of the sea, made by a painter who lived in a religious terror of the overwhelming sea surrounding his country on all sides: It is a design which is impressive by the sudden anger of its leap into the sky, by the deep blue and the transparent inner side of its curve, by the splitting of the crest which is thus scattered into a shower of tiny drops having the shape of animals' claws.[14]

Hokusai's *Wave,* nevertheless, has something rigid and static about it, revindicating Lucien Favre's statement, "La peinture est, si l'on veut, une musique des couleurs sans mouvement." (Painting is, if you will, a music of colours without movement.)

Music, instead, can be seen as the art closest to nature; music has a time dimension so that it can capture not only the sounds of the sea, its colours and textures, but their teasing changes and variations, their rhythms in time. "Music has this over painting," Debussy wrote, "it can bring together all manner of variations of colour and light – a point not often observed though it is quite obvious."[15] And Vallas, in his *Theories of Claude Debussy,* wrote:

Although they claim to be nature's sworn interpreters, painters and sculptors can give us but a loose and fragmentary rendering of the beauty of the universe. Only one aspect, one instant is seized and placed on record. To musicians only is it given to capture all the poetry of night and day, of earth and heaven, to reconstruct their atmosphere and record the rhythm of their great heartbeats.[16]

The playing of silvery ripples, the crashing of surf are easily located in orchestration; the swelling of storm and its exhaustion find expression in established modes of crescendo and decrescendo. The rolling of waves, their eternal cadences, are readily translated into the measures of musical time. The multiple layers of ocean space, from the mysterious sea floor through submerged waves, submarine rivers, to the bobbing scintillating surface, can be captured in counterpoint, vertically; its flux in time reflected in the duration of horizontal melodic development.

The sea is onomatopoetic to the highest degree, as generations of composers have known. Good examples are Richard Wagner's treatment of the sea, his musical characterizations of *The Flying Dutchman* – "And roaring and whistling and surging round them all is the Sea," as Ernest Newman observes, "not so much as the mere background of the drama as the element that has given it birth"[17] – the longing strains of *Tristan and Isolde* reflecting a leaden Irish Sea over which the vessel must come – "*das Schiff, sahst Du's noch nicht*" (the ship, do you not yet see it) – and the sensuousness of drowning in love, in the *Liebestod*, as in the sea:

Heller schallend,	The wafting sound,
mich umwallend,	Does me surround,
sind es Wellen sanfter Lüfte?	Is it a wave that me does lave?
. . .	. . .
Wie sie schwellen,	How they are surging,
mich umrauschen,	All around me,

soll ich atmen,	shall I breathe,
soll ich lauschen? Soll ich	shall I harken? Shall I slurp it,
schlürfen untertauchen?	dive into it?
...	...
In dem wogenden Schwall,	In the billowing surge,
in dem tönenden Schall,	in the sonorous sound,
in des Welt Atmens	in the flowing
Wehen, dem All,	of the breathing universe
ertrinken	Shall I sink
versinken	drown
unbewusst	unconscious
Höchste Lust!	Supreme joy!
...	...

In the long-drawn, single E-flat opening of *Rheingold*, water symbolizes the beginning of all things; water from which, through sequences of empty fifths, the flow of the Rhine takes its course, and which is the beginning of the gods and the creation of men in their complex interaction with eternity.

The onomatopoetic possibilities created by the new technologies of electronic synthesizers and concrete music are infinite. A good example is Alan Hovhaness's well-known *And God Created the Great Whales,* a composition counterpointing the lugubrious, lonesome, unearthly song of the humpback whale, in its manifold shades and modulations, with ominous pentatonic strains (of obvious Japanese inspiration); swelling, climaxing in confrontation and ultimate tragedy. Surprisingly, this effect seems not to have been intended. Throughout his work, prone to the seduction of Japanese styles of music, Hovhaness was apparently unaware of the drama he set up between Japanese whalers and their tragic victims. He wrote:

Pentatonic melody sounds openness of wide ocean sky. Undersea mountains rise and fall in horns, trombones and tuba. Music of whales also rises and falls like mountain ranges. Song of whale emerges like giant mythical sea bird. Man does not exist, has not yet been born in the solemn oneness of nature.[18]

Under the spell of developments in the International Whaling Commission, I hear the piece differently!

The composer who epitomizes the influence of the sea on music, in the broader context of the other arts (literature and painting), is Claude Debussy, whom Robert Godet defined as "an island, surrounded by water on all sides."[19] Debussy wrote of himself: "You

53

may not know that I was destined for a sailor's life and that it was only quite by chance that fate led me in another direction. But I always retained a passionate love for [the sea]."[20] Of his many major and minor works permeated by the sea, mimicking, reflecting the sea, certainly the most important, the culmination and synthesis, is *La Mer*. Harkening back to early impressions of the sombre North Atlantic and the more suave Mediterranean, this symphonic composition is articulated in three movements entitled *De l'aube à midi sur la mer, Jeux de vagues,* and *Dialogue du vent et de la mer* ("From dawn to noon at sea," "Play of waves," "Dialogue of the wind and the sea"). The last movement reflects, as one critic put it, "those ever delightful frolics in which [the sea] exhausts her divine energy, and the spell of foam and waves and spray, swirling mists and splashes of sunlight."[21] Music, as Baudelaire put it, ravishes you like the sea: *La musique souvent me prend comme une mer.*

We find music and the sea intimately linked in the writings of my father, Thomas Mann. Reminiscing on his childhood summers in the small Baltic town of Travemünde, he writes in an occasional essay,

In that place the sea and music entered a sentimental union in my heart, forever, and something was born of this union of feeling and ideas, and that is narrative, epic prose, Epic. For me, that always has been a concept closely linked to that of sea and music, in a way, composed of them, and as C.F. Meyer could say of his poetry that everywhere in it there was the great, calm light of the glaciers; so, I should think that the sea, its rhythm, its musical transcendence, somehow is present everywhere throughout my books – even then, often enough, when it is not mentioned explicitly. Yes, I should hope I have indicated my thankfulness to the sea of my childhood, the Bay of Lübeck. Maybe it was its palette that I used, and if my colours have been found opaque, without glow, abstemious – well, one may ascribe it to certain perspectives, through silvery beeches, to the pale pastels of sea and sky on which my eyes rested when I was a child and happy.[22]

Epic narrative, composed of sea and music! No wonder the annals of literature are as full of the oceans as those of painting and of music – from Homer and the Greek tragedians to Joseph Conrad, Baudelaire, Verlaine, Melville, Thomas Mann, and after. Religions have been the greatest inspirers of the arts. The ocean provides religious inspiration.

Although I was not conscious of it until much later, my father's love affair with the ocean must have influenced me powerfully. Rereading his works in my mature years, when I have myself become so deeply involved with the oceans, I find his analysis of the human relationship to nature, and specially the sea, the most profound I have come across. He recognized man's awe in face of the sea's infinity and wildness, in contrast to the constraints of civilization, both equally necessary and complementary; the sea as all and nothing, damnation and redemption, longing and fear; the sea as the dark and wild element within the artist, within his characters, within himself. "The sea," Mann wrote in another brief essay, was

Infinity! My love for the sea, whose enormous simplicity I have always preferred to the pretentious multifariousness of the mountains – my love for the sea is as old as my love for sleep, and I am fully aware of the common root of these two sympathies. I have within myself much that is Indian: a great deal of inert and heavy longing for that form or lack of form of perfection, called "Nirvana," or nought, and even though I am an artist, I have a rather unartistic inclination towards eternity, manifesting itself in an aversion against articulation and measure. What counteracts this inclination, believe me, is correction and discipline: or, to use a more serious term: it is morale ... What is morale? What is the morale of the artist?[23]

And on another occasion he wrote:

The sea is not landscape. It is the experience of eternity, of nothingness and death: a metaphysical dream; and the same wellnigh applies to the thin-aired regions of eternal snows. Sea and high mountains are not rural, not terrestrial; they are elementary in the sense of ultimate and savage, extra-human magnificence, and it would almost seem as though the civil, civic, urbane, bourgeois artist were inclined to skip over rural landscapishness and go directly for the elementary: for it is in the face of the elementary that he feels fully justified to confess and reveal his relationship to nature for what it really is, fear, alienation; illicit and wild adventure.

His feeling of awe, though tempered on many occasions, especially in *Travelling with Don Quixote*, by irony and self-irony, has no room for a utilitarian ocean: an ocean tamed to satisfy human needs, harnessed for progress:

It is nothing new to me that the sea, experienced from a ship, makes far less impression than experienced from the beach. The enthusiasm excited in me by the sacred crashing of its waves on the *terra firma* on which I stand, is lacking. There is a demystification. A spell is broken by the sobering of the element into the role of road, of highway for travellers. The ocean loses its character as spectacle, dream, idea, spiritual perspective on eternity, and it becomes "environment."[24]

What would Mann say to the raping of the ocean, its pollution by the penetration of the industrial revolution into its depth? How would he judge our attempts to cope with this new situation by imposing a new order on the oceans? Are not "order" and "oceans" antonyms in his grandiose perspective?[25]

There would be much room for irony over our "humanized ocean" but, in the last analysis, there could not be disapproval. For our humanizing efforts, our utilitarianism does not detract one whit from the concept of the enormity and wildness of the sea. It is not the oceans we want to dominate and regulate, it is human activities and human encroachment. The new ocean sciences do not demystify the oceans, just as the penetration of the universe by science does not diminish its mystery and majesty, and the greatest scientists often are the greatest mystics.

"I had a dream ..."

If the ocean has played an enormous role in the evolution of human life and culture, in the dreams of men, this influence is bound to grow in the coming period of history. Humankind is returning to the sea. Human dependence on the sea is increasing dramatically: for food, metals and minerals, energy.

We are likely to witness the transformation of a marine economy based on hunting and gathering (traditional fisheries) into one based on the cultivation of aquatic plants and the husbanding of aquatic animals. The emergence of aquaculture, including mariculture, may be a development no less important in anthropological, even evolutionary, terms than was the emergence of agriculture perhaps 10,000 years ago.

If it is true – as many technicians assert – that, in the long term, ocean mining of metals and minerals may be less expensive than land mining, while at the same time it offers other obvious advantages (such as the absence of conflict with competing land uses, less environmental impact, direct access to cheaper transportation), then we are likely to see a gradual shift from land-based mining to ocean mining. This is bound to cause displacements, internally within nations and between nations, but also to offer new opportunities and challenges.

Ocean energy resources – not only petroleum and natural gas, but the untapped, infinite, renewable, and non-polluting energy resources of the sea itself; the energy of tides and waves and currents, of thermal or salinity gradients, or of the huge and incredibly fast-growing biomass (kelp) of the sea – will make a major contribution to the satisfaction of the world's energy needs.

Be it on the basis of these economic-technological developments, be it on the foundation of immemorial dreams, or both, mankind has embarked on the task of building a new international economic order. This – not unlike the primeval earth in the dreams of men – appears to be emerging from the oceans. The adoption, in 1982, of the United Nations Convention on the Law of the Sea by an over-whelming majority of the international community, marks a break-through in this direction. Defective as it may be – and what is not defective in this world of ours? – and reflecting the dream of man only imperfectly, this convention offers a new platform to launch economic development, environmental conservation, and new efforts for peace.

In a final glance at the sea, at the sea of our dreams, we perceive the hoary concepts of ownership and sovereignty (on which the history of the last centuries was largely based) distorted and transformed in the reflection of teasing waves, broken up as in the scintillating col-ours of the Impressionists, the dissolved harmonies of Debussy. Now these concepts take the new form of the common heritage of man-kind, a notion transcending ownership and adding a new dimension to sovereignty: participation in common decision-making.

Based on the dream of common heritage, we see, emerging from the sea, a new "ecological consciousness," a different vision – new to us, though in some parts of the world ancient – of man's relationship to nature in general and to the sea in particular. All Eastern religions and mythologies, in fact, stress that everything on earth belongs to God; that the human being is a trustee and has to act according to God's will; that man has to harmonize his individual needs with those of society; that equity has to be attained through voluntary restraint in consumption. The Koran considers everything in nature as the common property of all creatures. Humanity's right to use natural resources is only in the sense of usufruct – which means the right to use another person's property on the understanding that we will not damage, destroy or waste what is in our trust. According to Islamic law the basic elements of nature such as land, water, air, fire, forests, sunlight, etc., were considered to be the common property of all – not only of all human beings, but of all creatures.

We see a vision of human evolution and history, not as confronta-tion with nature but as part of nature; not called by any god to subdue her, but led, by nature herself, to cooperate. This cooperation calls for interaction with nature, for cooperation among human beings. For the environment in general (not only the sea), both natural and social, is an extended mirror of man's soul. For better or worse, just as we perceive ourselves, so we see the world around, oceans and all.

Notes

1. This chapter is based on my essay, "The sea and the dreams of man," published by UNESCO, 1983, No. 3/4.
2. Bates, 1960.
3. Hardy, 1965.
4. Morven, 1980.
5. Saigal, forthcoming.
6. Saigal, *op. cit.*
7. Borgese, 1975.
8. Miller, 1966.
9. *Science* 279, 13 March 1998, "Ancient Island Tools Suggest *Homo erectus* Was a Seafarer."
10. Morven, *op. cit.*
11. Borgese, 1943.
12. See *The Ocean and the Agenda for Peace,* Paris: UNESCO/IOC, 1997.
13. Lockspeiser, 1962.
14. *Ibid.*
15. *Ibid.*
16. Vallas, 1967.
17. Newman, 1967.
18. A. Hovhaness, programme notes to *And God Created the Great Whales,* World Premiere Recording, Columbia Stereo Masterworks, M:30390.
19. Lockspeiser, *op. cit.*
20. Newman, 1967.
21. Lockspeiser, *op. cit.*
22. T. Mann, 1960.
23. T. Mann, "Süsser Schlaf," *op. cit.*
24. T. Mann, "Meerfahrt mit Don Quijote," Vol. IX, 1934.
25. For a recent, more complete analysis of Thomas Mann's relationship to the ocean, see E. Goebel, "Thomas Mann und das Meer," in *Mare,* I. 1. Hamburg: Dreiviertel Verlag, April, 1997.

3

Ocean perspectives: economic

"Ocean economics," obviously, is part of economics as a whole. But it is more than that. It is a source of concepts for shaping an economic framework for the next century. Human activities on the oceans or involving the oceans cannot be separated, in their impacts, from human activities on land, in the air, or in outer space; but the ocean forces us to think differently, to think anew.

The final decades of this twentieth century have witnessed the centrally planned economies becoming increasingly more dysfunctional; the economic system of the twenty-first century is likely to transcend the market system. The market system will still be there, but it will become more widely recognized as a sub-system. In "ocean economics," this has been anticipated with the adoption of the principle of the Common Heritage of Mankind. Branded as "socialism," or even "communism," by the conservative administrations of the United States and a number of other free-market countries, it is in fact as far removed from Karl Marx as it is from Adam Smith. It is neither a concept of private ownership nor one of state or world state ownership. It is a concept of non-ownership under which natural or legal persons have *user rights* and management prerogatives, but not ownership rights in the Roman Law sense. The Common Heritage principle has a fundamental ethical component: for both user rights and management prerogatives must be exercised with due consideration of the common good, which includes the rights of poor countries and poor people (intra-generational equity) as well as the rights of future generations with which it must be shared and for which it must be conserved (inter-generational equity). It has an economic development dimension, it has an environmental dimension, and it has a peace-building dimension: for, in the definition given by the Law of the Sea Convention, the Common Heritage of Mankind must be reserved for exclusively peaceful purposes.

The inclusion of resources that cannot be owned, as well as the inclusion of an ethical value system into economics, necessarily transcends an amoral market system. Add to this that the ocean – as, for that matter, the earth and heavens – is far more than an economic resource. It is, among other things, an essential part of our life support system, and indeed, of human "spirituality," dimensions which, I would submit, cannot be quantified or monetarized. Once we have included an ethical dimension into the economic system, market prices become less a dictator of policy and more a servant. Ethics cannot be translated into dollar terms, although they will certainly influence the direction of investments and consumer expenditures. Nor do ethics rule out the need to establish indicators in terms of welfare, happiness, efficiency (in a holistic sense) and "good" use of the oceans.

This chapter is organized under four main headings

1. First, the wealth of the ocean is described, and this is done in three sections. The first section, in table 3.1, presents an accounting of the total value of ocean-related or ocean-dependent goods and services, "Gross Ocean Product" (GOP), which can, at least in principle, be expressed in monetary terms. This GOP appears to be far larger than had been estimated in the past. By far the largest factors are sea-borne trade, which accounts for over 90 per cent of all international trade, and the explosive growth of ocean-related tourism, including cruise ship traffic. Another rapidly developing and staggeringly big factor is the undersea fibre optics cable industry. Not directly included are capital investments in ship construction, including tankers,[1] nor the huge amounts of funds involved in the insurance and counter-insurance industry.[2] While land-based (and drawing on "land-based resources,") they are obviously ocean-focused and ocean-dependent. Secondly, some indication is given of the market value of some of the new ocean industries likely to come to fruition in the next century; and thirdly, the value of the ocean as part of our life support system will be explored. It should be noted, however, that it is difficult to draw a sharp line between land-based and ocean-related or ocean-dependent industries.

2. An attempt has been made, under the second main heading, to

Table 3.1 **The economic impact of global marine industries**

Group	US$m	Activity	Economic impact (US$m)	Value added (US$m)	Value-added factor[1]
Oil and gas[2]	138,130	Natural gas	20,960	16,978	0.81
		Crude oil	117,170	94,908	0.81
		Total	138,130	111,886	
Ocean-related tourism[3]	423,000	Worldwide annual receipts	423,000	296,100	0.70
Sea-borne trade[4]	5,196,000	Total goods loaded	5,196,000	247,000	c. 0.05
Naval defence[5]	167,287	Navies	167,287	83,644	0.50
Fish[6]	183,535	Capture & culture	79,535	39,678	0.55
		Processing	100,000	21,000	0.21
		Seaweed	4,000	840	0.21
		Total	183,535	61,518	
Submarine telecoms[7] and fibre optics cables	1,000,000	Telephone service, internet	1,000,000	500,000	0.50
Ports and harbours[8]	?				
Marine tech. equipment[9]	?				
Coastal[10]	32,400	Construction	25,920	5,443	0.21
		Crossings	6,480	4,017	0.62
Environmental[11]	16,416	Waste disposal	14,976	5,391	0.36
		Survey	1,440	720	0.50
Safety and salvage[12]	9,984	Salvage	1,440	720	0.50
		Lighthouses	3,216	1,769	0.55
		Lifeboats	2,736	684	0.25
		Coastguards	2,592	648	0.25

Table 3.1 **(cont.)**

Group	US$m	Activity	Economic impact (US$m)	Value added (US$m)	Value-added factor[1]
Ocean-related education and training[13]	7,392		9,984	4,879	0.66
Marine research[14]	2,400	Marine research	2,400	1,584	0.66
Aggregates and placers[15]	756,000	Non-fuel minerals	756,000	196,560	0.26
		Submarine springs	365		
Fresh water[16]	11,965	Desalination	11,600	5,983	0.50
Tidal energy[17]	10,100	Annual estimated global potential	10,100	5,000	0.50
Total	7,198,609		7,198,609	1,706,230	

1. The adopted method of estimating the contribution of the marine sector to GDP has been based on the measurement of output values from each ocean sector activity, where the total output is then reduced by a value-added factor which varies between zero and one. The value-added factors are from J. Westwood and H. Young, 1997, *The Importance of Marine Industry Markets to National Economies*. Proceedings of the MTS/IEEE Oceans '97 Conference, Halifax, October 1997.
2. Data are based on the 1995 global offshore natural gas production of 35,892 million cu.ft./day and the 1995 average world price of US$1.60 per 1,000 cu.ft.; and the 1995 global offshore crude oil production of 19,200 billion barrels/day and the June 1997 average world price of US$16.72 per barrel. Sources: American Petroleum Institute and US Department of Energy, Energy Information Division. Value added is 81%.
3. Source: World Tourism Organization. The value added is 70% since this is a high labour-force industry.
4. Data are a 1996 estimate. The value of the goods (total output) is included in the 5,196 billion figure, so a value-added factor of less than 5% is used to reflect freight rates only. Source: Awni Behnam, UNCTAD, personal communication.
5. Naval expenditure is assumed to be 30% of the total 1996 world military expenditure of US$557,624m. (NATO military expenditure totalled $394,943m). Source: Stockholm International Peace Research Institute, 1997, *World Armaments and Disarmament: SIPRI Yearbook*. Cambridge, MA: MIT Press. The value added factor is 50%.

6. Capture and culture data is the 1995 estimated landed value less fresh-water production. Source: *FAO Yearbook Fishery Statistics: Commodities*, Vol 81. 1995. Processing data is the estimated world trade in marine fishery commodities. Seaweed data is from Westwood and Young (see note 1). The value added is 55% for capture and culture and 21% for processing and seaweed.

7. Data are based on 65% of the 1996 international telephone service revenue totaling US$69,000m, as 65% of international telecommunication traffic is carried by submarine cables. Sources: World Telecommunication Development Report 1996/97: *Trade in Telecommunications*, Executive Summary, International Telecommunication Union, Geneva, February 1997. On website ⟨http://www.itu.int⟩; and Westwood and Young (see note 1). A value-added factor of 50% is assumed for the manufacture and installation of cables. For the value of the submarine optic fibre industry, see *International Herald Tribune*, 10 March 1998, p.2, "A Wealth of Data on Ocean Floors," by Mike Mills.

8. According to the Tokyo-based International Association of Ports and Harbours, no system exists for valuing the economic impact of ports and harbours globally. The following figures may be indicative of orders of magnitude. The American Association of Port Authorities provides the following figures for 1994: 15.9 million jobs; a contribution of US$783.3bn to GDP; personal incomes of US$515.1bn; tax revenues at all levels of US$210bn; and business sales of US$1.623trn. Ninety-five per cent by weight of all US foreign trade moves through US ports. Rotterdam estimates that the port creates 70,000 jobs directly and 295,000 indirectly. For small countries like the Netherlands, Singapore, and formerly Hong Kong, their wealth is directly dependent on their port activities. The Canadian Ports Corporation gives the following summary of Canada's port system in 1990: 36,872 direct jobs; 28,876 induced jobs; 65,748 total jobs. Revenue impact: CA$5.7bn personal income impact: CA$3.2bn; tax impact: CA$1.2bn.

9. Marine and ocean technology is a difficult sector to estimate due to the lack of data relating specifically to *marine* equipment, since much equipment is produced with the manufacturer being unaware of its end use. Globally this sector generates billions of dollars in revenue.

10. The revenues in this sector have been extrapolated from the UK marine economy revenues calculated by Westwood and Young (see note 1). British revenues in this sector were converted to US dollars by the conversion of 1 £ = 1.6 US$ and multiplied by 30. Since the global monetarized marine GDP of US$1.5trn is approximately 30 times the UK marine GDP of US$44bn, this approach provides a reasonable approximation of the value this sector contributes to the global marine economy.

11. Borgese, 1986.

12. ibid.

13. ibid.

14. ibid.

15. Data are the production value at 1993 and 1994 year prices. Sources: Fillmore Earney. 1990. *Marine Mineral Resources*; David Cronan. 1992. *Marine Minerals in Exclusive Economic Zones*; Natural Resources Canada. 1995. *Canadian Minerals Yearbook*; US Bureau of Mines. 1995. *Minerals Yearbook*. A value added of 26% is assumed.

16. Data are the potential production in 1997 based on 2 million cu.m./day from submarine springs and 20.3 million cu.m./day from desalination, assuming an average cost of $0.50/cu.m. The desalination figure was provided by J.D. Birkett, West Neck Strategies, Maine.

17. Data are based on a potential 64 Gw global capacity × 8,760 h/yr × 20% efficiency producing 112,128 Gwh/yr, and uses the 1997 price of 1 Gw/h = $90,000. The site at La Rance, France, is a 240 Mw facility. The Annapolis Royal 20 Mw facility in Nova Scotia generates 2.5 Gwh/month (30 Gwh/yr), with annual revenue of CA$2.7m.

explore what might be appropriate indicators for assessing the real wealth of the oceans. There is a vast literature on social and environmental indicators today, but this literature concentrates on the terrestrial economy. The oceans have been sadly neglected, no doubt largely because they are not "owned by nations."

3. Under the third main heading, the chapter deals with the ethical or spiritual dimension of the emerging economics of sustainable development – in the oceans as a case study – which, however, would be applicable more generally. As Paul Wapner points out,

> While scholars of international relations have written on a wide range of topics – from environmental security and international environmental cooperation to the degree to which global environmental problems raise new challenges for international law – it is curious that they have generally failed to raise, in a sustained manner, issues of moral duty, principled understandings of appropriate conduct, or simply the challenge of moral deliberation as it relates to the causes of and responses to transnational environmental issues.[3]

The motto over his essay is a quote from Immanuel Kant: "A true system of politics cannot take a single step without first paying tribute to morality!"

4. In conclusion, the chapter will try to deduce some fundamental principles and practical guidelines from the previous sections.

The economic impact of global marine industries

Above, in table 3.1, is a detailed examination of the economic impact of these industries, with a comprehensive list of explanatory notes.

The total market value of ocean-related and ocean-dependent industries would appear, on the basis of the data in table 3.1, to be over 7 trillion US dollars per annum. This, it must be emphasized, is a "financial/product flow" or annual output number. As in the case of GNP, it is not a "stock" or "asset" number: the latter would be a somewhat meaningless estimate, since we still know so little about the wealth of the ocean. Moreover, without the oceans for the transport of land-produced products, trade would be significantly reduced and many of the benefits of international specialization would be lost.

Futuristic industries: quantifiable

The market value of the goods and services based on twenty-first century science and technology is yet more difficult to predict.

Table 3.2 **Sample pharmaceuticals and bioactive marine resources**

Class of organism	Example organism	Bioactive substance	Uses actual & potential	Comments
Tunicates Caribbean, Gulf of California, Medi-terranean	*Aplydium albicans*	Didermin B	Antiviral, anthelmintic, activity against leukemia & melanoma, ovary, breast, kidney, colorectal cancer	Potently antiproliferative, impressive cytotoxicity against lymphomas
Bryozoans	*Bugula neritina*	Bryostatin	Anti-tumour, anti-leukemia, anti-AIDS	
Echinoderms sea urchins, sea cucumbers	*Strongylocentrotus* sp *Holothurians* sp		Male contraceptive	
Nudibranches Guam, Marshall Islands, Australia	*Chromodoris elizabethiana*	Iatrunculin A	Antimicrobial (staph-ylococcus and candida)	
sea squirts	*Ecteinascidia turbinata*		Antineoplastic (cancer tumour)	"Striking," "remarkable," organism widely available
Fungi	*Cephalosporium acremonium*	Cephalosporin C	Antimicrobial	
Corals origin: Bahamian type: Gorgonian	*Pseudopterogorgia elisabethae*	pseudopterosin C	psoriasis and arthritis	"Resilience" (TM) skin care (Estée Lauder)
Hawaian coral skeletal coral	*Telesto riisei*		anti-cancer bone grafts	Remarkable cytotoxicity Provides "natural" structure
Fish and shellfish puffer fish		tetrodoxin	muscle spasms, palliative in terminal cancer	Traditional usage in the Orient

Table 3.2 **(cont.)**

Class of organism	Example organism	Bioactive sub-stance	Uses actual & potential	Comments
angler fish				Possible tissue rejection and organ transplant studies
Crustaceans horseshoe crab	*Limulus polyphemus*	crab blood	coagulant, detect meningitis and septic shock bacteria	
Molluscs squid		axon studies	nerve cell skeleton studies	Parkinson's and Alzheimer's, epilepsy
blue mussel (edible)	*Mytilus edulis*	adhesives	cornea and retina repair, dental work	
sea hare Indian Ocean	*Dolabella auricularia*	dolastatin-10	anti-tumour, melanoma	high life extension for patients at low dose levels
Algae Porphyra "red seaweeds"				Possible activity irrespective of depth or latitude of source organism
Japan	*Halichondria okadai*	Halichondrin B	Ovarian cancer, melanoma, leukemia	Very promising anti-cancer drug
New Zealand Palau Caribbean	*Ircinia variabilis* *Luffariella variabilis*	Manoalide Cytarabine	Antibiotic, antiviral Analgesic, anti-inflammatory Antiviral	"Bee stings to arthritis"
Bahamas	*Discodermia dissoluta*	Discodermolide	Immunosuppressive	Organ transplant tissue anti-rejection
chondrus crispus (Irish moss)	*Chondrus* sp	Carrageenan	Anti-peptic, anti-ulcer	
	Digenea simplex	Kainic acid	Anti-parasitic	

Brown (laminarians)	Stypropodium sp Laminaria sp		Anti-tumour, hypotensive, anti-fungal, anticoagulant, cervical dilation (physical, not chemical action)
Diatoms and dinoflagellates	Nitzschia sp	Domoic acid et al.	Central nervous system studies
	Dysidea sp	"Iolide pump"	Helpful in understanding thyroid action

Source: W. Irwin Judson, "Marine Pharmaceuticals: A Special Case of the Common Heritage of Mankind," unpublished.

Marine biotechnology is still in its infancy. It is a well-protected baby, growing rapidly in the secrecy of highly competitive, mostly private industries. New discoveries are being made daily, mostly in tropical seas, although bioactive substances may be present in the flora and fauna of colder waters as well. Thousands of substances have been identified thus far, and financial rewards for developing even one successful product can be considerable. Many sources cite potential sales of US$1 billion or more annually for a successful product, particularly if it is an antiviral or anti-cancer drug. The antiviral compounds Ara-A and Ara-C, derived originally from a Caribbean tunicate, have been used for a number of years in the treatment of herpes, and currently maintain sales of US$50–100 million a year.

Besides its multi-billion-dollar economic potential, this new industry has complex political, legal, institutional, and ethical implications if it is to be adapted to the goals of sustainable development. To this we shall return in the final chapters of this volume.

A special case is constituted by the industrial utilization of the genetic resources, in particular the thermophile bacteria, of the deep seabed. The industries utilizing this genetic resource are more extensive than the pharmaceutical industry. They comprise waste treatment, food processing, oil-well services, paper processing, and mining applications, together with the pharmaceutical industries. From another aspect, the case is more limited as it is restricted to the deep sea-bed. The potential market for industrial uses of hyperthermophilic bacteria has been estimated at US$3 billion per year.[4]

In his carefully documented paper Glowka continues:

Hyperthermophilic bacteria are just one example of the commercial potential of microbial genetic resources from the Area; as research continues, other commercially interesting organisms may also be discovered. For example, there may be organisms that orchestrate processes for minerals transport and bioaccumulation of metals. These could be useful in bioremediation of hazardous waste. Other organisms could be useful in biomining applications. Viruses associated with the organisms of the Area, in particular hyperthermophilic bacteria, may provide new vectors useful in biotechnological applications. Researchers may also be able to isolate potential anticancer and antibiotic compounds from deep seabed bacteria or fungi associated with other macroorganisms, as they have in more accessible areas of the ocean. In short, the biodiversity of the seabed has hardly been explored, and we simply do not know what may exist.[5]

The present and future value of these resources can be gauged by the brazen intransigence with which the United States, in particular, under pressure from its bio-industries, is keeping the item off the agenda of the meetings of states parties to the Biodiversity Convention, even though it is not even a party to this convention!

A third example of industries likely to considerably increase the "quantifiable" contribution of the ocean to the global GDP is the production of renewable energy from the ocean. Turbines to extract a tiny portion of the enormous amount of energy produced by ocean currents – updating projects that were on the drawing board 20 or 30 years ago – are in the headlines today. Tests recently conducted on the Florida Current (part of the Gulf Stream) have demonstrated that a 1-megawatt unit could be built for just under $3,000/kilowatt and that the power from this unit could be supplied at a rate of $0.085/kWh.[6] Ocean Thermal Energy Conversion, also long on the drawing boards, is still considered to have great potential. The market for this technology, in the Pacific and Caribbean, is estimated to be, by the year 2015, about US$18.5 billion a year.

No figures at all are as yet available for the methane hydrates of the deep sea-bed which may become another source of energy during the next century. During recent years, the US Geological Survey has stressed the importance of the methane hydrates of the deep sea, describing them as "a new frontier." "The worldwide amounts of carbon bound in gas hydrates is conservatively estimated to total twice the amount of carbon to be found in all known fossil fuels on earth."[7] A great deal of research is being devoted to these hydrates, in the USA and in other industrial countries, and fascinating futuristic scenarios are already on the table. Dillon writes:

For example, fuel cells eventually might be placed on the sea floor to use hydrate-derived methane as an energy source to generate hydrogen, which could be piped ashore to support a nonpolluting, hydrogen-based energy distribution system and the waste carbon dioxide might be disposed of as a sea-bottom gas hydrate (carbon dioxide also forms gas hydrate at sea-floor conditions).[8]

Hydrates are considered a future source of energy as well as a threat to the environment.[9]

From the above we can speculate that the annual "Gross Oceanic Product" could double, in real terms, over the next century.

The ocean as life support system: non-quantifiable

Disciples of the market system have made very interesting attempts in recent years to define, and express in monetary terms, the "eco-system services" performed by the oceans and other eco-systems. A group led by Robert Costanza has come up with the figure of some US$30 trillion for 17 categories of "goods and services"[10] – including protection against storms and floods, nitrogen fixation, or plant-derived pharmaceuticals – provided by 16 specialized "biomes," such as oceans, estuaries, tropical forests, etc. The calculation was based on a "witches' brew" of market prices, people's estimated willingness to pay, and the cost of replacing services. Considering the size of the ocean and coastal system, and the intensity of its interaction with the atmosphere, it is not surprising that US$21 trillion of that amount was estimated to be contributed by it.

Costanza's calculations have been widely criticized. A Cornell University ecologist, David Pimentel, and his colleagues argued that the figure is far too high. According to their estimate, these "goods and services" amount to no more than US$3 trillion.[11] The mere fact that such calculations may diverge by such orders of magnitude must make us wonder if such efforts at measurement could ever become of practical value. But the same thing, of course, was said of GNP measures in the early days of national accounting. Such magnitudes may not be helpful of themselves but they can provide frameworks for important questions on further definitions of "ocean economics." For example, from the work on GNP there came recognition of the importance of social factors in generating output (e.g., education's impact on productivity, quality of life measures, etc.). Then the United Nations pioneered the Human Development Index. As will be indicated, this touches on the ocean environment, but considerably more work will be needed. The essential question must focus on "sustainability." In the case of fisheries, resources, quite blatantly, are not sustainable – given the way they have been used: "guided" by the market system. Moreover, the current "contribution" of US$42 billion to the global GDP does not take into account the US$52 billion which, according to FAO, is paid annually in subsidies to the fishing industries globally; nor does it recognize stock depletion (from whatever causes). It does not take into account the impacts of over-investment in high-tech fishing vessels, large trawlers, and factory ships on debt-ridden countries, where the pressure of debt repayment is forcing fleet owners to deplete stocks more and more; and that stock depletion, for whatever complex reasons, makes us poorer in the longer term, albeit richer in the very short term. Giarini's model, measuring stocks rather than flows and taking into account not only gross value added but also deducted value, i.e., genuine net value added, is more responsive to contemporary reality.

As Giarini put it,[12] when the essence of the process in wealth production is centred around the *sustained performance of a system*, then the value of maintenance activities (particularly those related to the control of vulnerabilities within the functioning system as well as the management of risks) can be of critical importance. In a conventional cost-benefit framework, they will, of course, be factored in as costs. But will they be costed in a manner that makes provision for "lumpy" future (longer-term) cost elements – e.g., eventual decommissioning of a nuclear power plant – or will they only estimate shorter-term "operational and initial capital recovery costs?" The need to manage risks and vulnerabilities becomes an additional reason for designing complex systems in a manner and at a level at which risks can be spread in an optimum way.

It is clear that the problems linked to the correct valuation and operations of longer-term risk management of the oceans are key elements in our efforts to protect the ocean environment against pollution and depletion. It is here that we encounter fundamental questions linked to the preservation and development of the oceans as a fundamental life resource.

In sum, the necessity of integrating monetarized and non-monetarized values implies an integration of the economic *and* the ecological view of the notion of value. This, in the new perspectives of the service economy, provides a new approach to the question of measuring and managing the common heritage of mankind as represented by the oceans.

Ocean-related indicators

Our first Report to the Club of Rome[13] concluded its discussion on the "economics of the common heritage" with the following recommendations:

A great deal of research will be needed in this new field on, for example, the need for and the cost of subregional, national, regional, and global services. Research will also be needed on deducted values arising from negative synergisms of conflicting uses of ocean space and resources; from present technological gigantism, risk management, and pollution economics; and from conflicts between military and peaceful uses of the marine sector of the economy. In addition, investigators must examine the utilization value of services provided and production created (for example, by aquaculture facilities and technologies, mining ships and technologies and OTEC plants); the generation of secondary and subsidiary industries (e.g., canning, construction, pharmaceuticals, petrochemicals, land-based transportation); and above all, *how to define a set of usable social indicators that will properly assess and monitor the generation of real wealth.* The latter research would help point out inadequate economic policies and organize actions toward specific as well as general goals. It should be a feasible exercise to select the most adequate indicators, even considering the delicate political problems likely to be encountered in gaining their acceptance. A recognized institute could then issue periodic verifications of the changes brought about in the level of wealth, with reference to the indicators, and stimulate the appropriate actions.

A great deal of work on social and environmental indicators has been done since the writing of these recommendations. It is deplorable, however, and almost beyond belief that most of this work has concentrated on terrestrial systems and activities. The oceans have been sadly neglected. In this section we are trying to contribute to closing this lacuna.

Indicators in fact are needed to perform measurements of monetarized and non-monetarized resources in a more comprehensive theory of wealth and welfare, rooted in the concept of the Common Heritage of Mankind.

Traditionally, indicators are defined as information which (a) is a part of a specific management process and can enable comparisons of results to be made over time and between policies; and (b) has been assigned a significance beyond its face value. Indicators can be developed (and distinguished) from general-purpose statistics that have important applications in their own right, and then be used for problem-solving of given issues.

This section presents in the first part ongoing initiatives relevant to ocean-related indicators, discusses in the second part gaps in ocean-related indicators, and explores in the third part the validity of ocean-related indicators in the light of the new economics of the Common Heritage of Mankind. Conclusions round up the analysis.

Ongoing initiatives about ocean-related indicators

We call the explicit development of indicators "indicator movement."

Greener national accounts are being developed in a variety of

In considering ocean indicators, one might start by reflecting on indicators in general – on how they are arrived at and on what is done with them. Four axioms might launch the discussion:

1. *Indicators follow theories.* We do not count pebbles on a beach or sheep in a field without some rationale – even if the rationale might be as flimsy as "it will help put one to sleep!"

2. *Indicators do not have to be numbers.* In a numerate world that might sound unorthodox. But it does serve to remind us that not everything can be tidily measured and turned into dollar signs, weights, or other quantifiable dimensions. Just as snow can have many names and characteristics to an Inuit, so the ocean has many colours and sends many signals to a Bajo fisherman in rural Sulawesi. The more mechanized we become, the more readily we lose sight of the messages of non-numerical indicators.

3. *Data awaits human insights to recognize their shapes and to interpret their meanings.* Data, of themselves, can signify much. To an animist, the sound of rain on a rock or the colour of a stream bed might evoke concepts of gods or demons, of spirits past or future. To a geologist, those same sounds and sights can suggest gold or copper, iron-ore or coal within the rock face.

4. *Indicators are, in a world of some uncertainty, frequently couched within frameworks of probability.* The likelihood of an individual having a disease, when particular measures of heat, blood contents, or visual characteristics fall within such and such a range, might be 20 per cent or 50 per cent or whatever...

Over time the importance of particular indicators has changed. The significance of the sighting of Haley's comet is considerably different today than was the case at its first recorded sighting. Knowledge can reduce uncertainties: but it can also limit a more holistic understanding of life. Who is to suggest that a modern composer can plumb the emotional or spiritual depths of a Beethoven or Mozart? Could a Leonardo da Vinci have ever emerged in twentieth-century North America?

The oceans remain a realm of the still largely unknown.

One of the accomplishments of twentieth-century humanity has been the delineation of a number of land-bases shapes, albeit very imperfectly and haphazardly. National accounts provide some shape to the size and broad past behaviour of nation states in the context of production and consumption – at least when such activities fall within a market place that allots prices or weights. The Human Development Index, despite many limitations, parallels the GNP indicators in the context of "human welfare." The oceans are practically ignored. They rarely fall into nation states – they fringe them; they rarely, indeed are treated "in their own rights" but almost always as adjuncts: as if their claims for recognition were directly dependent on land-oriented policies.

Ian McAllister

shapes and forms and deserve attention by consumers and producers of indicators alike. They are being built upon the legacy of traditional national accounts, but are extending the framework to respond to the challenges of "sustainable development." Similarly, attempts to take into account social and environmental factors through cost-benefit analysis and environmental impact assessment (CBA/EIA) brought about a development of methodologies and applications useful to the indicator movement.

Descriptive indicators
In his Report to the Club of Rome, Giarini[14] introduces Dowry and Patrimony, that is, the global stock of wealth, as a combination of natural (e.g., physical and biological) and man-made (e.g., cultural, human skills and "man-enriched" capital). Similarly, the United Nations Commission on Sustainable Development distinguishes social, economic, environmental and institutional aspects of sustainable development.[15] Uncertainty and changing values have to be factored into assessments of each component of sustainable development. In shorthand, we call these parameters "the SEEIU (*Social, economic, environmental, institutional, uncertainty*) dimensions."

Social indicators
Social indicators for large series of countries are elaborated and routinely presented by the UNDP, e.g., in its Human Development Report and by the World Bank, e.g., in its World Development Report.[16]

UNDP's Human Development Report (described in the box below) specifies a number of welfare indicators and brings them together into a Human Development Index. These are meant to measure the social and economic situations in some 175 countries and to enable country comparisons to be made.

Human Development Indicators inevitably must have some relevance to the use and health of the oceans. The same is true for indicators such as GDP/GNP. Thus the aggregate levels of a nation's output will often give some proxy indication of the pollution that is likely to pour down its rivers, the pressures on fish stocks, the volume of international transoceanic trade, and so on. Employment and unemployment indicators can give an indication of how seriously environmental factors, likely to impinge on the oceans, may be taken. (In times of high unemployment, environmental protection groups tend to be marginalized by groups promoting growth and higher

UNDP's Human Development Report with the Human Development Index (HDI)

UNDP's Human Development Report, annually published since 1990, presents Human Development Indicators and the Human Development Index for each of 175 countries, for some aggregates (regional, developing and industrial countries, North-South, rural-urban) and for the world as a whole; also, efforts towards further subnational disaggregations are ongoing.

The set of over 200 Human Development indicators concerns the human development/deprivation profile, wealth, and economic performance.

The Human Development Index reflects achievements towards a long and healthy life, knowledge, and a decent standard of living. Initially, descriptive steps are produced for the country's estimates for life expectancy, educational attainment (depending on adult literacy and school enrolment), and GDP per capita (adjusted for the local cost of living and for the diminishing utility of higher levels of income). In the following normative steps, minima and maxima identical for every country are stipulated in each of three components; each country's descriptive indicators are then compared to the corresponding minima; finally, the previously obtained measures are put into relation with the new ones, i.e. with the corresponding difference between the two extremes. The resulting dimensionless relative values then indicate how far that country already has gone towards the attainment of certain defined goals: the closer its indicators are to 1, the shorter is the remaining distance that country has yet to travel. Finally, a simple average combines the three dimensionless indicators into one single HDI.

The HDI accounts for the social and the economic dimension. Proposals to include material weight of economies, to adjust existing components of the HDI, or to construct an all-new Green Index to stand alongside the HDI would introduce an environmental dimension.

Source: UNDP, 1997.

employment "at any cost.") Land-use and income distribution data, urban population densities in coastal cities, annual marine fish catches and numbers and size of protected areas – such indicators provide clues to the intensity of use and abuse of the oceans and ocean resources.

For other variables, such as life expectancy, the linkage with ocean development may be less direct, but even in such numbers clues may be encountered. For small island developing states (SIDS), the social and economic situation can centrally be a result of ocean development (or non-development); for them, almost all nationwide social and economic indicators are "ocean-related." Large coastal countries like Argentina or Canada, on the other hand, depend for much of their social and economic development on interior land resources as well as on marine activities. For them, indicators such as GDP and life expectancy will impinge less heavily on the oceans, albeit many interior mined or manufactured products find their ways across the oceans through international trade arrangements. Large countries must develop meaningful ways for disaggregating economic and social indicators in a manner that will show their impact on the oceans.

Economic indicators

Ocean-related goods and services fall into many categories. Thus, for example:
- offshore oil, gas and non-fuel minerals;
- man-made capital (built infrastructure such as ports and harbours, ships, oil-rig installations);
- sea-borne trade, services and institutions; and
- coastal and marine-associated tourism.

Such factors were referred to in the previous section reporting production (flow) estimates. We now turn to considerations about stocks and their impacts.

Global data on energy and mineral reserves are regularly compiled by specialized institutions including the World Energy Council, the International Energy Agency, the US Bureau of Mines and the World Bureau of Metal Statistics.

Offshore reserves and their depletion (or growth) are not, however, identified in the major data reports (nor in the two sustainability indicators about fossil fuel energy and mineral reserves proposed by UN-CSD; see below). Stock of built infrastructure should, in principle, be embedded (over time) in the national accounts and capital depreciation/accumulation processes should also be detectable (but far from readily). Input-output matrices provide indications of inter-industry flows, and specialized publications (e.g. *OECD Maritime Transport* for the world fleet and FAO yearbooks for the fishery fleet) provide further pieces of the complicated and far from fully understood picture.

Environmental indicators

Environmental indicators reflect stock and/or flow realities of marine resources, with man-made and natural additions and deductions

76

(flows) modifying the initial into a final stock. As with economic indicators, stock has a quantity and a quality aspect: such as size of species population and contaminants in fish. Flows result from *"uses"*, e.g. sustainable harvesting, and *"abuses"* of natural resources, i.e. over-exploitation of renewable and depletion of non-renewable resources; pollution resulting in environmental expenditures and non-compensated economic costs; as well as loss of ecological functions and immaterial welfare (e.g., damage to landscape and cultural patrimony).

Overall, the UNDP/CSD indicator menu lists approximately 130 indicators used in the UN-CSD proposal for sustainability indicators, and the Core Data Sets Matrix, some 170 parameters/data sets used for the first UNEP Global Environmental Outlook (GEO-1[17]). Of the latter, about 30 can be considered social and 40 economic indicators; this leaves about 100 environmental indicators; of these we consider up to one-quarter being ocean-related, more than half terrestrial and the remaining quarter general (climate, institutional support).

As recalled in the previous section, sea water is used for desalination and for producing renewable energy from the ocean (including tidal energy for the production of electricity). Indicators of bathing quality, metal content and coastal marine water quality, litter in marine environment (quality of stock) reflect pollution through dumping, discharges and, as proposed by UNDP/CSD, releases of nitrates, phosphates and oil discharges; GESAMP offers an overview over the respective and more general indicators.[18]

Within our category of natural areas, small islands indicators are reported *inter alia* in UNEP's Island Directory[19] and in UNDP's Small Island Developing States Network. Interesting in the present context also is UNEP's Barbados Programme of Action for Small Island Developing States (SIDS), to be fully reviewed in 1999. Besides the length of coasts (stock quantity), GEO-1[20] gives estimates about pollution and the resulting stock quality. The Barbados International Coral Reef Initiative for small islands may complement existing data about reef disturbances and reef uses. As for protected parks and reserves, the standard inventories (IUCN, WCMC) identify marine sites and are the basis of a proposed sustainability indicator (stock quantity).[21]

GEO-1 reporting on flora, including mangrove loss, and an algae index, proposed as a sustainability index, concern stock quantity. Algae Catch (World Resources Institute: flow) relate to the uses for pharmaceuticals/food mentioned in the previous section. A sustainability indicator for threatened species as a percentage of total native species is proposed for vascular plants and vertebrate species; however, no distinction between marine and terrestrial is mentioned (IUCN, World Conservation Monitoring Centre).

Other sources for fauna include the UNEP/FAO Marine Mammal Action Plan and the International Whaling Commission. For fish and other marine animals, estimates for stock quantity, stock quality (contaminants), catch and accidental kills (mainly FAO, including mariculture) are available. The UN-CSD list includes an indicator for maximum sustainable yield for fisheries.

Some indicators exist already for taxonomic, genetic, ecosystem, and environmental function diversity including threatened and endemic species, protected areas, and percentage of developed coast. The Global Biodiversity Forum's Dialogue on Biodiversity Indicators and Implementation Targets should provide impetus for a systematic treatment within the implementation of the Biodiversity Convention. UNEP's Biodiversity Programme and Implementation Strategy gives priority to marine biodiversity, included in SIDS.[22]

Uncertainty

"Owing to the complexity of the mechanisms that affect biological capacity and fish populations, estimates of commercial fish stocks are uncertain at the present time."[23] This statement in UNEP's latest Environmental Data Report recalls the "limits to certainty" inherent in every indicator or index, be it descriptive of the present state or future-oriented.

Uncertainties exist: with regard to the measurements and resulting statistical data, the causal relations, and the models used to represent reality; and no probabilities can be calculated and assigned to outcomes. Therefore a vulnerability index may be developed and merged with the more traditional social, economic, and environmental indicators. Thus the UN Department of Economic and Social Affairs (DESA) has initiated work on the development of a Vulnerability Index in support of the Programme of Action for the sustainable development of SIDS and has suggested that an economic vulnerability index and an ecological vulnerability index be constructed. Already in its Island Directory[24] UNEP has proposed an index for important islands at risk, underlining the importance of marine conservation, human impact, and data reliability. More recently, Briguglio[25] addressed the issue of SIDS, in an attempt to quantify factors enhancing their economic vulnerability (dependence on external economic conditions, remoteness and insularity, disaster proneness). On this basis he attempted to construct a composite index of vulnerability. For one out of three analysed SIDS, the switch from the present GDP-based ranking to the ranking based on the vulnerability-adjusted development index would have immediate conditionality effects. In another example, vulnerability to anthropogenic change of tropical coastal ecosystems was calculated as a function of GNP per capita and population density, and the resulting normalized vulnerability index was plotted against a normalized resource abundance index for mangroves, sea grasses, and coral reefs.[26]

Indicators for sustainable development

Agenda 21 emphasizes the need for indicators in chapter 40, requesting the United Nations system to create, with other relevant organizations, a set of indicators reflecting developments towards sustainability. Subsequently, the UN Commission on Sustainable Development adopted a Work Programme on Indicators of Sustainable Development, whose primary purpose is to make internationally consistent ISDs accessible to decision makers at the national level. On an international level, it is especially the Department for Policy Coordination and Sustainable Development (UN-DPCSD) of the UN Division for Sustainable Development which is dealing with this issue. A provisional core set of ISDs was published in 1996 with the approval of the Commission on Sustainable Development under the title *Indicators of Sustainable Development – Framework and Methodologies.*[27] Preparatory activities of the UNEP/EAP Environment Assessment Programme in this ISD process included an overview of environmental indicators (1994), a SCOPE-Belgian-Costa Rican workshop held in January 1995 in Ghent, and the SCOPE scientific workshop on ISDs in Wuppertal, Germany, of November 1995.

In the published core set of ISDs the dimensions are social, economic, environmental, and institutional; although holistic, the approach does not include moral/ethical/spiritual sustainability, defining acceptable behaviour and motivating people to act in the common interest. Descriptive methodology sheets for every ISD (with no estimates for the time being) are presented according to the dimensions, the chapters of *Agenda 21*, and the indicator type (driving force, state, or response indicator).

In principle, an ISD results from the national descriptive indicator discussed earlier in this section, from the corresponding international

sustainability target (e.g., the critical stock or level of a coastal resource) and from comparison between the two. Environmental targets or limits may have an objective, scientific basis; social and economic targets/limits are much more value-loaded and hence subject
to each society's concepts, goals, and values. This may explain why,
for most of the indicators, international targets are not yet available.

A dozen ISDs can concern ocean development, such as indicators
about income inequality, the environmentally adjusted net domestic
product EDP, mineral reserves, fossil fuel reserves, lifetime of proven
energy reserves, population growth in coastal areas, discharge of oil,
nitrates, and phosphates into coastal waters, maximum sustainable
yield for fisheries, existence of algae, threatened species, and protected areas. Within this dozen ocean-related indicators, one is
expressed in monetary terms, namely EDP. Targets are defined for
only three: for sustainable yield for fisheries, for threatened species,
and for the protected areas. Finally, one third of the ocean-related
ISDs are "under development" altogether. This reminds us of the
fact that the CSD core set of ISDs still is in development.

Other relevant initiatives
Greener national accounts, functions of nature (ecosystem services)
services and cost-benefit analysis support the indicator movement in
several ways.

GREENER NATIONAL ACCOUNTS At a conference at the European
Parliament, the Club of Rome and WWF-International called for
a modification of the UN System of National Accounts (SNA)[28]
framework and boundaries leading to a new, nature-adjusted single
measure, incorporating the value of nature's resources and services.[29]
Satellite accounts offer a mid-way solution in that without modifying
the SNA they complement it with estimates of stocks of natural
resources, environmental non-market services, and damages due to
economic activity. In its Satellite System for Integrated Environmental and Economic Accounting (SEEA), UNSTAT[30] offers a menu of
five alternative versions, Version IV being concerned with satellite
accounts. Pilot country applications of parts of SEEA exist, for
example, for Colombia, Mexico, Papua New Guinea, and Thailand.

Ocean-related explorations of greener accounts include:
– accounting for the depletion of natural resources: e.g. the World
  Bank's Genuine Saving (output minus net depletion of natural
  resources);

- estimates in several developing and industrial countries for offshore minerals and oil; for the recreational value of marine resources; for wetlands, mangroves, and marine wilderness areas; for fishery and national patrimony;
- more adequate treatment of "defensive" expenditures: in Germany in general and in Mexico for environmental protection services; in half a dozen industrial countries the development of an Index of Sustainable Economic Welfare (ISEW) covering, *inter alia*, costs of pollution and non-renewable natural resource depletion; and
- accounting for the degradation of environmental quality; e.g., of the Yellow Sea off Korea with oil spills and hazardous substances, of the Chesapeake Bay due to herbicide pollution.

The UN Satellite System for Integrated Economic and Environmental Accounting can also be used to calculate linkage environmental indicators. In a pilot study for 11–13 developing and industrial countries, the World Resources Institute formulated a macroeconomic Index of Resource Depletion measuring the value of the decline in natural resource stocks relative to the value of gross investment in man-made capital during the given year. The Institute also produced a disaggregated Resource Depletion Index for the agriculture-forestry-fisheries sector measuring the ratio of the SEEA environmentally adjusted domestic product combined to the standard GDP for these resource sectors.[31]

Green accounting supports the indicator movement by generating relevant quantitative data and methodologies, representing the linkage between economy and environment on which to base macroeconomic indicators, offering the input needed to develop environmental ISDs. Hence it is not surprising that countries including Finland, France, the Netherlands, and the United Kingdom are integrating, in one way or another, the efforts towards greener national accounts and the generation of indicators in practical applications.

FUNCTIONS OF NATURE It is in line with the present context of the Common Heritage of Mankind concept and the modern service economy to consider the studies dealing with functions of nature as further initiatives helpful to the indicator movement. Costanza's attempt to measure the "ecosystem services" performed by the oceans has already been mentioned in the previous section. Here, attention is drawn to the system of some 50 functions of the natural environment developed by de Groot.[32] They are grouped in regulation functions for essential ecological processes and life support systems, carrier functions providing space and a substrate or medium for human activities, production functions covering the provision of many resources, and information functions offering opportunities for reflection, spiritual enrichment, cognitive development, and aesthetic experience.

De Groot has applied this system to the Galapagos National Park (table 3.3) and the Dutch Wadden Sea. Other ocean-related applications include regulation functions (e.g. waste treatment services provided by wetlands compared to restoring a wetland); nursery function of estuaries and wetlands; primary productivity of some coastal marshes supporting offshore commercial and recreational fishing industries; carrier functions (the value of wildlife-related recreational activities; in Canada they exceed by far the economic value of sport fishing or hunting); production functions (the contribution of wildlife to the US economy, including fisheries, biological diversity, ecological services, recreation, and marine medicinal resources).

COST-BENEFIT ANALYSIS AND ENVIRONMENTAL IMPACT ASSESSMENT Over the past decade, significant progress has been achieved in the development of techniques for the monetary valuation of environmental damage and benefit. In its Cost-Benefit Analysis/Environmental Impact Assessment Programme, the OECD has published a comprehensive survey of existing techniques and data as well as an analysis of some 50 case studies from six member countries.[33]

In the Netherlands, for example, the value of water quality for recreation was estimated using the market price of entry to commercial swimming pools and the value for navigation was calculated based on savings in sludge removal. In a series of valuations of user and non-user benefits from Norway, the total cost and the contingent valuation method were applied.

This OECD programme illustrates an initiative supporting the indicator movement with new methodologies and other applications examined later.

Gaps in ocean-related indicators

General

Ethical values/consciousness dimensions of human life, leading to efficiency, vitality and harmony are missing. With respect to Agenda 21, Earthwatch[34] mentions as gaps local population programmes (3C), establishment of global marine databases and better quality

Table 3.3 **Socio-economic value of the functions of the Galapagos National Park (based on maximum sustainable use levels)**

Environmental functions			Types of values			
	1 Conservation	2 Existence value[1]	3 + 4 Social values[2]	5 Consumptive use value	6 Productive use value	7 Value to employment (people)[2]
Regulation functions						
Water catchment/erosion prevention	>63.00	++	++		++	>833
Bio-energy fixation	0.30	+	+		*	+
Storage/rec./human waste	(1,200.00)[3]		+		*	772
Biological control	58.00[4]	+	+		*	61
Nursery f./migration hab.	++	++	++		*	>160
Maintenance of biol.diversity	7[4]	++	++		*	156
Carrier functions					>45.00	+
Aquaculture	4.90				0.02[4]	4
Recreation	0.50	++	+		45.00	+
Nature protection	0.55	++	++		*	+
Production functions					>8.00	+
Food/nutrition			++	+	0.70	
Genetic resources			++	+	+	
Raw materials for constr.					5.20	
Biochemicals					++	
Energy resources					1.50[2]	
Ornamental resources					0.40	
Information functions					>3.00	>67
Aesthetic information	0.50		++	++	+	
Spiritual information	0.52		++	++	*	
Historic information			+	++	*	

83

Table 3.3 **(cont.)**

Environmental functions	Types of values					
	1 Conservation	2 Existence value[1]	3 + 4 Social values[2]	5 Consumptive use value	6 Productive use value	7 Value to employment (people)[2]
Cultural/artistic insp.			+	+	0.20	+
Educ. and scientific inf.				+	2.70	67
TOTAL ANNUAL RETURN	>64.00	++	++	++	>56.00	(1.060)

Note: (Values are expressed qualitatively (++) or in US$/ha/year) except column 7 (Total surface area of the study area = 1,150,000 ha)
1. Social values consist of the importance of environmental functions to human health and the option value placed on a safe future.
2. This function applies to the terrestrial area only (720,000 ha).
3. If a figure is given between brackets it was not used in calculating the total value because the calculation is too speculative.
4. This function applies to the marine area only (430,000 h of which 4,100 intertidal zone).
* These functions do contribute to economic productivity, either directly or indirectly, but no market or shadow price could be determined due to lack of information and/or shortcomings of the market mechanism.
Source: De Groot, 1992, p. 235

fishery data at the national level (17), and consistent georeferencing of data. Also, a specific northern orientation of indicators should be avoided.

Downstream of indicators, detailed statistical analysis of the ocean relevance of potentially pertinent variables like coastal population or regional income are needed. Concerning the marine sector's contributions to GNP, the European Union's Environmental Assessment Report[35] considers information for transport, tourism and fishing/ aquaculture as weak, and UNEP has prepared guidelines, with pilot applications in Gambia and Tanzania.

In specific sectors
"Many highly aggregated economic and social indicators have been widely adopted, but there are virtually no comparable national environmental indicators to help decision-makers or the public evaluate environmental trends."[36] At the level of disaggregated environmental indicators, main data gaps concern marine renewable energy technology; fish stocks and aspects such as trends in fishing techniques, employment levels and productivity; biodiversity. A distinction between the terrestrial and the marine part of phenomena should be aimed at whenever appropriate, and lessons gained with like-minded initiatives (greener national accounts, functions of nature, CBA/EIA) in methodology, data generation, and applications should systematically be exploited. Also, inter-dimensional linkage indicators are needed, as well as introducing some environmental aspects into the Human Development Index (HDI).

The Brent Spar affair in 1995 confirmed the general level of ignorance of matters oceanic. The oceans remain a realm of the still largely unknown. Indicators of vulnerability and indicators couched within frameworks of probability should systematically be developed.

We have gone a long way since the publication of my first report on the oceans to the Club of Rome. We still have a long way to go – and will, forever. Completeness and international acceptance of the methodology sheets for ISDs still need scientific input, efforts of the agencies involved and inter-cultural cooperation of all governments. In fact, the Work Programme sets out a number of activities including:
– further identification and assessment of linkages between economic, social, institutional, and environmental aspects of sustainable development and the development of linkage-based, policy-relevant indicators;
– further work on highly aggregated indicators; and

– completion of the national testing phase, during which a few selected countries have volunteered to test and evaluate the use of ISDs.

Inconsistency of present indicators with Common Heritage economics

The validity of present and projected ocean-related indicators in the light of the new economics of Common Heritage must now be explored.

Requirements for consistent indicators

Orio Giarini[37] repeatedly insists on the fact that a more comprehensive theory of wealth and welfare, in the context of the economics of the Common Heritage of Mankind, encourages utilization of indicators. They must address the following points:

(i)   indicators are needed especially for non-marketed and non-marketable goods and services;

(ii) wealth and welfare is a combination of natural or physical and biological, of man-made (cultural tools) and of monetarized (capital) phenomena; this holistic view reflects our social, economic, and environmental dimensions;

(iii) stock rather than flow magnitudes must be addressed; the value-added accounting system is based on *flow*. What is needed *is* the effect on *stock*;

(iv) utilization instead of exchange value is relevant; exchange value, up to a certain point, is a sub-system and can be used as a part of utilization value, provided that deducted value is taken into account;

(v)   non-remunerated work, i.e. work not exchanged and work exchanged, but not paid with money, must be included;

(vi) deducted value, i.e. costs of man-made pollution and over-exploitation of ocean resources, must be taken into consideration; and

(vii) uncertainties inherent in complex systems have to be taken into account.

Stock and flow magnitudes (iii) relate thus: during a given period, man-made and natural additions and deductions modify the opening into a closing stock; hence methodologies for compiling stock and flow indicators have to be compatible. Moreover, national accounts link (v) and (vi): today's GDP is too low since it excludes non-remunerated work, and too high since it includes environmental costs. As for unpaid work (v), the value of non-SNA production in industrial countries is at least half of GDP, and in developing countries it is even higher. It accounts for more than half of private consumption; at world output basis, unaccounted household and voluntary community work including the informal sector adds about 70 per cent to the officially estimated US$23 trillion of global output.[38]

Inadequacy of today's indicators
Some examples will show how ocean-related indicators do not fulfil all of these requirements.

MULTIDIMENSIONAL PROGRAMMES A holistic approach is attempted by the UN-DPCSD core set of indicators for sustainable development and WRI's World Resources Report. They both cover the social, the economic, and the environmental dimension. Other sets of indicators concentrate on only two dimensions, e.g., SEEA, the UN system for integrated economic and environmental accounting, and the Human Development Index with social and economic indicators. Still other initiatives cover mainly one dimension, such as the UN System of National Accounts (the economic dimension) or UNEP's GEO-1 and the Environmental Data Report (environmental dimension); or they deal in depth with one sector, such as FAO for fishery. In the marine sector, however, multidisciplinarity is not applied adequately.

WEALTH FROM MARKETED AND NOT-MARKETABLE NATURAL RESOURCES The estimated value of marketed marine natural resources such as fish or offshore oil depends on the estimated quantity and on the valuation method. The quantitative estimates depend on the choice between stock (e.g., stock of fish; man-made capital) or flow (e.g., fish catch; GNP) and hence concerns point (iii) above. The stock approach has already been fully adopted in some areas, such as IUCN's threatened species reports, and is now being proposed in some others, especially in national accounts with SEEA and in UN-DPCSD's ocean-related ISDs.

The valuation, moreover, is based on net prices, that is, market prices minus external costs, or on user-costs (based on the value-added element [true income] and the user-cost element [depletion costs]). These valuation methods should respect the point (iv) above – utilization instead of exchange value, point (v), they should include non-remunerated work; and (vi) they should exclude deducted values or external costs. Acceptance of these requirements is growing,[39] but application has by no means been generalized. The suggestion, by the CSD core set of ISDs, of an indicator EDP, is therefore of great importance.

The valuation of non-marketable marine resources like mangroves or wilderness areas depends on a delicate choice between methods developed in the area of CBA/EIA. Relevant are the different motivations people have in valuing natural resources: for an actual use (use value), for preserving the option to use it (option value), for the environment's own sake or intrinsic value of species and ecosystems (existence value). The use value is estimated via surrogate markets like travel costs to recreational sites, the option value via experimental markets with the contingent valuation method, i.e., asking people what they would be willing to pay for the conservation of a certain asset, the existence value with the replacement, avoidance, and maintenance cost approach. Total economic value of natural resources then corresponds to actual use + option + existence value. The recognition of these different forms of values is a contribution to developing the concept of utilization value in wealth and welfare, which will help develop the new Common Heritage economics.

A systematic treatment of uncertainty (point vii) is still lacking.

Turning to like-minded initiatives, we are reminded of SEEA in National Accounts and of the functions of nature approach. SEEA Version IV deals with valuation methods without, however, giving clear-cut guidelines for the valuation of depletion and degradation. Table 3.3 on the socio-economic value of the functions of Galapagos National Park on the other hand gives estimates for the types of values mentioned above for the regulation, carrier, production, and information functions. This remarkable application is instructive; a detailed analysis however would show where the requirements from Common Heritage economics are not satisfied.

Quantitative and aggregated indicators?
Point (i) calls for indicators; but do they have to be quantitative and aggregated? Indicators do not have to be numbers. In the Global Environment Outlook,[40] for instance, we find a graphical representation of seven environmental issues (including biodiversity as well as marine and coastal zones) in seven world regions in four different colours according to intensity of concern. Regional environmental trends are represented in an analogous way, and both summaries are concise and informative.

Indicators may have many components, but the final indices must be few in number; otherwise decision makers and the public will not readily absorb them.[41] This requires aggregation within each of the three dimensions – social, economic and environmental, applying natural weighting based upon physical and chemical properties, weighting proportionally to economic consequences or assigning weights by experts or by citizen. The resulting three partial indices may remain disaggregated (ISDs, the GEO-1 or the HD Report indicators) or else be aggregated if dimensionless or expressed in a common term (e.g., with the HDI and the vulnerability index).

Hence, indicators exist in non-numerical, physical and in monetary terms, and also aggregated to an index, and this is consistent with the requirement of point (i).

Conclusions

Much work is going on in the indicator movement in general. An indicators website will provide users with the latest news related to the CSD indicators programme.[42] Renewed impetus will also come from the agreement reached at Earth Summit+5 to strengthen efforts towards a sustainable use of the oceans. Lessons learned from like-minded initiatives (greener national accounts, functions of nature, CBA/EIA) in methodology, data generation and applications, however, should more systematically be exploited.

Gaps in ocean-related indicators exist in general, specifically in descriptive social, economic, and environmental indicators, in coping with uncertainty and concerning indicators for sustainable development.

Much of what exists has to be thought through in the light of the new economics for Common Heritage. Concerning the holistic, multidisciplinary approach required, attempts are being made to bring more disciplines together; however, this does not satisfactorily extend to the marine environment.

As far as the evaluation of marketed marine resources is concerned, acceptance of principles of the new economics (utilization value, deducted value, non-remunerated work) is growing, but their application is by no means generalized. In any case, at the Earth Summit (Rio+5) governments agreed to promote internalization of environmental costs in prices of energy and other goods and services.

Efforts to apply cost-benefit analysis to ocean-linked activities has revealed, as in the case of land activities, the importance of not being

89

mesmerized just by marketable and measurable costs and revenues, but also the necessity to consider intangibles and externalities. At the same time, the same kinds of traps (such as the temptation to "double count" to make a case more or less attractive) are lurking for the ocean project analyst, just as for the terrestrial.

To promote the further development of ocean-related indicators, consistent efforts should be undertaken especially by the task forces for sustainability indicators and for biodiversity indicators as well as by the regional training workshops on CSD indicators (like the workshop conducted in June 1997 in Accra, Ghana, for Africa or the initiative of the Mediterranean Action Plan). Also, the greening of national accounts should extend to marine resources. At the same time, however, as Giarini put it, a new theory of value (utilization value) must be developed. This will undoubtedly enhance the development of a new economics for the Common Heritage.

The ethical dimension

The final link between economics and the spiritual aspects is that people have the right to live under the best possible minimal economic conditions to respect their physical and consequently also their spiritual identity. It is here that economics becomes ethical because it deals with the respect of people and their right to develop their physical well-being, which is inevitably linked to emotions, dreams, and spirituality.

Orio Giarini

Cultural indicators are as important as environmental and social ones. There is a consensus today that socio-economic systems are embedded in cultural systems that are largely shaped by value systems, determined, in the last instance, by religions.

Modern economic theory, whether Marxist or capitalist, was generated by the first phase of the industrial revolution in Europe, in the eighteenth and nineteenth centuries. It is embedded in the Judaeo-Christian value system, elevating human beings to the status of lords over nature, and demeaning nature to the status of handmaiden to serve at the pleasure of human beings. It is based on Roman Law and its hard and fast concept of individual private property. It constitutes a dualistic system of thought, opposing "I" and "other"; individual and collective; culture and nature; matter and energy; space and time; scientific truth and untruth; good and evil.

Dualism, in a way, is the simplest form of "specialization," and specialization, indeed, has evolved in the context of European culture, at the price of losing a vision of the whole. Specialization has isolated economics as a separate sector, divorced from other cultural values, divorced from science, which has transcended Newton's paradigm of linearity, certainty, and predictability towards Heisenberg's uncertainty and Prigogine's chaos; while economics has largely remained in the previous, Newtonian paradigm.

Industrialized states have entered a new phase of the industrial revolution, based on high technology, qualitatively different from the technologies of earlier phases of the industrial revolution. They have moved from an economy dominated first by agricultural, then by industrial production, to an economy based essentially on service.[43]

New economic protagonists, rooted in different cultures and value systems, have come front-stage. Eurocentric values of past centuries can no longer dominate.[44] They may still make contributions, but they must blend with other value systems, including those of the new economic giants of Asia.

In a forthcoming book,[45] Krishan Saigal has examined the value systems of the major Asian religions and tried to extract some guiding economic principles from them. Their concepts of individual and community, of property, of humans and nature are different from the Western concepts. They could make important contributions to the shaping of the economics of the Common Heritage and the implementation of sustainable development. The following observations are based on this work.

Comparing the Eastern and Western "paradigms," Saigal comes to the conclusion that the wealth of the oceans looks different depending on the paradigmatic glasses through which you view it. In the Western paradigm, the wealth of the oceans is what humanity can get from them: resources, food, energy, space.

The Eastern paradigm looks at ocean wealth as "value-in-existence," that is, the life-giving value of the oceans – and this is something that cannot be mathematically or statistically determined. The national system of accounts (which is what GNP flows from) can capture neither the global, planetary dimension of the oceans nor its inestimable value to humanity as the sustainer of life. The Western paradigm aspires to be objective, value-free, based on science, technology and economics; the Eastern paradigm is, in various ways, value-loaded. The Western mind is excessively individualistic; the Eastern world view is holistic, conceiving the individual as "illusion," unless integrated in the community, in nature, in the universe. The integration of individuality and community has implications for the concept of "ownership" or "property." Thus the Lord Buddha taught, "It is because people cherish the idea of an ego-personality that they cling to the idea of possession, but since there is no such thing as an 'ego,' there can be no such things as possessions. When people are able to realize this truth, they will be able to realize the truth of 'non-duality.'" In contrast to the Roman Law concept, the Eastern paradigm conceives property as a *trust*, to be managed responsibly for the good of the community as a whole and with due respect for nature, of which the human community is part.

Hindu economics

The value premise underlying Hinduism is a mixture of materialism and spiritualism. Economics would thus have to take note of non-material values, thereby grounding its core elements in the Vedic holistic view of what constitutes human nature. Economics has to be a subset of social and political systems. To the Hindu, human beings not only have the need to survive, implying the need for food and shelter, but they also have the need to care for others. A harmonious balance thus needs to be struck between selfishness and selflessness, or between the needs of the individual and those of others; between spirituality and materialism.

The production system, run by managers and entrepreneurs imbued with Hindu ethics, ideally would not produce articles that are harmful to others. Thus the production of armaments, toxic materials, drugs, films showing violence and sex, etc., would not take place. Industries that pollute the air, water or the soil would not be set up. Firms would not create unnecessary wants through high-pressure advertising.

Besides, there would be no laying-off of workers or impacting on the livelihood of traditional communities for the sake of profit. For *artha* and *kama*, earning of wealth and attainment of happiness, have to be not at the expense of others. To deprive others of their livelihood would be ethically unacceptable.

The goal of economics would be the maximization of happiness combined with full spiritual, mental, and moral growth. The welfare function would thus radically differ from the neoclassical one. Unlike the single-order neoclassical Pigovian welfare function, it would be a multi-order function: if a person looks after his own interests he derives a certain order of utility; if he looks after the interests of his family, he derives a higher order of utility; if he cares for the society in which he lives, he derives an even higher order of utility; if his vision and goal embraces the entire collection of living beings, human and others, he derives the highest order of utility. This concept of welfare would modify the acquisitive society by shifting acquisition of wealth from the purpose of private gain to that of societal or universal gain.

There would be no intellectual property rights like patents, copyright, etc. As the Veda says, "all knowledge comes from God."[46]

Hindu society would ideally be based on the following principles:

- Ethics, politics, economics, and societal structure constitute an indivisible whole leading to a unified society.
- Economics is essentially the science of human happiness. Its goal is the welfare of all. Implicit in the above is the basic presumption of equal dignity of and respect for the life and welfare of every individual. Translated into the sphere of economic policy, it entails top priority for meeting the most basic material needs (water, food, shelter) of everybody.
- The supreme consideration of economics has to be the human being. Economic systems that ignore humanity and its needs – material, mental, moral, spiritual – are meaningless.
- Human welfare economics focusing on man requires a decentralized social economy. The ideal is a communitarian economy allowing for living interaction, mutual access, and voluntary cooperation of all its members.
- Three-quarters of society (the student, the social worker and the *sannyasi*, according to the social scheme of Hinduism) would be in the non-profit, voluntary sector of free education, social service, and service to humanity through the realization of truth. This would reduce the pressure regarding employment (for money) on the remaining quarter and also require changing the concept of national wealth to include non-monetized work as well.
- There would be no absolute right to property but only to its usufruct as a trust of the Divine.
- There would be full employment in society as everybody would be "employed," whether for earning one's livelihood or for doing service.
- There would be no hoarding of wealth and the economy would have fast circulation of money as the method for attaining development, both material and spiritual.

The Hindu system would also be in perfect harmony with nature. Based as it would be on the concept that the divine is immanent in the universe, it would to that extent make nature sacred and treat it with respect and consideration. The objective would be to take from the earth as much as it can sustainably give and not to exploit it beyond limits for the attainment of a material affluence.

Buddhist economics

The value systems of Hinduism, Buddhism, and Gandhiism, in Saigal's analysis, are closely interrelated. In Buddhism, one could stress particularly the emphasis on peace, to be attained through non-violence and truth. Peace and security must be the basis of societal growth and happiness.[47]

Neoclassical theory is based on the premise that all human beings in the economy act rationally, and the concept of "perfect competition" assumes that all have perfect information and anticipations of the future. In narrow terms of the efficient allocation of resources, "imperfect competition" was a variant. This "ideal" makes the actions and perspectives of the human elements of the economy uniform and homogeneous, thereby leading to unique equilibria. It was, of course, quickly realized by a substantial number of economists that this, while useful up to a point, had very severe limitations (see, for example, the work of John Maynard Keynes).

Buddhist society, on the other hand, is by its very nature non-homogeneous and diverse. Every human being has his own *karma*, his own debts to pay. The differing initial conditions for everyone lead to great diversity of actions and behaviour. This induces intensive non-linear interactions among the large number of "non-rational" agents in contrast to neoclassical theory, where rational agents operate in a linear and statistically predictable environment.

Non-homogeneity and the inclusion of moral, psychological, and sociological factors in the economic system inevitably lead to multiple equilibria, thereby making impossible the prediction of unique future states. Different socio-cultural environments therefore determine different evolutionary economic paths. We thus get economic diversity in the world. Also in the Buddhist context, none of the states are considered superior or can dominate over the others, as this would be against the doctrines of peace, harmony, and non-exploitation.

The Buddha, of course, was fully aware of this and it is for this reason that he laid down values for guiding the actions of different individuals rather than categorical directions of what to do or what not to do. This flexible and adaptive approach led to the flowering of many Buddhist doctrines in different socio-cultural environments. This approach makes a Buddhist economy a learning and adaptive system.

Western economics, as described in the previous section, tends to distinguish two kinds of values: values-in-use and values-in-exchange – in Giarini's terminology, utilization value and exchange value. Gross National Product (GNP), in neoclassical economics, measures only values-in-exchange since they are the only ones marketed. Values-in-threat, that is those which threaten human happiness like armaments, drugs, etc., are subsumed under the values-in-exchange and are included in GNP because they are marketed. A Buddhist economy would not only *not* include value-in-threat in GNP but would *deduct* it from GNP as it is not a "good" but a "bad"(Giarini's "deducted value").

Buddhist concepts of economic development are driven by morality and not technology as is the case with the modern system. At the time of the Buddha technology was not as pervasive in society as it is today. But one can be reasonably certain that if he were to rule on technology in today's circumstances he would want it to be such as can only be used for peaceful purposes, does not harm the environment, or lead to poverty, unemployment, and exploitation.

Certain kinds of activities which harmed society were prohibited. During the simple economy of the Buddha's time, the teaching was:

There are five trades that a lay follower should not ply. What five? They are: trading in weapons, in breathing things, meat, liquor, and poisons.[48]

The main features of the Buddhist economy may now be briefly enumerated:
- The basic unit of the system is the human being who is conceived as being multidimensional and having multiple orders of utility.
- The goal of the system is the maximization of human happiness, combined with full mental and moral growth, and the optimization of health and welfare.
- The societal structures have to be such as to be non-exploitative and non-violent.
- The overall direction of the economy is determined by the interaction of many dispersed units (human beings) acting in parallel. The action of any one unit depends on the state and actions of a unlimited number of other units.

- There are very few external controls on interactions – controls are provided by an internal set of values ("self-awareness") and the desire of all to reach the state of *nirvana.*
- The economy has many levels of organization and interaction: family, community, society, humanity. Units at any one level serve as "building blocks" for the next level but in a non-hegemonic manner.
- The building blocks are continuously being revised and recombined as the system accumulates experience: the system is flexible and adapts.
- The units are not hierarchically arranged and all are free to follow their own way to the goal: the goal is one but the paths are many.

The Buddhist economy thus, in a way, converges with what some contemporary Western economists[49] have defined as an "adaptive non-linear network."

The following of this path would lead to an ideal economy which is:
- flexible, adaptive, and creative;
- non-exploitative, so that assets and income get equitably distributed;
- in harmony with the natural environment;
- self-regulated, leading to restraint on unnecessary consumption; and
- culturally determined.

The Buddhist economy thus ideally meets all the dimensions of eco-development as defined, e.g., by Ignacy Sachs, namely, sustainability of society, economy, ecology, and culture.[50] In addition the Buddhist economy would lead to the maximization of happiness in society and to a peaceful and stable world order.

Gandhian economics

There is now a considerable literature on "Gandhian economics"[51] and, indeed, it converges with the economics of the Common Heritage.

The production goal of a Gandhian economic system has been stated by Huq as "the maximization of socially necessary goods and services, and the minimization of luxuries and superfluous goods, constrained not only by the availability of scarce resources but also by an overriding moral purpose." The production and consumption of luxuries to stimulate effective demand was repugnant to Gandhian economic philosophy. He was opposed to such "conspicuous consumption" on both moral and economic grounds.

Another parameter of Gandhi's model was localized production or *swadeshi.* Modern economics stresses individualistic mobility and competition on the basis of self-interest. Gandhi's doctrine of non-self-interest, on the other hand, emphasizes the social virtues of loyalty and cooperation. No other Gandhian concept illustrates this better than that of *swadeshi*, the spirit in us which restricts us to the use and service of our immediate surroundings to the exclusion of the more remote. It would give preference to locally grown and manufactured goods. This applies also to the labour market: employers are to exhaust first whatever pool of local and unemployed workers there is before hiring more suitable labour from other towns or regions. Similarly, the workers would be more reluctant to leave a local employer in spite of more attractive job offers elsewhere. In short, economic agents living together in a community, region, or country, should first and foremost explore all possibilities to do business with each other before going outside in order to get a better deal. *Swadeshi* demands the sacrifice of utility.

The convergence with contemporary sustainable development theory and its stress on community-based production and consumption is obvious.

Gandhi's fundamental principles, as summarized by Saigal, are seven:

– Non-violent ownership – *trusteeship*: trusteeship recognizes the right to private property in the means of production as long as it is responsible to the needs of the community. It is *sarvodaya* extended to the firm. Absentee ownership of capital and land, investment, and production violating *swadeshi*, excessive salaries and expense accounts are not consistent with trusteeship. Trusteeship is also consistent with workers' self-management provided they act as trustees.

– Non-violent production – *appropriate technology*: the term "appropriate" is used to designate the production function that maximizes human needs satisfaction. According to Gandhi no technology should be used which economizes on manual labour while there are unemployed workers in the community. This clearly flows from his concepts of *sarvodaya*, *swadeshi*, conscience, and trusteeship. In addition appropriate technology should do no harm to the body, mind, or soul. Machinery, according to Gandhi, should not be turned into a craze. Mass production, yes, but in people's own homes.

– Nonviolent consumption – *non-possession*: non-possession follows strictly from the principle of non-violence. The less you possess, the less you want, the better you are. And better for what? Not for enjoyment of life, but for enjoyment of personal service to fellow beings; service in which you dedicate yourself, body, soul, and mind. Everyone is entitled to the consumption of the basic necessities but the golden rule for the élite and those in power is to refuse to have what millions cannot have and not multiply their wants.

– Non-violent work – *bread labour*: throughout Gandhi's writings runs the thread of the importance of work in humanity's personal growth. The doctrine of bread labour was inspired by Ruskin, Tolstoy, and the *Gita*. According to Gandhi:

> I cannot imagine anything nobler or more rational than that, say one hour in the day, we should do all the labour that the poor must do and thus identify ourselves with them and, through them, with all mankind.[52]

Gandhi stressed, however, that bread labour could never be forced on anybody, otherwise it would breed poverty, disease, and discontent.

– Non-violent allocation – *cooperation*: Gandhi was no believer in competition, which more often than not led to violence. He saw in competition the culmination of a materialistic and sensuous paradigm that degraded the population. Competition predicated on fear and insecurity bred greed and violence. Cooperation, on the other hand, appeals to the human element, our need to serve others. Yet Gandhi felt it important to stress that true (non-violent) cooperation could only take place after provision of the most essential material needs. This is true of the individual (bread labour) as well as of the local, village (*swadeshi*) levels. The problem of scarcity would also be largely dealt with by the institutional features of bread labour and localized economy with both acting to internally reduce wants, thereby leading to a harmonious society.

– Non-violent distribution – *equality*: equality meant to Gandhi primarily two things: first, everybody has a basic right to live, i.e., to meet the basic vital needs and live a dignified life integrated in the community with one's fellows. As means to such a goal he strongly denounced charity, the flinging of free meals at people unable to find work, but advocated guaranteed employment for everybody who wants to work. Secondly, equality is absence of exploitation. He endorsed non-exploitative capital labour relations as well as non-exploitation of manual by intellectual labour and, above all, non-exploitation of the countryside by the city.

Here, again, there is a convergence between Gandhi's approach to the problem of labour, sustainable employment, and the dignity of work, and the post-industrial approach as elaborated by Giarini postulating a minimum of guaranteed work, paid sufficiently to guarantee satisfaction of basic needs (shelter, food, health, education), complemented by "free enterprise" and/or (unpaid) service to the community.

– Non-violence – *reforming economic systems*: Gandhi was no friend of capitalism. On the contrary, he dedicated much of his life to its destruction. But the destruction of an ideology could not be done with violence. The capitalist had to be redeemed and converted to trusteeship.

Gandhi also clearly has an ecological orientation. He was led to ecology through his emphasis on non-violence. Peace in his view was a universal concept. It was not attainable unless harmony – not only in the social sense between individuals but also in the larger sense as between humans, animals, and plants – was attained. He was sensitive to the bringing about of a balance between individuals and their environment. His encouragement of the Indian masses to spin cotton for their personal use was not only aimed at instilling self-reliance and self-dignity among them, but also to preserve the environment while using a minimum of capital. His concept was to shift the emphasis of economics from capital to labour.

Islamic economics

Saigal's conclusion with regard to the teachings of the Koran reconfirm those of a previous study undertaken by IUCN. Islamic culture, based on the Koran, has a great deal to offer to a development of the concept of economic/ecological sustainability.

The Koran considers everything in nature as the common property of all creatures. Humanity's right to use the natural resources is only in the sense of usufruct, which means the right to use another person's property on the understanding that we will not damage, destroy, or waste what is in our trust. According to Islamic law the basic elements of nature such as land, water, air, fire, forests, sunlight, etc., were considered to be the common property of all – not only of all human beings, but of all creatures. The Islamic juristic rules and legal principles on this issue are very specific and clear and are based on the Koran, such as:

> For the earth is God's
> To give as a heritage
> To such of His servants
> As He pleaseth; and the end
> Is [best] for the righteous (7:128)
>
> To Him belongs all that is
> in the heavens and on earth (22:64)

This is what an early Muslim legal scholar, Abu al-Faraj, says:

People do not in fact own things, for the real owner is their Creator; they only enjoy the usufruct of things, subject to the Divine law.[53]

Then the Koran tells us how to use the resources of nature; in moderation and without wastage:

> But waste not by excess,
> For God loveth not the wasters. (7:31)

Everything on earth, perhaps the only living planet in the universe, is interwoven into a beautiful and extremely intricate and complex balance of nature.[54] The Koran repeatedly enjoins humanity to maintain that balance and not to upset order in nature. For upsetting the balance could lead to the extinction of humanity and its replacement by another creation. The Koran says:

> See they not how many
> Of those before them
> We did destroy?
> Generations We had established
> On the earth, in strength
> Such as We have not given
> To you – for whom
> We poured out rain
> From the skies in abundance,
> And gave [fertile] streams
> Flowing beneath their [feet]:
> Yet for their sins
> We destroyed them,
> And raised in their wake
> Fresh generations
> [To succeed them] (6:6)

The concept of man's role as a trustee is intended to remove the wide disparity between the rich and the poor. The theme of trust (*amanah*) rests on the belief that capitalists and landlords should transfer the accumulated wealth into a trust for the common use of society. In an Islamic society food, clothing, provision of pure drinking water, shelter, security, peace, and sufficiency are, says the Koran, the inalienable rights of all its members.

In Islam one is to share one's wealth with those who are of limited means and share in the works that benefit the society as a whole. Surplus wealth should go for the collective welfare of society. The message of the Koran in this regard is categorical and unqualified. It upholds the rights of the needy and destitute, even to those who do not ask, in the wealth of the rich.

Certain commercial practices are, however, forbidden. These are, in the first place, practices that are in one way or another fraudulent, together with trade in goods regarded by religion as impure: wine, pigs, animals that have died otherwise than by ritual slaughter, or in goods that are considered to be common to everyone: water, grass, fire. Prohibitions are also directed against various practices that prevent the free working of the economy. Thus, any speculation in foodstuffs, and especially the hoarding of them, is forbidden. Above all, however, what is involved is prohibition of any selling in which there is an element of uncertainty. For instance, sale by auction, since the seller does not know what price he will get for the object being sold, or any sale in which the merchandise is not precisely, numerically defined (e.g., the fruits growing on a palm tree) although the price is expressed in definite terms.

Islam also prohibits what it calls *riba*. The Arabic word *riba* literally means excess or addition. The orthodox view is that this prohibition applies to interest of all kinds while a revisionist view is emerging that this only applies to profiteering and that the Koranic injunction "God hath permitted trade and forbidden usury" (2:275) does not imply abolishing interest but of replacing it by a legitimate financial mechanism that does not perpetuate, or create, distributional inequalities.[55]

The matter is controversial. Saigal tends towards the orthodox view that interest is not allowed and evaluates its impact on sustainable development on this basis.

The non-charging of interest has been considered as a sign of "backwardness" by those professing the mainstream (modern) economic doctrine. But Islamic banks have been opened and are flourishing not on the basis of interest but equity participation in investments. This interestingly is very much like modern venture capital institutions which are the main means in modern society of encouraging innovative developments. In this context, the Islamic system, and the Koranic exhortation to the adventurous and enterprising, would seem to be more in line with post-industrial society, where production and innovation are considered to be the main driving forces in the economy.[56]

These principles, obviously, would lead to a system in which no one "owns" wealth and property and which, therefore, would be equitable, entrepreneurial, and charitable. Society emerging from such an economic system would be a brotherhood of equals, non-exploitative and peaceful. The non-charging of interest would also not discount the future as against the present and so lead to the interests of future generations being taken into account.[57]

Ideally, therefore, any system claiming to be Islamic would have to work within the following parameters:
- the essential unity of all creation subject only to God's laws;
- humans act as trustees, or are even able to achieve the exalted status of God's vice-regent when they act for the betterment of the global society;
- the least-privileged members of society have the first claim on its resources so that economic progress and social harmony are simultaneously attained;
- the Divine Law has to be interpreted within different societal contexts and according to the changing needs of time, thus leading to cultural diversity;
- man does not have unlimited licence in the exercise of private rights: he has to keep in mind the needs of society, especially the least privileged, and the fact that he has to refer all matters to God whose trustee he is;
- economic growth and the distribution of wealth are not two distinct processes but are tightly intertwined so as to form a seamless net of causes and effects;
- every human being has the right to a full life of self-fulfilment and happiness;
- all creatures have a right to the bounties of the world; other creatures have to be loved and cherished in the same way as is done by God.

Principles and guidelines for the economics of the Common Heritage for the twenty-first century

Thus there are deeply rooted differences in the ethical dimensions of economic thought between different cultures. There are, for that matter, important differences *within* each culture. Urban ethics differ from rural ethics. The ethics of the poor differ from those of the rich; the ethics of the old from the ethics of the young; the ethics of women from those of men. To find a common denominator is not an easy task. Basically, however, it would appear that the very nature of the world ocean, where everything flows and interacts with everything else, where uncertainty prevails and by far the largest part of value is unquantifiable, forces us to think anew and brings our Western concept of ownership closer to that of the majority of humankind throughout most of history. This is what the Common Heritage of Mankind concept is doing or could do, if properly developed as a common denominator and a basis for sustainable development in a new economic system for the next century.

Clearly, that common denominator, the basis of a Common Heritage manifesto, must be simple, but it must be the highest, not the lowest common denominator. The simpler its statements, the wider they will be shared and the longer they will last.

Here are some of the principles which we could tentatively draw from the considerations of this chapter.

1. The holistic approach[58]
Economics has social, political, environmental, cultural, and ethical dimensions. Its focus must be the whole human being; its goal, the welfare of all.

2. Decentralization, community-based co-management
The impact of high technology and the principles and methodologies of modern management converge with the ideas and ideals of the non-Western religions in their emphasis on communitarianism and a decentralized social economy, as espoused by Gandhiism. This implies:
- resource saving through greater discipline on the part of consumers, improving energy efficiency, reducing traffic at peak hours, and better organization of the production and distribution system;
- a reduction in consumption standards through "voluntary simplicity" and self-restraint;
- acceptance of substitutions between material and non-material consumption: fewer goods and more services or less time spent in market-oriented economic activities and more time allocated to non-economic activities and/or small-scale environmentally benign material production for self-consumption;

- reducing the demand for intra-urban transportation by redesigning cities; and
- reducing long-distance transportation of materials and goods by better integration of local and regional economies.

3. Equity

The goal of economics is not the greatest good for the greatest number (which might leave 51 per cent of the population free to exploit the remaining 49!) but the welfare of all. Implicit in the above is the basic presumption of equal dignity of and respect for the life and welfare of every individual. Translated into the sphere of economic policy, it entails top priority for meeting the most basic material needs (water, food, shelter, health, education) of everybody.

4. Intellectual property

Intellectual property rights may have to be reviewed and revised in the context of the economics of the information age and sustainable development.[59]

5. Uncertainty

Decisions on socio-economic policy will have to be made forever in the light of uncertainty inherent in the system. Uncertainly can be reduced, not eliminated, through applying the *precautionary principle* and new concepts of *risk management* as developed by contemporary insurance economists. It can be further reduced by blending insights gained through improved scientific and technological methodologies with those gained through ancient wisdom and experience, in community-based co-management systems.

6. Work

Work, as expression of self-development and fulfilment, is a basic human right. Theories of the post-industrial society and the ideals of Eastern cultures converge in distinguishing "work" from "paid employment" and stressing the importance of "service." This would imply:

- guaranteed minimum paid employment for everyone, sufficient to assure the basic necessities of life: shelter, food, health care, and education;
- self-employment and "free enterprise" for the free time left by the part-time employment, to increase income and generate savings;
- a period of life to be devoted to unpaid service to the community,

thus enhancing the common heritage and repaying what the community has provided at an earlier stage of life; and
- such a scheme to be realized at the local community level, on the basis of co-management.

7. Wealth
- Wealth is a composite of resources, whether living, genetic, non-living or spiritual, capital, labour or services; and
- wealth is in *stock*, not in *flow*. It is to be measured by human development indicators, including economic, social, cultural, and environmental indicators, not by GNP or GDP, and after taking "deducted value," resulting from activities which do not contribute to the creation of real wealth and welfare.

8. Value
- The value of goods is not their "exchange value" ("market value") but their "utilization value." The longer the duration of products through inputs, paid or non-paid, of services such as training, maintenance, repairing, rebuilding, recycling and disposal services, the greater their value.

9. Ownership
The seas and oceans and their resources are the Common Heritage of Mankind:
- "resources" means non-living, living, and genetic resources, and whether they are in areas under national jurisdiction or in the high seas or in or under the International Seabed Area, they must be managed sustainably, keeping in mind the needs of future generations, with special consideration for the needs of poor countries and poor people, aiming at the eradication of poverty. They are reserved for peaceful purposes, peace and security being basic for sustainable development; and
- the principle of the Common Heritage of Mankind thus becomes the foundation of sustainable development, not only in the oceans, but globally. In accordance with the cultures of the vast majority of humankind, its application must be extended from the wealth of the oceans to wealth in general, not to be "owned" by humankind, whether individually or collectively, but to be held in trust, and to be administered on the basis of cooperation between civil society and the institutions of governance, at local, national, regional, and global levels.

10. Internal/international revenues

- Taxation may be shared between municipal, national, regional and global levels of governance, in accordance with the levels of services required;
- gradually, a development tax might be levied on all commercial uses of the global commons, starting with the oceans; and
- taxes might be levied on activities generating deducted value, converging with the ethical postulate of the prohibition of trade in weapons, drugs, etc.

11. Adaptive non-linear network

- The overall direction of the economy is determined by the interaction of many dispersed units (human beings). The action of any one unit depends on the state and actions of a unlimited number of other units; leading, inevitably, to a system of multiple equilibria thereby making impossible the prediction of unique future states;
- the units are not hierarchically arranged and all are free to follow their own way to the goal: the goal is one but the paths are many;
- the following of this path should lead to an economy which is:
    flexible, adaptive, and creative;
    non-exploitative, so that assets and income get equitably distributed;
    in harmony with the natural environment; and
    self-regulated, leading to restraint on unnecessary consumption; culturally determined.

12. Non-violence

- The socio-economic system for sustainable development is based on non-violence as applied to ownership, production, consumption, work, allocation, distribution, and in reforming economic systems; and
- all disputes are to be settled peacefully and appropriate mechanisms must be established as needed at all levels of governance.

Notes

1. These numbers, however, will be "factored in" by prices charged for ocean transport.
2. This, too, should be included in the transport cost.
3. Wapner, 1997.
4. Glowka, 1996.
5. The World Conservation Union has estimated that the deep sea may be home to 10 million species.

6. Venezia and Holt, 1995.
7. Dillon, 1992.
8. bdillon@nobska.er.usgs.gov
9. See Englezos, 1993.
10. R. Costanza, R. d'Arge, M. van den Belt. "The value of the world's ecosystem services and natural capital." *Nature*. May 15, 1997. vol. 387, no. 6630. pp. 253–260.
11. Roush, 1997.
12. Giarini, 1987. Abstract in Giarini and Börlin, 1991.
13. Borgese, 1986.
14. Giarini, 1980.
15. UN, 1996.
16. UNDP, 1997; World Bank, 1997.
17. UNEP/DEIA/MR. 96-3. A core data working group (1996), six regional consultations held in 1996, and a model-based analysis supporting GEO-1, were preparatory initiatives of DEIA, UNEP's Division of Environmental Information and Assessment. Our following review is also based on: UNEP/UN System-wide Earthwatch Coordination, 1995; *UN system-wide Earthwatch Programme Document*. The mission of Earthwatch is to coordinate, harmonize and integrate observing, assessment and reporting activities across the UN system in order to provide environmental and appropriate socio-economic information for decision-making on sustainable development, including information on the pressures on, status of, and trends in key global resources, variables and processes in both natural and human systems and on the response to problems in these areas.
18. GESAMP, 1990. "The State of the Marine Environment." Regional Seas Reports and Studies No. 115. Nairobi: UNEP. p. 111.
19. UNEP, 1991.
20. UNEP, 1997.
21. For a detailed table from national and international systems for protection of natural areas, including separate data for marine and coastal protected areas, see the bi-annual *World Resources* of the World Resources Institute.
22. See also UNEP, 1995; *The UNEP Biodiversity Programme and Implementation Strategy* and UNEP, 1995; *Global Biodiversity Assessment*, an over-1,100-page report about the present state of knowledge, gaps in understanding, and areas where further research is needed.
23. UNEP, 1993. See also Giarini and Stahel, 1989.
24. UNEP, 1991.
25. Briguglio, 1995.
26. World Resources Institute, 1986.
27. UN, 1996.
28. UN Statistical Office, 1994.
29. Sheng, 1995. van Dieren (ed.), 1995.
30. UN Statistical Office, 1993.
31. Hammond, 1995.
32. De Groot, 1992.
33. Barde and Pearce (eds.), 1991.
34. UNEP/Earthwatch Coordination, 1995.
35. European Environment Agency, 1996.
36. Hammond, 1995.
37. Giarini, 1980; Giarini and Börlin, 1991.
38. UNDP, 1997.
39. Think, for example, of SEEA for external environmental costs and of the Human Development Report for wealth not covered by SNA.
40. UNEP, 1997: GEO-1, pp. 6–7.
41. Hammond, 1995, is of the same opinion.
42. Address: http://www.un.org/desa/dsd/isd.htm

107

43. "We tend today to analyse the US economy in industrial terms. Even though 50 per cent of employment, 67 per cent of GNP, 90 per cent of new jobs and much of the dynamics of the economy are in the service sector." John Reed, Chairman of Citicorp.
44. "Eurocentrism" of course includes "America-centrism" which, with its economization of life and globalization of economized life, is its apogee.
45. *Sustainable Development: The Spiritual Dimension*.
46. *Sama Veda*, 1462, *Yajur Veda*, 3.17. Both are available from Motilal Banarsidas, Delhi.
47. Today new, interesting theories are being developed in the West on the linkages between property, governance, and security. See Prins, 1998. Also Gray, 1993.
48. *Anguttara Nikaya*, note 13, V.177.
49. Holland, 1988, pp. 117–123.
50. Sachs, 1992.
51. E.g., Huq, 1985, p.68.
52. *Ibid.*, p.42.
53. Quoted in *Islam and Ecology*, Khalid and O'Brien, eds. 1992, p.7.
54. See, for example, Lovelock, 1979.
55. See for example, Naqvi, 1995. For a contrary view see Ahmad, 1974.
56. See for example, Drucker, 1992, pp. 21–26.
57. The importance of the "discount factor" in the ongoing efforts to integrate "economy" and "ecology" in "sustainable development" is stressed increasingly by resource economists.
58. "Holistic" is about overcoming specialization. "Inclusive" is about overcoming specific interests.
59. Harlan Cleveland deals with the impact of the information revolution on intellectual property. Information is "shared," not "exchanged," he points out, and this explains "why, since information can't really by 'owned,' the phrase 'intellectual property' is a contradiction in terms." Cleveland, 1996. Sustainable ocean development requires technology cooperation on a large scale. Without the necessary technologies, poor countries will be unable to fulfil their new responsibilities. Current trends to reinforce patent and other intellectual property rights may complicate the issue. Thus the Biodiversity Convention states: "The Contracting Parties, recognizing that patents and other intellectual property rights may have an influence on the implementation of this Convention, shall cooperate in this regard subject to national legislation and international law *in order to insure that such rights are supportive of and do not run counter to its objectives* (Art. 16.5)." This means: "If there is a conflict between the requirements of sustainable development and established intellectual property rights, it is the former that will prevail."

Recently, the developer and owner of a major software programme, Richard Stallman, gave an interview to the *International Herald Tribune* (14 March, 1998) suggesting that software should be free and shared. "Our software is copyright, but we give the user permission to give away copies and to make changes and publish a changed version ..."

4

Ocean perspectives: legal

This chapter will confront "land perspectives" with "ocean perspectives." A medium quite different from the earth, the oceans force us to think differently. Just as one cannot apply the laws of gravity in outer space, many "terrestrial" concepts simply will not work in the ocean medium. These concepts include property in the Roman Law sense; sovereignty in the sense of the "Westphalian era"; and "territorial boundaries," which neither fish nor pollution will respect. The chapter will focus on the concept of the Common Heritage of Mankind, with its economic, environment, and disarmament dimensions and its relations to "sustainable development" and "comprehensive security."

It will begin with a very succinct analysis of the United Nations Convention on the Law of the Sea, with only cursory attention to legal and perhaps transitory details, while emphasizing the truly innovative concepts and principles of this "Constitution for the Ocean" which are "systems-transforming" and have provided the foundation for the whole process emanating from the United Nations Conference on Environment and Development (Rio de Janeiro, 1992). All this will be seen in the broader perspective of the restructuring of the United Nations system.

The Convention: A bird's-eye view

The United Nations Convention on the Law of the Sea was adopted in Montego Bay, Jamaica, in 1982, after five years of preparatory work by the Committee on the Peaceful Uses of the Sea-bed and the

Ocean Floor beyond the Limits of National Jurisdiction (1968–1973) and nine years of the Third United Nations Conference on the Law of the Sea (UNCLOS III, 1973–1982). The Convention marks a point of breakthrough in the history of international law and relations. It is the beginning of a process, continued and developed through the United Nations Conference on Environment and Development (Rio, 1992) and its many follow-up conferences, conventions, agreements and programmes,[1] and pointing towards the new political, social, and economic world of the twenty-first century.

The Convention, which consists of 17 Parts in 320 Articles, plus 9 technical Annexes, can roughly be divided into three major divisions. The first division, comprising Parts I–X of the Convention, is territorial in character. It redefines the spacial organization of the ocean, and the rights and duties of states in each space. It closes some of the gaps left by the First and Second United Nations Conferences on the Law of the Sea (UNCLOS I, 1958; and UNCLOS II, 1960) by determining the limits of the territorial sea (12 nautical miles measured from the baselines), the contiguous zone (an additional 12 miles), the continental shelf (maximally, 350 miles from the baseline), and the high seas with its freedoms, much reduced in size by the expansion of national jurisdiction in ocean space. It creates three new types of ocean space: the Exclusive Economic Zone (200 miles, measured from the baselines), with a most original combination between a functional and a territorial regime about which more below; the archipelagic state, with its archipelagic waters – vast expanses of formerly high seas now enclosed by baselines linking the outermost islands and reefs of the state; and, perhaps most important for the future, the international sea-bed area – "the Area" beyond the limits of national jurisdiction, which is governed by "the Authority" on the basis of the principle of the Common Heritage of Mankind.

Part XI, the centrepiece of the Convention, defines this regime with its combination of functional and territorial characteristics. "Territorial," in so far as the Area is a territory to be delimited by "boundaries" by the year 2004, 10 years after the entry into force of the Convention. As the drawing of these boundaries is a very complicated task, it will be accomplished with the assistance of a Commission on the Limits of the Continental Shelf; "functional" in so far as the Authority exercises limited functions through exclusive rights (controlling and managing the exploration and exploitation of the mineral resources of the Area and related activities) that cohabit in the area with shared jurisdictions (scientific research) and with the rights of states in the Area (e.g., prospecting). The Area is reserved for exclusively peaceful purposes.

In the Convention, as adopted and signed by 117 states and 2 non-state entities in 1982, the Authority consisted of:

– an assembly, representing all states parties, the supreme and policy-setting organ of the Authority,
– a Council of 36 carefully balanced members, elected on the combined principles of regional representation and interest representation – the executive body of the Authority. It is advised and assisted by two commissions of experts, the Economic Planning Commission and the Legal and Technical Commission, of 15 members each.
– a Secretariat, headed by a Secretary-General, the Chief Executive Officer of the Authority;
– an Enterprise, the operational arm of the Authority, which was to engage directly in exploration, mining, processing and marketing activities, on behalf of humankind as a whole, with particular consideration of the needs of poor countries. It was through this Enterprise that developing countries hoped to be able to participate in this high-tech activity, otherwise open only to the industrialized countries.

The exploration and exploitation of manganese nodules was to be based on the so-called *parallel system*, meaning that it could be conducted, on the one hand, by the Enterprise, and on the other, by states or companies on the basis of licences against payments of royalties to the Authority. A third mode of conducting business, although ardently advocated by a number of developing countries, was sketchily indicated, and that is operation through joint ventures.

The parallel system was a concession to the USA, which proposed and imposed it in 1976. It may not have been the best of all ideas as it set the industrial states and the private sector up in competition with the Enterprise, which caused infinite problems especially with regard to payments to the Authority and technology transfer. Production limitation during a first, transitional period, to protect land-based producers of the minerals to be mined from the sea-bed (nickel, copper, cobalt, and manganese) from loss of their export earnings, was another thorn in the eyes of the champions of free enterprise.

A review conference was to take place 15 years after the start of the first commercial mining operation, to assess whether the parallel system was functioning properly – with the Enterprise keeping pace

111

with the private sector, whether the Area was in fact used exclusively for peaceful purposes, and other fundamental issues. If there were failures, amendments would have to be made.

Part XI was fundamentally flawed: shaped by political and ideological compromise rather than responding to the needs of a modern high-tech undertaking. It was based on certain premises – that manganese nodules were the only economically interesting resource on the deep sea-bed; that they were all located in the international Area; that commercial mining would start in the 1980s; that the industrialized states would be the only ones capable of exploring and exploiting these resources, which all turned out to be wrong. But it was the best the international community could come up with in the 1970s, and the Authority as designed in Part XI was the only existing model for an institutional embodiment of the Common Heritage of Mankind principle.

As the ratification process languished through the decade of the 1980s and, furthermore, remained restricted to the developing countries, the Secretary-General of the United Nations initiated, in 1990, a process of "informal consultations" on Part XI in an attempt "to make the Convention universally acceptable," especially to those who had refused to sign it in 1982, led by the United States. The result was the "Implementation Agreement" of 1994, which entered into force, on a provisional basis, together with the Convention on 16 November 1994; then permanently, having received the necessary number of ratifications, in July 1996.

The Implementation Agreement addressed the ideological phobias of the 1970s, not the real problems of the 1990s and the next century. It wiped out all the benefits the developing countries thought they had conquered in the 1970s: The Enterprise was put on ice *sine diem*; the production limitation was abolished; technology transfer was cancelled, left to the good will of partners to Joint Venture agreements; balanced decision-making in the Council was manipulated in such a way that now three rich countries ("investors") could veto any decision to be made by the Council; and a powerful "Finance Committee" was established which could decide, in due time, that the sessions of the governing organs of the Authority were not "cost-effective" and thus should not be held any more.

The Agreement did not address the real problems: that, on the one hand, there would be no commercial nodule mining for the next 20 years; and that, on the other, science and technology were rapidly moving and new resources were being discovered for which the

Convention and the Implementation Agreement did not provide any management regime.

The Authority was established in Jamaica on 16 November 1994, on the basis of the Implementation Agreement. Its budget for 1998 is above US$4.6 million. Its agendas dwell in the 1970s. They diligently avoid looking beyond. The future of the Authority is uncertain.

The third major division of the Convention consists of Part XII through XV. This division is distinctly non-territorial. It deals with the marine environment as a whole; with marine scientific research and technology development transfer on a global, regional, and national basis, and with the peaceful settlement of disputes in a most comprehensive way.

Part XII contains what is still today the only existing comprehensive, universal, binding and enforceable international environmental law, covering the ocean environment globally, dealing with pollution from all sources, whether oceanic, atmospheric, or from land-based sources, and including pollution of all kinds, whether oil or industrial or agricultural wastes, chemicals or other hazardous substances. Environmental issues are subject to binding settlement procedures, whether through the International Court of Justice, the International Tribunal for the Law of the Sea, Arbitration or Special Arbitration by technical experts. Enforcement is the responsibility of coastal states, flag states, and port states. "Port states" are a new concept in international law, and they are beginning to play an increasingly important role in the enforcement of environmental and fisheries regulations.

Part XII provides a framework, to be filled in by literally hundreds of geographically or functionally sectoral Conventions or Agreements, already in existence or yet to be created: Conventions either limited to a specific geographic region, or covering one specific pollutant or type of pollutant.

Part XII is therefore the mother of the great United Nations Conference on Environment and Development (UNCED, Rio de Janeiro, 1992) which could not have happened without it. All conventions, programmes, and agreements emanating from UNCED, in turn, have important ocean components, which now interact with the provisions of the Law of the Sea Conventions. The task before us is to use all these instruments in such a manner that they reinforce one another in the process of building a better world order for the next century.

Part XIII creates a new regime for marine scientific research. This part has three outstanding merits. First, the Convention, in this part and throughout, gives to science and technology the importance they need in modern governance systems. Many national constitutions could learn from this perception. About 100 of the 320 Articles of the Convention – nearly one-third – touch in one way or another on science and science-based technology. Here again, it is not by chance that the Law of the Sea is playing a pioneering role. Science and technology are today of fundamental importance for decision-making in all sectors. Economic development is unthinkable without them. Suffice it to recall that between 85 and 90 per cent of economic growth is due to science-based technological innovation, not to additional inputs of material or capital. But many countries are sluggish in recognizing that science and technology are not a luxury which they may begin to indulge in after satisfying their basic needs, but that they will be able to satisfy their basic needs only if they do something to close the science and technology gap, which is the worst of all development gaps. Thus there is indeed a danger inherent in the strong emphasis on science and technology. In ocean governance, given the imbalance between "North" and "South," this emphasis could reinforce the dominance of the North. Unprecedented efforts are needed therefore to close the development gap in science and technology.

It is the nature of the oceans that pushes science and technology into the foreground. Without marine science and technology we would be blatantly unable to explore, exploit, manage, and conserve marine resources or to navigate safely or to protect our coasts. And it is the nature of the marine environment that forces us to recognize that this science must be interdisciplinary, integrating physical, chemical, biological, and social sciences, and that it must be international, to cover the global dimension of the ocean and its interaction with the land and the atmosphere.

The second merit of this part, following from this first, is its consistent emphasis on international cooperation, on bilateral, regional, and global levels. Cooperation, in fact, is made *mandatory*: states *shall* cooperate: not "states *should* or *might* cooperate." Provisions of this kind have led one expert, Ambassador W. Christopher Pinto of Sri Lanka, to postulate the emergence of a new international law of cooperation.

The third special merit of Part XIII of the Convention is that it establishes that marine scientific research is "reserved for peaceful purposes"; a provision as interesting as those reserving the high seas and the Area for peaceful purposes. This, obviously will not deter the Pentagons of this world from continuing or even intensifying their marine scientific research for war purposes, but if read together with the emphasis on cooperation mentioned in the preceding paragraph, it follows that the more the new international law of cooperation is developed, the more marine scientific research will be applied and reserved for peaceful purposes. Marine scientific research is costly. It can be financed either by Ministries of Defence or through international cooperation. What is financed through international cooperation will not be used for purposes of war-making.

These are aspects of the Convention which may open new ways for the future. It is already clear that marine scientific research is given more attention by governments than ever before. The number of oceanographic institutions in all parts of the world is fast growing; new interdisciplinary institutes are established in many universities; ocean universities are being established; training, diplomas and degrees in ocean affairs, quite unknown 30 years ago, have been introduced in institutions all over the world. At the same time, however, some aspects of Part XIII have been overtaken by scientific/technological developments and are obsolescent.

Part XIII establishes what has been called a "consent regime," i.e., states wishing to conduct research in areas under national jurisdiction – one-third of ocean space – need the consent of the coastal or island or archipelagic state under whose jurisdiction the research is to be carried out. As a rule, and barring certain exceptions, this consent should be given. The researcher state assumes certain obligations in return, such as taking observers on board the research ship and sharing data and samples.

In the 1970s it looked like a good solution, beneficial to poor countries who would be able to share in the results of the research. During the past decades, however, remote sensing technology has made giant steps forward and perfected resolution to the point that many research projects and projects of resource exploration which formerly had to be carried out *in situ* can now be conducted through remote sensing from high-flying planes and from satellites. Reliance on the consent system for the protection of economic interests or national security has thus become unrealistic. The further internationalization of marine scientific research through regional and global cooperation, and the participation of developing coastal states in the management of international projects, is a far better guarantee.

Part XIV, together with the original Part XI, provides the best available institutional framework for technology cooperation, development and "transfer"[2] at the national, regional, and global levels. It makes it incumbent on the UN system as well as on donor states to assist developing countries to improve their scientific/technological infrastructures. At the regional level, it establishes centres for scientific/technological development and "transfer"; a provision that, thus far, has not been implemented and whose time has come. At the global level the Convention assigns increasingly important roles to the "competent international organizations." These organizations – FAO for fishing; IOC for marine scientific research; IMO for shipping; UNEP for the conservation of the environment; ISBA (International Sea-Bed Authority) for mineral mining – are given additional and new responsibilities.

The system for the peaceful settlement of disputes designed in Part XV and annexes has been widely and rightly hailed as the most comprehensive and most binding system ever accepted by the international community. Its main merit is that it is not an optional protocol to be signed by states or not to be signed; it is an integral part of the Convention, and by becoming a party to this Convention, a state *eo ipso* accepts in advance binding third-party settlement of disputes. That is a big step forward in the development of international law, peace, and security; and as the Secretary-General of the United Nations pointed out, this principle should be taken over by the United Nations as a whole.[3] At the same time, Part XV is extremely flexible when it comes to the particular way or the particular forum which states may choose to settle their disputes. They are exhorted to settle them bilaterally through negotiation; if this fails, they may resort to conciliation which is not binding; and if this fails they may choose to submit their case to the International Court of Justice in the Hague or the newly established International Tribunal for the Law of the Sea in Hamburg, or to arbitration by an arbitral tribunal, the rules for which are laid down in the Convention. The Convention introduces two new concepts: "mandatory conciliation," on matters, such as determining the total allowable catch within the Exclusive Economic Zones, where the coastal state has sovereign rights exempted from binding dispute settlement. "Mandatory conciliation" means that, in spite of this exemption, the litigating states *must* go through a process of conciliation. They are not bound, however, to accept the opinion of the conciliation tribunal. The second innovation is "special arbitration." Issues on technical matters, regarding fisheries, shipping, marine scientific research, or the environment, may be submitted to "special arbitration" by an arbitral tribunal consisting not of judges, but of experts, selected from lists to be kept by the "competent international organizations" upon nomination by governments. It is the first time that these organizations are involved in any way in the process of dispute settlement. Issues arising from the interpretation or implementation of Part XI (sea-bed mining) are to be dealt with by the Sea-bed Dispute Chamber of the International Tribunal. This is a part of the Tribunal which is of particular interest, because, in consideration of the nature of the disputes to be settled, it is not only states that have a standing in this chamber, but non-state entities, such as mining companies, NGOs, or even individuals.

Part XV, in a way, is the part that draws the whole structure of the Convention together and integrates it as a whole. The 21 judges are elected by a meeting of the states parties. Since the judges are elected on staggered terms, one-third to be renewed every three years, this meeting takes place every third year. Its functions are limited to this election and to reviewing and adopting the budget for the Tribunal. Quite possibly, these functions should be extended in the future to reviewing and revising the Convention as a whole and including Part XI. It is in fact surprising that the Convention made no provision for regular review conferences that are normally part of any modern Convention and are essential to keep Conventions alive and able to respond to rapidly changing circumstances. Since the Review Conference for Part XI has been abolished, it would be opportune to reinstate it as part of the review process of the whole Convention.

The final Parts (XVI and XVII) contain mostly routine matters such as provisions for the entry into force of the Convention; amendments; etc., and provisional measures. One provision, however, should be mentioned in particular, and that is para. 6 of Article 311, which states that states parties agree that there shall be no amendments to the basic principle relating to the Common Heritage of Mankind set forth in Article 136, and that they shall not be party to any agreement in derogation thereof. This paragraph elevates the principle of the Common Heritage of Mankind to the status of *jus cogens* which indeed it should have and which will be important for the future.

Sovereignty

In chapter 3 an attempt was made to show how the nature of the ocean has changed the Western concept of "ownership," which has dominated the global economic system for some centuries. Through the concept of the Common Heritage of Mankind, the ocean is taking us closer to a concept of ownership as trusteeship, held by the majority of humankind throughout the larger part of history.

In this chapter we will examine the impact of the ocean on two other, related, time-hallowed concepts: sovereignty and territorial boundaries. Value- and emotion-laden, these concepts are perhaps even more controversial and conflictual than the concept of ownership, for while there is broad agreement that "sovereignty" is in crisis in our age of growing interdependence and "globalization," the vast majority of humankind, i.e., the developing nations, are adamant in its defence, which is of course understandable, inasmuch as they have just recently acquired it and they view it as an inalienable right and an indispensable defence against new forms of post-colonial exploitation.

There never has been a precise or universally agreed definition of sovereignty. Looking at its evolution in time, one might make three observations.

First, that sovereignty has always had two faces, an internal and an external one. Internally, it was the sovereignty of the ruler over the ruled; externally, it was the sovereignty of the state in relation to other states. The internal face, historically, has been the more important one. Jean Bodin, in the sixteenth century, used internal sovereignty to defend the power of the French king over the rebellious feudal lords.

Both faces of sovereignty are under attack today. States are breaking up under the pressure of ethnic, linguistic, or religious forces that may have remained dormant since the beginning of the age of nation states some 300 years ago. At the same time, states are entering new types of union and creating international if not supranational institutions, under the pressure of economic, environmental and technological forces and to solve problems which clearly transcend the boundaries of national jurisdiction and therefore cannot be managed by national institutions. These two trends are often considered as puzzlingly contradictory. They are not. They both are consequences of the disintegration of sovereignty in its two faces.

The second observation is that, over time, sovereignty has moved from the status of a unitary concept to that of a multiple concept. The French Constitution of 1791 states: "Sovereignty is one, indivisible, unalienable and imprescriptible; it belongs to the Nation; no group can attribute sovereignty to itself nor any individual arrogate it to himself." Democracy, internally, and the increasingly denser net of international treaties and conventions, externally, soon started to erode this unitary concept. Federalism proposed the theory of "shared sovereignty." Harold Laski, among others, went further, advancing the theory of "pluralistic sovereignty," shared by political, economic, social, and religious groups that may dominate governments at various times.

Thirdly, through this disaggregation, "sovereignty" moved from the status of a *territorial* concept to that of a *functional* concept.

Basing himself in particular on the work of John Gerard Ruggie, F. Mikis Manolis[4] elucidates the particular role of oceans and transborder waterways in this process.

The establishment of territorially fixed state formations brought with it what Ruggie refers to as the "paradox of absolute individuation." That is,

having established territorially fixed state formations, having insisted that these territorial domains were disjoint and mutually exclusive, and having accepted these conditions as the constitutive base of international society, what means were left to the new territorial rulers for dealing with problems of that society that could not be reduced to territorial solutions?[5]

With regard to ocean space, Manolis points out, the solution to this problem was developed by Hugo Grotius through the doctrine of the freedom of the seas. In this he sees "an attempt to attenuate the paradox of absolute individuation through the complete negation of mutually exclusive territoriality in the elaboration of ocean space as *res communis* or an all-inclusive common space not subject to appropriation by any state." This, he asserts, involved the "unbundling" of territoriality, as the means of situating and dealing with those dimensions of collective existence that tend to be "irreducibly transterritorial in character." There are other forms of "unbundling the unitary concept of sovereignty," such as common markets, political communities, and functional regimes. To this we shall return below.

The Exclusive Economic Zone is an advanced example of a functional regime.

In terms of unbundling or disaggregation of the traditional package of sovereign territorial rights, it would seem that the EEZ involves a partial negation of mutually exclusive territoriality in that inclusive rights of use, with respect to such activities as navigation and overflight, are incorporated in the same geographical area in which the adjacent coastal state enjoys exclusive rights with respect to certain resources and economic activities, such as the exploitation of living and nonliving resources.[6]

Beyond that, as I elaborated elsewhere,[7] the 1982 United Nations Convention on the Law of the Sea, limits, transforms, and transcends the concept of sovereignty.

It *limits* sovereignty

– by making peaceful settlement of disputes mandatory and creating a comprehensive dispute settlement system, not as an optional protocol but as an integral part of the Convention binding on all parties;
– by subjecting "sovereign rights" over resources to the duty of conservation, environmental protection, and, to some extent, even sharing;
– by imposing the duty to cooperate in matters concerning the environment, resource management, marine scientific research, and technology development and transfer; and
– by imposing international taxation, not only on resource exploitation in the international area but even in areas under national jurisdiction (continental shelf beyond 200 miles).

It *transforms* sovereignty

– by disaggregating the concept into a bundle of rights ranging from "sovereign rights"[8] to "exclusive rights,"[9] "jurisdiction and control,"[10] and "jurisdiction,"[11] which is shared. The cohabitation of sovereign rights and shared jurisdiction in the same space (the EEZ, continental shelf, archipelagic waters) adds a new dimension to Laski's "pluralistic sovereignty."

Furthermore, the Convention accords equal, or almost equal, treatment to states and non-state entities. Reference is made, throughout, to "states and competent international organizations" – again, an application of "pluralistic sovereignty." Non-state entities, companies ("juridical persons"), even individuals, have a standing before the International Tribunal for the Law of the Sea (Sea-bed Disputes Chamber).[12] Non-state entities, like the European Union, are parties to the Convention and subjects of international law.

The parification of states and non-state entities has progressed even further during the decade and a half since the adoption of the Law of the Sea Convention. It was enhanced by the Rio Conference on Environment and Development, 1992, and the series of post-Rio Conferences, through the important role played by the non-governmental organizations; it progressed further with the establishment of the Mediterranean Commission on Sustainable Development, where non-governmental organizations enjoy equal rights (including voting rights) with states,[13] and it will be completed by the forth-coming UNCTAD Conference in 1998.

Another interesting example of the growing interaction and par-ification of governments and non-governmental organizations is the International Union for the Conservation of Nature (IUCN) which comprises a membership of both governments and non-governmental organizations.

Finally, the Law of the Sea Convention *transcends* the concept of sovereignty through the concept of the common heritage of mankind, a concept of non-sovereignty as it is a concept of non-ownership. Article 137 declares that

1. No state shall claim or exercise sovereignty or sovereign rights over any part of the Area or its resources, nor shall any state or natural or juridical person appropriate any part thereof. No such claim or exercise of sovereignty or sovereign rights nor such appropriation shall be recognized.
2. All rights in the resource of the Area are vested in mankind as a whole on whose behalf the Authority shall act ...

One might indeed go so far as to claim that this article bestows sovereign rights on mankind as a whole, which was the position taken by the late Jean René Dupuy,[14] and makes it a subject of interna-tional law: the ultimate transcendence of the concept of the sovereign state.

Lessons from the past

As noted above, there are different but converging ways of dis-aggregating sovereignty such as functional regimes; common markets; political communities; and one could indeed establish certain anal-ogies between the regime of the European Coal and Steel Commu-nity, or the Schuman Plan, and the ocean regime, and lessons to be learned therefrom.

Coal and steel were important for economic development. They were also strategic resources. The genius of Jean Monnet was in the perception that the establishment of an international regime for the control and management of these resources would serve two pur-poses: to enhance economic recovery and development in war-torn Europe; and to promote European security by eliminating the German war-making potential. If these strategic industries were internationalized, they could not be used for war-making.

In the context of the new phase of the industrial revolution, the mineral resources of the deep sea-bed could be seen as the equivalent of coal and steel during the preceding phase. They, too, had an economic development as well as a strategic importance. Arvid Pardo foresaw that the internationalization of these resources, and of the high technologies to be developed for their production, would enhance both economic development and maritime security, preventing an arms race and the carving-up of the deep sea-bed.

The lesson to be learned from the coal and steel experience is that it turned out to be impossible to detach one sector of the economic system from the rest of it, or detach economics from politics. The coal and steel regime was a trigger mechanism that initiated the unification of Europe. The sea-bed mining regime may be destined to play a similar role in the world at large.

We raised this issue of the Coal and Steel Community and its common features with the nascent International Sea-bed Authority as early as 1970, at Pacem in Maribus I.[15] Scheingold ascribed the success of the Coal and Steel Community, at that time, to two factors: first, the then-ruling Christian Democratic leaders, though committed to a market economy, decided to pool these industries rather than leave them to the vagaries of free trade. "Free trade arrangements were too ephemeral: what was needed was the kind of industrial interpenetration which would inextricably link these basic industries of the member states." Secondly, those leaders were united in the belief that an organization was needed that would be headed by an agency with the authority to make decisions binding not only on states but on juridical persons as well.

The International Seabed Authority, based on the principle of the Common Heritage of Mankind, would have satisfied both these conditions.

Although the market-oriented Implementation Agreement of July 1994 made the Authority inoperable, it is hoped temporarily, the principle of the Common Heritage of Mankind is here to stay. With its four dimensions – economic development; conservation of environment and resources; equity; peace and security – it constitutes a basis for sustainable development that simply cannot be implemented on any other basis. It builds a bridge to the non-Western cultures – a bridge that is needed at a time when Western hegemony must come to an end. And it is a principle of non-sovereignty as it is a principle of non-ownership, suited to the scientific, technological and environmental needs and recognitions of the post-industrial society and to the positive aspects of "globalization." It is the nature of the ocean, so different from that of the land, that forced humankind to embark on a course of innovation, just as the havoc left by World War II forced Europe to innovate – in a different but somewhat analogous way.

Territorial boundaries versus joint management zones

It seems paradoxical that just as territorial boundaries are becoming obsolete on land, we are trying to impose them on the oceans! Even though the air, whether fresh or polluted, flows freely over land, and birds cross boundaries in their migrations, or even in their daily search for food, it is nevertheless possible to mark a state boundary with barbed wire, or even a Chinese Great Wall or an "Iron Curtain." Rivers and mountain chains have been barriers deterring infantry or cavalry attacks: shields behind which cultures might follow their divergent paths. All this is becoming meaningless in the age of air- or satellite-borne weapons of mass destruction and of economic, technological, financial and environmental interdependence and interpenetration. Land boundaries have fallen within the European Community, and they will fall elsewhere.

In the seas and oceans, where everything flows, everything interacts with everything else, and resources are "straddling," the notion of hard and fast "boundaries" is rather meaningless to start with. It is impossible to manage resources or to protect the environment even within the largest Exclusive Economic Zone, if there is no management beyond the boundary. Ecological space and political space do not coincide.

It is one of the characteristics of the Law of the Sea Convention that it reflects, in its provisions, a compromise between the old and the new; the territorial and the functional; the terrestrial and the oceanic. The establishment of boundaries between the maritime zones of adjacent or opposite states, or between coastal or island or archipelagic states and the high seas or the legal continental shelves and the International Sea-bed Area, causes more problems than it solves, and there is a growing recognition that *joint management systems* are more important than political boundaries. Boundary claims may be frozen, for determined periods or indefinitely, in favour of functional cooperation which may extend to one or more or all functions. Although the principles involved have already a fairly long history, going back to the years after World War I, the joint management or joint development zone concept has developed, one might say, dramatically during recent decades, based on the simple provision, in Articles 74 and 83 of the Law of the Sea Convention, suggesting that "pending agreement [on the final settlement of the boundary dispute], the States concerned, in a spirit of understanding and co-operation, shall make every effort to enter into provisional agreements of a practical nature and, during this transitional period, not to jeopardize or hamper the reaching of the final agreement. Such arrangements shall be without prejudice to the final delimitation." In plain language, this suggests a freezing of claims and the establishment of joint development or joint management zones. We have selected three examples, from different parts of the world.

The establishment of the Saudi-Sudanese Red Sea Commission, by an agreement of 1974, was remarkably successful. In this agreement, the two states recognized each other's exclusive sovereign rights up to the 1,000-m isobath and established a common zone composed of the seabed of the Red Sea between their exclusive rights areas. The Joint Commission had the task of controlling the exploration and exploitation of the metalliferous muds of the so-called "Atlantic II Deep" which lies in that area. The Commission contracted the German firm, Preussag AG, for the technical work of exploring, mining, and processing the metals. The sediments occur at a depth of about 2,189 m, covering a surface of about 60 sq km. According to a rough estimate made by the scientists of the Woods Hole Oceanographic Institution in the USA, these muds contain about 2.5 million tons of zinc, half a million tons of copper, and about 9,000 tons of silver worth $6.7 billion at 1976 prices. In addition they contain quantities of lead, cadmium, cobalt and gold, which at some time in the future can also be extracted.

In this rather exceptional international joint venture, the Sudan and Saudi Arabia provided the resource, Saudi Arabia provided the capital, and Germany provided the technology organization and know-how. All partners profited from the deal. Saudi Arabia should have benefited from industrial diversification and a decrease in its dependence on oil exports; the Sudan from the acquisition of technology and know-how; the Federal Republic of Germany from the utilization of its technology.

An elaborate long-term research, R&D, and production programme was adopted and carried out. It included a large segment of environmental studies. A vast number of data were accumulated. Production was to start by 1980, but the collapse of metal prices, together with increasing environmental concerns and uncertainties, led to an indefinite postponement of the commercial phase.

Our second example is the Timor Gap Cooperation Treaty of 1989, between Indonesia and Australia. As summarized by *International Legal Materials*,[16] this Treaty, the product of 10 years of negotiations (1979–1989), is the most substantial bilateral agreement concluded between Australia and Indonesia. It establishes a unique and complex regime to develop areas of mutual interest and mutual profit. The whole area of the Zone of Cooperation is about 61,000 sq km. Areas of cooperation include petroleum exploration and exploitation, fiscal administration, environmental protection and pollution control, search and rescue, customs, employment regulation, scientific research, health and safety regulations, and security against terrorism.

It is in full accord with the Law of the Sea Convention, to which reference is made in the Preamble. It is longer and far more complex than Part XI of the Law of the Sea Convention, which, at a future stage of its evolution, could learn a lot from it.

The Treaty establishes a Ministerial Council and a Joint Authority, responsible to this Council. The Council consists of those ministers who may from time to time be designated for that purpose by the contracting states. There will always be an equal number of ministers designated by each contracting state. The ministers meet annually or as often as required. Decisions are to be taken by consensus. The functions of the Ministerial Council are very comprehensive and include approval of all activities of the Joint Authority. The functions of the Ministerial Council, in a way, are similar to those of the Council of the International Sea-bed Authority under the Law of the Sea Convention.

The Joint Authority has legal personality and such legal capacities under the law of both contracting states as are necessary for the exercise of its powers and the performance of its functions. It is responsible to the Ministerial Council. In a way, its functions are similar to those of the Enterprise of the International Sea-bed Authority, but the pitfall of the "parallel system" has been avoided, and the Joint Authority functions as a "unitary enterprise system," on the basis of production sharing contracts for each undertaking.

The Joint Authority consists of executive directors appointed by the Ministerial Council comprising an equal number of persons nominated by each contracting state. There are three Directorates – a Technical Directorate, a Financial Directorate, and a Legal Directorate – responsible to the executive directors. There is also a Corporate Services Directorate, to provide administrative support to the executive directors and the three other directorates and to service the meetings of the Ministerial Council.

The executive directors and the four directors constitute the Executive Board. Decision making is by consensus. Where consensus cannot be reached, the matter shall be referred to the Ministerial Council.

The directorates are located in two offices, a head office in Indonesia, the other in Australia, which includes the Technical Directorate.

The Cooperation Zone is divided into three areas, A, B, and C. Area A is the most important one as it is exploited jointly. Area B, closer to Australia, but extending up to 200 nautical miles from Indonesia (the boundary of Indonesia's EEZ), is managed by Australia, which, however, has the obligation of notifying Indonesia of any developments and of paying to Indonesia 10 per cent of the taxes it collects from its contractors.

Area C, closer to Indonesia but extending to the maximum Australian claim line, is administered under Indonesian law, again with the duty of notification to Australia and of payment of 10 per cent of the tax collected from contractors.

The Treaty has four annexes containing a detailed description of the area, a Petroleum Mining Code for Area A, a Model Production Sharing Contract for Area A, and a Taxation Code for the avoidance of double taxation concerning activities in Area A.

A development of this type is hard to imagine without the precedent of the International Sea-bed Authority and the years of work preceding its establishment. The Timor Gap Treaty, however, is more advanced, coming later in time. It is more empirical and practical and holds a number of lessons for a future restructuring of the Sea-bed Authority.

The Treaty also offers some broader lessons, beyond sea-bed mining, particularly with regard to regional organization and development.

Two features should be emphasized: one is the variability of the Ministers who are to attend the Ministerial Council, depending on the decisions to be taken. If environmental issues are the subject of decision-making, it will be the Ministers of the Environment who will attend. If science and technology are the subject, it will be the Ministers of Science and Technology. We shall return to this concept in the next chapter.

The second feature to which attention should be drawn is that the Treaty *integrates resource management with security management*. To my knowledge, this is the first time this has been done in an international ocean treaty. The United Nations has consistently avoided it, dealing with "peaceful uses," including resource management in one forum, and with security separately in another. However, since security is a basic component of sustainable development, the time may have come to draw the institutional implications from it. This issue too will be taken up in the next chapter.

Solutions such as those reached in the Timor Gap Treaty could hardly have occurred on land. It was the nature of the oceans and the unsuitability of territorial boundaries in the oceans that generated them. Joint development zones are based on a dynamic concept, not a static one, like territorial boundaries. They reconcile managerial needs and political needs with the nature and the requirements of the ocean environment.

A third extremely interesting example comes from Africa: the Agreement on Management and Cooperation between the Government of the Republic of Senegal and the Government of the Republic of Guinea Bissau of 1993.

This again represents an advanced form of a comprehensive international ocean regime, with competence over the management of living and non-living resources, either directly or through contracts or licences; scientific research; data exchange, the protection of the marine environment and the prevention of pollution; shipping; search and rescue; surveillance and enforcement and the maintenance of security. The zone of cooperation covers the entire area between the territorial seas of the two states. This zone is governed by the Management and Cooperation Agency, which has the additional task of promoting cooperation between the two states in a general way.

The Agency has two components, the High Authority and the Enterprise. The High Authority is the political organ, which lays down the policies for the Enterprise. It is composed of the heads of state or heads of government or persons designated by them, and the Secretary-General. The President of the High Authority holds office for two years. The heads of the two states parties, or persons designated by them, hold this office alternately. The High Authority meets as often as necessary, but at least once a year. During his term of office the President of the High Authority exercises, additionally, the function of President of the Administrative Council of the Enterprise. The High Authority has to ensure that the activities of the Enterprise are in conformity with the 1993 Agreement, that exploration and exploitation of the resources are optimized, conforming to the best mining and drilling practices and with due consideration for the protection of the environment and the conservation of the living resources. The High Authority may also adopt amendments to the rules and regulations regarding the exploration and exploitation of the resources of the zone. It is, furthermore, responsible for surveillance (security) and scientific research, and makes recommendations thereon to the Administrative Council.

The Enterprise has a legal personality of its own. It is governed by the Administrative Council, consisting of a minimum of 3 and a maximum of 11 members, representing the states parties as well as the shareholders.

The Enterprise is organized in various directorates. There is a directorate for general administration; one for the exploration and exploitation of minerals and hydrocarbons; one for fisheries – exploration as well as surveillance. There is also a directorate on finance. The heads of these directorates are appointed by the Director General of the Enterprise, upon consultation with the Administrative Council. The Secretary General exercises the normal functions of a Chief Executive Officer. In the exercise of his functions he is responsible to the High Authority.

The capital fund of the Enterprise, fixed at US$100,000, is provided by the two states parties, 67.5 per cent by Senegal, 32.5 per cent by Guinea Bissau. 51 per cent of the shares are reserved to the two states; 49 per cent may be sold to private persons or entities. Additional funding comes from rents, taxes, and royalties collected from mining and oil companies, and licence fees, etc., from fishing companies.

Oil and mining companies as well as fishing enterprises, international organizations and funding agencies are also expected to contribute to scientific research and training.

This Agreement, again, would have been unthinkable without the precedent of the Law of the Sea Convention, but it brings a considerable development of its concepts. The organization of the Enterprise and its scope of activities is far superior. The financial provisions are businesslike. Public and private sector are harmonized. Had the Law of the Sea Convention provided for an Enterprise of this sort, we would not have needed the Implementation Agreement on straddling stocks and highly migratory stocks on the high seas.

One of the advantages of this ocean-inspired concept of good neighbourliness and cooperation is its flexibility and adaptability to specific needs and circumstances. It might thus lend itself to expansion to larger areas as well as to areas straddling "boundaries," not between states but between states and international areas, whether high seas or the International Sea-bed Area.

The entire Aegean Sea might become a joint development zone, based on the freezing of national territorial claims for a period, let us say of 50 years; and perhaps the inclusion of the hinterland countries of Bulgaria and Macedonia. The freezing of territorial claims, borrowed from the Antarctic Treaty system and the conflict between "claimant" and "non-claimant" states, can evidently satisfy the pride and save the face of the most ardent patriots, for it implies no renunciation, but merely a postponement of claims. The inclusion of hinterland countries is advisable for two reasons. The growing emphasis on "coastal management," the ongoing integration of fresh-water and sea-water management,[17] and the prevention of river-borne and atmospheric pollution from land-based activities requires the cooperation of hinterland countries; and, secondly, more partners in the arrangement make negotiations easier, not harder, as they deflect from the confrontational approach that might stifle the efforts of two opposing countries to settle their problems.

The scope of the joint management regime, in a wider area such as the Aegean Sea, should be multifunctional or comprehensive, covering the management of living and non-living resources, the protection of the environment, marine scientific research and technology cooperation, coastal tourism and navigation as well as regional security. It could learn from the Senegal-Guinea Bissau Agreement.

The Spratley Islands, contested by China, Taiwan, Vietnam, the Philippines, Malaysia and Brunei, are another case where there is now widespread agreement that a joint development zone, freezing all territorial claims, would be the only practical solution.[18]

Thinking ahead, into the next century, the joint development zone might cover the entire South China Sea. The UNEP-initiated Regional Seas regimes, in general, might eventually evolve into regional, multifunctional joint development zones. The lesson on how to integrate resource management and security should not get lost.

Conclusion

The brief (one-page) Preamble to the United Nations Convention on the Law of the Sea, this monumental document, contains the cornerstones of the world-ocean or ocean-world order for the coming century:

- Peace
  Aware of the historic significance of this Convention as an important contribution to the maintenance of peace ...
- Equity
  Bearing in mind that the achievement of these goals will contribute to the realisation of a just and equitable international economic order
- The Common Heritage of Mankind
  Desiring by this Convention to develop the principles embodied in resolution 2749 (XXV) of 17 December 1970 in which the General Assembly of the United Nations solemnly declared inter alia that the area of the sea-bed and ocean floor and the subsoil thereof, beyond the limits of national jurisdiction, as well as its resources, are the common heritage of mankind, the exploration and exploitation of which shall be carried out for the benefit of mankind as a whole ...
- The Interdependence of Issues and Spaces
  Conscious that the problems of ocean space are closely interrelated and need to be considered as a whole ...

Each one of these statements has institutional implications to which we shall turn in the next chapter.

Notes

1. The Biodiversity Convention; the Climate Convention; *Agenda 21*; the Desertification Convention; the Programme of Action for Small Island Developing States; the Implementation Agreement on straddling fish stocks and highly migratory stocks; the Global Programme of Action on the prevention of pollution from land-based activities; the Programme of Action on Integrated Coastal Management; Habitat; the Social Summit.
2. "Transfer" is set between quotation marks, because, in my opinion, it does not exist any more in the traditional sense. The nature of high technology is qualitatively different from that of traditional technology. It is based far more on software, on knowledge and information than on hardware, capital, and material. It cannot be "bought"; it must be learned. The institutional implications of this change will be examined in chapter 5.
3. Boutros-Ghali, 1993.
4. Manolis, 1996.
5. Ruggie, 1993.
6. Manolis, 1996.
7. Borgese, 1995.
8. Article 60.
9. Article 81.
10. Article 94.

11. Article 79.
12. Individuals have no standing at the International Court of Justice. At the global level, this is an innovation. At the regional level, individuals do have standing at the European Courts. The implications for the concept of sovereignty can be gauged from the following quote from a 1963 Decision of the Court of Justice of the European Communities (*American Journal of International Law* 58(1)): "The Community constitutes a novel juridical order of international legal character for the benefit of which the states, though only in limited areas, have limited their sovereign rights and the subjects of which are not only the member states but also their nationals; consequently, Community law, independent of the legislation of the member states, creates not only burdens upon the individuals as such but, conversely, is also apt to entail rights which enter into their legal patrimony."
13. Although selected by governments, following the pattern first established as early as 1918 by the ILO.
14. Personal communication.
15. Scheingold, 1972.
16. ILM, Vol. XXIX, No. 3, May 1990.
17. UNEP, the World Bank, UNDP, and the Global Environment Facility have all restructured their internal organization and their project management systems integrating fresh-water and sea-water management. In the coastal area, in fact, the two interact in a number of ways. Desalination of sea-water contributes a growing proportion of water for irrigation and even drinking water; rivers and estuaries act on coastlines (erosion, silting) and coastal waters, including the EEZ.
18. In April, 1991, the Chinese premier reaffirmed explicitly that "we are willing to discuss the question of joint development of the Nasha [Spratley] Islands with the countries concerned through peaceful and amicable consultation." See Jagota, 1992.

5

Ocean perspectives: institutional

The world's problems cannot be solved by designing institutions. They must be solved by people. People will design the institutions they think they need; and the kind of institutions they will build will depend on the kind of culture they were born into. But without building institutions, people would not be able to solve their problems, and if institutions are out of phase with the problems of the real world, an "institutional gap" will open. The likely response of people to the appearance of an institutional gap is violence.

We have lived through a period of institutional gaps. The real world has gone through incredible dynamic changes during the past half-century – and institutions, both national and international, have remained basically static and unchanged. But we have reached a point where the shapes of a new institutional order are becoming recognizable. Pieces of it are emerging here and there, filling the gaps.

Everything touched on in the preceding four chapters has institutional implications. In this chapter we will try to spell them out.

What we see emerging is the majesty of the oceanic circle.

Gandhi's vision was inspired by the ocean. Would he be surprised therefore, if it were to be implemented and realized, to start with, in structuring the relations between humans and the oceans? Is it not the very nature of the ocean – as we have seen throughout the preceding chapters – that forces us to think differently? There must not be a gap between the institutions we build and our ocean-inspired perspectives of the world, whether physical, cultural, economic, or legal.

> Life will not be a pyramid
> with the apex sustained by the bottom.

> But it will be an oceanic circle
> whose centre will be the individual

The individual, however, is not conceived as an ego whose interests or whose growth is limited or in conflict with the interests of the community (the dualistic view) but as part of the whole: deriving his/her strength from the strength of the whole, comprised by the outermost circle, just as the whole derives its strength from the strength of the individual. What is most intimate and personal is also most universal, and the whole will only be as strong as its weakest part (the non-dualistic view).

This concept of the individual and his/her relationship to the whole contains within itself the two fundamental principles on which the new Law of the Sea is founded: the principle of the Common Heritage of Mankind,[1] and the principle of the close interrelationship of all problems of ocean space, which need to be considered as a whole. It also accords with the guidelines for institution-building laid down in *Our Common Future*[2] and *Agenda 21*.[3]

These guidelines can be summed up under four headings: The institutional framework must be (i) comprehensive; (ii) consistent; (iii) trans-sectoral or multidisciplinary; and (iv) participational, bottom-up rather than top-down.

"Comprehensive" means that it must reach from the local level of the coastal community through the levels of provincial and national governance to regional and global levels of international organization. This, in response to the fact that, as the Brundtland Report puts it, the boundaries between levels of governance – local, national regional, global – have become transparent: in the oceans, obviously, even more so than on land.

> In this structure, composed of innumerable villages,
> there will be ever-widening, never ascending circles.

"Consistent" means that regulation and decision-making processes and mechanisms at all levels of governance must be compatible. The importance of this principle was highlighted in the discussions on straddling fish stocks and highly migratory fish stocks in areas under national jurisdiction and in the high seas, but it is equally important for all other aspects of sustainable management in the oceans.

> Till at last the whole becomes one life
> composed of individuals,
> never aggressive in their arrogance,

but ever humble,
sharing the majesty of the oceanic circle
of which they are integral units.

"Trans-sectoral" or "multidisciplinary" means activities in the ocean environment cannot be considered separately, sector by sector, but must be seen in their interaction, which may be positive or negative. The recognition that "the problems of ocean space are closely interrelated and must be considered as a whole" has institutional implications of some magnitude. For, if these problems must be so considered, there must be fora or institutions or decision-making mechanisms or processes capable of doing it, whether at the local, the national, the regional, or the global level. Councils, committees or commissions comprising all actors in the marine environment, and the governmental as well as the non-governmental sector, are needed at the municipal level; inter-ministerial and inter-departmental mechanisms, headed by a lead agency or by the Prime Minister, are beginning to appear in many states. As the Brundtland Report has it, boundaries are becoming transparent, not only between levels of governance, but equally between departments and disciplines. Scientific institutions must be placed in a position where they can make their needed input into decision-making and management; social and natural scientists must learn to dialogue; science and politics must enter a new relationship.

"Participational" means that regulation must not be imposed by central or federal governments, then to be ignored or flouted by local communities whose livelihood depends on the ocean, but that these communities must be involved in the making of regulation and in management. Thus the notion of "co-management" is gaining ground in countries as far apart, culturally, as Canada and India.

Institutional arrangements, based on these four principles, will vary from community to community, from country to country, depending on existing local infrastructure, level of economic and technological development, resource base, cultural tradition, etc., but this is undoubtedly the general direction of the evolution of ocean governance or coastal and ocean management.

The village

In many parts of the world, a new concept of "governance" is emerging: the concept of *co-management*. Co-management is a response to the failure of regulation by central governments and the crisis of fisheries, entailing the social and cultural disintegration of coastal communities or else very high costs to central governments. It also responds to the more general current trend towards decentralization and local cultural, and in many cases ethnic, autonomy. Co-management is a consequence of the "transparency of boundaries" between levels of governance – local-provincial-national. It is an example of the new relations between the governmental and non-governmental sectors. Where it blends with the concept of "community-based management" it also reflects the "transparency of the boundaries" between disciplines and departments. It embodies a bottom-up approach. It thus responds to several of the guidelines of the Brundtland Report and *Agenda 21*.

In South Africa co-management is evolving in the context of post-apartheid democratization. Fishing and coastal zone policy forums, local and regional government forums, involving consultations between all "stake holders," are being established at various levels through Reconstruction and Development Programmes (African National Congress, 1994).[4] Co-management and community-based management are merged, providing a possible model through which South Africa can restructure the coastal zone equitably and sustainably. Hasler describes it as "multi-tiered co-management," in which national control of resources is maintained but participation of local communities is maximized. As he points out, competing vested interests within the fishing industry and other competing activities such as mining, heavy industries, and luxury housing developments, suggest that a very dynamic definition of "local community" and proper linkages to the regional and national levels are requirements for effective management. Such a definition may be provided by the introduction of democratic and representative local government structures which started to emerge in 1995.

Local community participation in coastal and ocean management thus must be conceived as a multi-tiered co-management regime linking national, provincial, and local government and incorporating "civil society" structures (industry, labour, the nongovernmental sector) under the umbrella of local government and through new alliances between the governmental sector and fishing corporations/cooperatives representing the apartheid disadvantaged sector.[5]

Legislation will have to be modified to allow for the transfer of control to local authority in cooperation with other civil institutions: local councils, forums, local natural resource management cooperatives, municipalities, NGOs, trusts and collective property rights associations are now evolving in South Africa.

There are examples of highly developed forms of co-management in Latin and Central America and the Caribbean, in China, in Norway, Australia, Canada, and also the South Pacific. In some cases, e.g., Norway, the South Pacific, and Japan, co-management has a very long history. Two particularly interesting examples – Belize in Central America, and the autonomous Nunavut region in Canada – may be sufficient to illustrate the concept.

Co-management in Belize goes back some 75 years, during which the fishery seems to have been managed equitably and sustainably. The system is based on fishing cooperatives of which, at present, there are seven, each serving a specific geographic area along the country's coastline.[6] These cooperatives have exclusive rights, by legislative authority, for the marketing, processing, and export of fish products by their members. They conduct basic and industry-related research, including the collection of catch and effort data; they exercise quality control of all marine produce, they train fishers and provide technologies, insurance, and access to credit; and they determine the quantity and quality of marine produce for each year. They also determine how profits are to be distributed. The government's role is limited to establishing the necessary legislative framework to protect the marine environment. It also administers the Fisheries Act under which fishing licences are issued. The Act specifies that 25 per cent of all profits made by the cooperatives must be utilized for the enhancement of the industry, as determined by the memberships.

Each cooperative is represented on the Fisheries Advisory Board as well as the Belize Fishermen's Cooperative Association, which makes policy recommendations to the Minister of Agriculture, who is responsible for fisheries, including enforcement. Through their active participation on the Fisheries Advisory Board, cooperatives direct policy decisions affecting the industry, and government has come to rely on this relationship, especially with respect to information concerning the status of the stocks.

The Nunavut Final Agreement, ratified by the Canadian Parliament in 1993, provides for the establishment of a complete co-management regime for Nunavut. The Agreement provides (section 15.4.1.) that:

The Nunavut Impact Review Board (NIRB), the Nunavut Water Board (NWB), the Nunavut Planning Commission (NPC) and the Nunavut Wildlife Management Board (NWMB) may jointly, as a Nunavut Marine Council, or severally advise and make recommendations to other government agencies regarding the marine areas, and Government shall consider such advice and recommendations in making decisions which affect marine areas.

Each one of the bodies mentioned in this paragraph is itself a co-management body having equal government and Inuit representation.[7] Bruce Gillies adds: "In practice, the consensus-building approach of institutions like the marine council would mean that their recommendations should carry the day." Article 15 of the Agreement recognizes that "there is a need for Inuit involvement in aspects of Arctic marine management, including research."

One beneficial aspect of co-management is greater involvement of fishers in scientific research providing a broader base of information and knowledge.[8]

Until land-claims agreements installed meaningful co-management structures, traditional knowledge had little chance for expression in government policy. Now that aboriginal people have equal representation on management boards, traditional knowledge and beliefs are incorporated into management decisions.[9]

The reverse side of the coin is that it makes science available to fishing communities so that they can use it as a tool along with their indigenous knowledge.

The same applies to technology. Co-management provides the best institutional framework for the blending of native skills and indigenous technologies, contributed by the local community, and high technology which may be provided by the central government. The blending of traditional wisdom and high technology (especially micro-electronics and genetic engineering) into "ecotechnologies" is an important contribution to sustainable development in coastal areas.

Co-management, of course, is not a panacea. Its applicability is limited. Its take-off point is rather high on the scale of social development. It presupposes the existence of infrastructure – cooperatives, village councils, organized user groups, etc. Poor coastal villages in poor countries do not have this sort of infrastructure, and the task of making them active partners in integrated coastal management is daunting. And yet if integrated coastal management does not include them, integrated coastal management is neither integrated nor sustainable. The upgrading of livelihoods in poor coastal villages is also essential if migration of the poorest people to the shanty towns of

What is co-management?

Cooperative management, joint management, and *collaborative management* are all terms synonymous with co-management. These terms are used to define:
- an institutional arrangement in which responsibility for resource management, conservation and/or economic development is shared between governments and user groups;
- management systems in which users and other interests take an active part in designing, implementing, and enforcing management regulations;
- a sharing of decision-making between government agencies and community-based stakeholders;
- management decisions (policy) based on shared information, on consultation with stakeholders, and on their participation;
- the integration of local-level and state-level systems; and/or
- institutional arrangements in which governments and other parties, such as Aboriginal entities, local community groups, or industry sectors enter into formal agreements specifying their respective rights, powers, and obligations with reference to, for example, environmental conservation and resource development.

Source: National Round Table on the Environment and the Economy. *Sustainable Strategies for Oceans: A Co-Management Guide*, 1998. Ottawa.

coastal megacities is to be halted and further urban sprawl, entailing further degradation of the coastal environment and exposing swelling masses of poor to the hazards of natural or anthropogenic catastrophes, are to be prevented. Ways must be found to include the inhabitants both of poor villages and coastal megacities in integrated coastal management.

An excellent beginning was made, in recent years, by the S.M. Swaminathan Research Foundation in India with the so-called "bio-villages" by selecting a number of rural villages, inhabited by landless and extremely poor populations, upgrading their livelihoods through the introduction of "ecotechnologies," and enhancing their capacities for social organization. The International Ocean Institute has extended this project to coastal and fishing villages where conditions are desperate. Water management; desalination of mismanaged soils; the planting of halophile crops; improved fish processing and the prevention of post-harvest waste; shrimp waste recycling; creation of new jobs through adapting some of the new bio-industrial processes

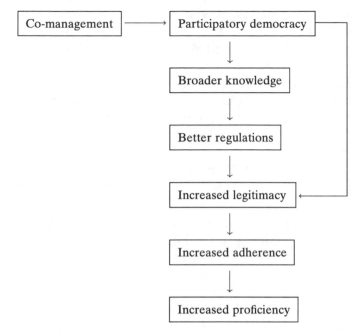

Source: Svein Jentoft and Knut H. Mikalsen, *loc. cit.*

Fig. 5.1 **Benefits of Co-management**

to village and household levels; the enhancement of social organization and managerial skills are goals which cannot be reached in the very short term, but, from a certain point on, the process can be accelerated through co-management.

In a previous book[10] I tried to envisage some general features of an institutional framework for ocean governance at the village level, which ought to be secured through national legislation, here updated.

Such legislation might read as follows:

Coastal communities

1. The municipal council of a coastal village or town shall elect a Marine Resources Council, composed of representatives of the port authority, shipowners, fishing associations, maritime industries, the tourist board, research institutes, non-governmental organizations, and consumer cooperatives.
2. The Marine Resources Council shall deliberate on all matters

139

affecting the sustainable development of marine resources, the protection of the marine and coastal environment, research and training in ocean affairs, and shall prepare legislation thereon for the Municipal Council.

3. The Marine Resources Council shall prepare short-term (one year) and medium-term (five years) plans for sustainable resource development and the protection of the marine environment, and submit them, through the Municipal Council, to the Provincial Government.

4. The Marine Resources Council shall be responsible for the local implementation the Law of the Sea Convention, of Chapter 17 of the Agenda, of the marine-related parts of the Biodiversity and Climate Conventions, the Agreement on Straddling Stocks and Highly Migratory Stocks in the High Seas, the Global Programme of Action on the Prevention of Pollution from Land-based Activities, the Regional Seas Programme and other ocean-related agreements and programmes.

5. The Marine Resources Council shall meet as often as necessary.

6. Municipalities, through their Marine Resources Councils, shall cooperate, within their Province and with the municipalities of neighbouring Provinces as well as with municipalities of neighbouring countries on matters affecting their common ecosystem. Appropriate provincial, national, or international conferences shall be arranged for this purpose.

The nation

Also at the national level institutional arrangements will vary, depending on existing infrastructure – e.g., whether federal, confederate or unitary, democratic, monarchic or dictatorial, small or large, continental, insular, or archipelagic; and it will also depend on the stage of economic development, on culture, etc.; but there are at least two features which all national ocean regimes will have in common.

There must be effective linkages between the "circle" of the coastal community, and the wider "circle" of the national government. In small countries, this linkage will be direct; in large, or federal or confederate states, there will be an intermediate "circle": that of the province, state, or *land*, with effective linkages both to the local community and to the national government.

And, secondly, there must be effective linkages between all government departments or ministries involved one way or another in ocean affairs; and almost all departments or ministries are in fact involved:

- Foreign Affairs is involved through legal affairs and treaty divisions as well as through international trade, foreign aid and cooperation in ocean affairs;
- Environment is responsible for the protection of the marine environment, including marine protected areas;
- Transport has to regulate shipping, ports and harbours;
- Tourism handles coastal tourism;
- Agriculture, in many countries, regulates fisheries, while in some others there is a separate department/ministry for fisheries;
- Energy and Resources or, in some countries, the Ministry for the Interior, is responsible for offshore oil and gas as well as non-fuel minerals and metals;
- Labour and Health are involved in labour and sanitary conditions on vessels and platforms;
- Science & Technology and Education are of primary importance as they are responsible for building the scientific-technological infrastructure which is of crucial importance as a basis for ocean management and development;
- The Department of Justice will have to be involved for the peaceful settlement of disputes;
- Defence regulates navies and coastguards and is responsible for surveillance, enforcement and maritime security.

The ocean-related responsibilities of all these departments and ministries overlap and often conflict, and the framing of a consistent and integrated oceans policy requires interdepartmental cooperation of a kind not achievable within the traditional sectoral structure of traditional governance.

Some countries – e.g., France, India – have tried to respond to the new challenge through the establishment of a new Ministry for the Ocean or Department for Ocean Development; but these attempts have not really been successful anywhere, since the traditional departments involved sectorally in ocean affairs were not willing anywhere "to yield turf." In France, the Ocean Ministry was abolished after a short trial period; in India, the functions of the Department for Ocean Development were restricted to activities which fell outside the responsibilities of the traditional ministries, i.e., developing programmes for Antarctic research and exploration and for deep sea-bed mining. All other ocean activities remained largely uncoordinated.

Other states have developed policy integration through inter-ministerial councils under the responsibility of a lead agency or, frequently, of the Prime Minister or his deputy. This appears to be the more promising route, although by itself it does not ensure "co-management," or the input from the "village circle." The most complete national institutional framework for integrated ocean and coastal management that I have come across is that designed by the Netherlands for the administration of the Dutch part of the North Sea.

The Dutch model provides for wide participation and an effective decision-making system linking government, research institutions, and interest groups. At the political level, there is a Board of Ministers under the Chairmanship of the Prime Minister. The Board is advised by a Parliamentary Commission on ocean affairs as well as by a Non-governmental Advisory Council comprising industry and science. The work of these advisory bodies is coordinated by the Minister of Transport and Public Works. At the bureaucratic level there is an Interdepartmental Commission, composed of senior officials of 13 departments and usually chaired by a former Prime Minister. It is its responsibility to prepare the work for the Ministerial Board. Decisions by the Board are made by consensus.

The Netherlands is not a very large country. Coastal management, including the management of the dikes to control flooding, is of primary importance for the whole country. "The village circle" could be structured into the Non-governmental Advisory Council (fig. 5.2).

Another excellent model has evolved in Brazil. The National Coastal Management Plan (PNGC) of Brazil was established in 1988 by the Inter-ministerial Commission for Sea Resources (CIRM), a governmental agency headed by the Ministry of the Navy which includes representatives of 11 federal ministries. The programme, drawing on the participation of 17 coastal states, is supported by an elaborate institutional structure involving governmental agencies at various levels, scientific institutions and non-governmental organisations.

The political/administrative structure of the programme is organized at three interactive levels. There is a Secretariat for the Inter-Ministerial Commission (SECIRM) which provides technical and financial support to the states, regional, and municipal agencies, encouraging them to generate and adopt their own management plans, applying a common methodology designed by a coordinating group comprised of a number of governmental agencies at the federal

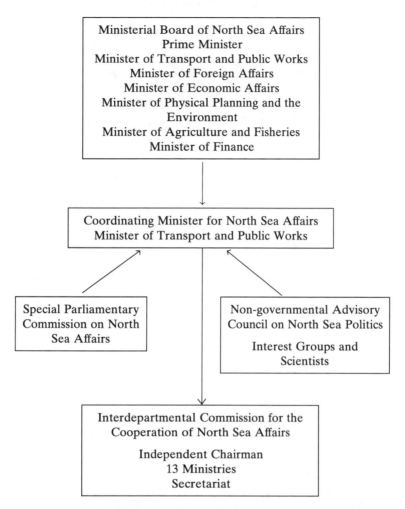

Fig. 5.2 **A Model of the Non-governmental Advisory Council**

level. The participation of the local governments and municipalities is the third level in the entire cycle of the political administrative process, providing the feedback necessary for the revision of national priorities and guidelines.

These new structures keep evolving, changing in details, adapting to local and national needs and conditions.

A great deal of training and education, of a new, genuinely interdisciplinary type, is required to make the system work. In fact, a new type of civil servant is required, not narrowly specialized in the "sector" of this or that government department, but at home in both

143

Fig. 5.3   **The National Coastal Management Plan (PNGC) of Brazil**

the natural and the social sciences, and in all major uses of the seas and oceans. Such persons must be on the staff of every one of the ministries and departments involved, to make inter-ministerial cooperation effective.

As one follows the widening oceanic circle, from the local to the provincial to the national range, and from there to the regional and global one, two axioms emerge. I like to call the first one the Aurelio Peccei axiom. Peccei expounded it during a seminar he led at the Center for the Study of Democratic Institutions in Santa Barbara, California, in the late 1960s. It can be found in the center's archives. The axiom asserts that planning at the narrowest circle, the village circle, will be most effective in the short term. Longer-term planning at the village circle is likely to be frustrated by externalities. The wider the circle, the greater the need for longer-term planning. Planning, within the circle of the nation, must be medium-term – at least 5 to 10 years. Planning for the circle of the region, conforming closer to ecosystemic conditions, must be longer-term while planning within the global circle must be very long-term, looking forward over the next 50 or 100 years.

The second axiom I like to call the Jovan Djordjević axiom. It, too, was expounded at a seminar of the Center for the Study of Democratic Institutions, during the same period, by Djordjevic, one of the great theoreticians of the Tito/Kardelj era of Yugoslavia's evolving self-management system. That axiom asserts that the longer the planning period, the broader must be people's participation in the planning process. Short-term local planning can be decreed by government. Planning for periods longer than the time between one election and the next cannot. Politicians come and go, but people remain. Therefore, the wider the circle, the longer the planning period, the more active and intensive must be people's understanding of and participation in the planning process, which must be bottom-up, not top-down.

Incidentally, it was during that same period that the ocean regime project, which generated Pacem in Maribus and the International Ocean Institute, was born at the Center for the Study of Democratic Institutions.

The region

The Regional Seas Programme provides the most comprehensive institutional framework for regional cooperation in the seas and oceans. Initiated by UNEP following the Stockholm Conference on the Human Environment, it was one of the success stories of the United Nations system.

- However, it necessarily reflected the sectoral approach which still prevailed in the early 1970s. Stockholm generated the establishment of sectoral ministries of the environment at the national level, the Regional Seas Programme for the Protection of the Environment at the regional level, and UNEP, as a sectoral programme, at the global level.
- Between 1972 (Stockholm) and 1992 (Rio) global awareness moved from a sectoral to a comprehensive approach, from the protection of the environment to sustainable development. This change has a number of institutional implications, which the parties to Regional Seas Conventions, Protocols, and Action Plans have now to face. A most promising beginning has already been made with the revision of the Barcelona Convention and Action Plan in 1995.
- The updating and restructuring of Regional Seas Programmes is absolutely essential, not only to save that useful programme by itself, not only for the implementation of the Law of the Sea Convention, but of all the post-UNCED Conventions and action programmes as well as for the strengthening of regional security, including economic and environmental security. All these new instruments call for and rely on regional cooperation and organization as an essential element: whether one looks at the Climate or

Biodiversity Conventions, *Agenda 21*, the Barbados Action Plan for Small Island Developing States; the Nordwijk recommendations on integrated coastal management, the agreement on straddling stocks and highly migratory stocks, the Global Plan of Action on Protection of the Marine Environment from Land-based Activities, or the Secretary-General's Agendas for Peace and for Development.

· The restructuring of Regional Seas Programmes must be based on the same principles as the structuring of national and local governance: comprehensiveness, consistency, interdisciplinarity, and participation. If there is a mismatch between the oceanic circles, they cannot properly interact, and compatibility between rules and regulations at the national and regional level is impossible.

The change from a sectoral to a comprehensive approach, the new tasks arising from the implementation of Chapter 17 (and others) of Agenda 21, the Climate and Biodiversity Conventions and the Global Programme of Action, as well as the new emphasis on integrated coastal and ocean management, clearly *broadens the mandate of the Conventions*. This mandate now must cover all peaceful uses of the regional sea, including fisheries management, surveillance and enforcement; shipping, minerals, and offshore oil, as well as coastal management, tourism, port management, etc.

This does not mean that UNEP's Regional Seas Programme should try to duplicate what other organizations, such as FAO, IOC, UNDP, etc., are already doing in the region. It means that a framework has to be established where all such organizations, including also regional development banks and UN Regional Commissions as well as science, industry, and the NGO sector, can cooperate.

UNEP has already begun to create such an institutional framework for the implementation of the Global Programme of Action on Protection of the Marine Environment from Land-based Activities.[11]

The Proposal, in fact, repeatedly emphasizes that it should serve to "Revitalize the UNEP Regional Seas Programme, in particular by facilitating appropriate activities of the regional programmes."

The Proposal states:

The collaboration of UNEP and its partner agencies as well as relevant global and regional programmes, structures and agreements, will be essential for successful implementation of the Global Programme of Action. *Such collaboration will ensure that implementation of the Global Programme of Action will be approached in a wider context, encompassing, inter alia, concern for human health (WHO), productivity of coastal areas (FAO), loss of biodiversity (CBD and others), radiation protection and marine pollution monitoring (IAEA), retarded development and poverty (UNDP), shifting democratic patterns (UNCHS/Habitat), declining food security (FAO, WFP), global environmental change (IGBP of ICSU), nature conservation (WWF, IUCN), marine pollution monitoring and radiation protection (IAEA and others).* (Italics added)

The proposal also envisages the establishment of an inter-organizational steering group which will be chaired by UNEP and will meet on a regular basis.

The proposal foresaw 10 regional workshops in 1997. Due to budgetary and other constraints, most of these workshops have not yet taken place: They should – as early as possible. More than that, the type of forum, or "regional ocean assembly," created for this purpose by UNEP, should be *institutionalized.* It should take the place of the biannual meetings of the Contracting States of the Regional Seas Convention, with the mandate to cover not only the Global Programme of Action, but the whole broad new range of ocean and coastal issues of the regional "circle," set into the broader intersectoral context of sustainable development, including the mandates of UNEP's partner agencies such as food security (FAO); eradication of poverty (UNDP), scientific cooperation (IOC), etc. The Parties to the Barcelona Convention have already initiated this development.

Building firmly on the basis already laid by UNEP and the Contracting States of the Barcelona Convention and generalizing the institution of this sort of regional "Ocean Assembly" for all Regional Seas, one might suggest the following Article to be included in revised Regional Seas Conventions:

The Contracting Parties shall hold ordinary meetings once every two years, and extraordinary meetings at any other time deemed necessary, upon the request of the Co-ordinator or of any Contracting Party, provided that such requests are supported by at least two Contracting Parties.

The meetings of Contracting Parties shall be attended also by competent regional and international organizations, including regional economic integration organizations, regional economic commissions of the United Nations, regional development banks, and non-governmental organizations ...

The scope of activities of this kind of "ocean assembly" will be broad, even though different in different regions. But, again, there will be elements they all have in common.

Integrated coastal and ocean management covers ecosystems including the EEZ on the seaward side and the watershed on the landward side. It necessarily includes the management of rivers which may originate in land-locked countries. It will therefore become necessary to include land-locked countries of the hinterland in the membership of regional seas programmes.

Integrated coastal management thus necessarily includes integrated water management. Fresh-water and sea-water systems in the coastal zone interact. The recent reorganization of divisions for integrated water management within UNEP, UNDP, the World Bank, and the Global Environment Facility (GEF) is a promising first step in this direction.

In these pages we shall focus on three innovations, universally required at the regional level at this stage of the evolution of regional cooperation and development.
– The first concerns technology cooperation.
– The second one, the establishment of Regional Commissions on Sustainable Development, providing the necessary linkage between the regional and the global "circle."
– The third concerns regional security.

Technology cooperation

The Law of the Sea Convention as well as each one of the post-UNCED Conventions, Agreements and Programmes recognize the fundamental importance of technology cooperation and technology sharing if poor countries are to fulfil their responsibilities and enjoy their rights under these new instruments. This recognition is progressive, gaining strength. The provisions in the new conventions impose greater obligations on the industrialized states than the Law of the Sea Convention. And this is logical: while powerful states, with powerful fleets, could still think they could rule the waves by waiving the rules and marginalizing weak and fleetless states, it is blatant that they cannot deal with global climate, the ozone hole, and global biodiversity without the cooperation of two-thirds or three-quarters of the people on this earth. The new global concerns have put bargaining chips into the hands of developing countries. They should use them effectively.

The weakness of the system lies in the fact that *each one* of the conventions, agreements and programmes has *its own* provisions for technology cooperation and sharing as each one attempts to create its own regime, at national, regional, and global levels.

This obviously is a colossal waste, implying, more than a duplication, a multiplication of effort – especially considering that the technologies involved are largely the same.

If now we see the emergence of comprehensive regimes, responsible for the implementation of *all* the new instruments within the local, national, and regional "circles," it becomes logical to think in terms of setting up one single system of technology cooperation serving the needs of *all* the conventions, agreements and programmes in the region. Obviously this would be more cost-effective, and far more could be done with far less.

In creating such a system, a second fundamental point should be kept in mind but is often forgotten: "technology transfer" is not what it used to be. This obviously derives from the changed nature of contemporary technology. Technology today is not what it used to be.

Traditional technology was "hardware" that could be "transferred" from "producer" to "user" or "consumer" through a self-contained commercial transaction. The new technology is information, knowledge, development; it is process rather than product, a process that involves the consumer together with the producer and transforms the roles of both into what Alvin Toffler has called the "prosumer" – with profound effects on international trade and the "transfer of technology." Technology today can no longer be "bought." It must be "learned." Each transfer becomes a kind of joint venture, involving long-term agreements with regard to training, maintenance, repair, upgrading, etc. Or, as Orio Giarini put it, "... the notion of transfer of products or technologies has therefore to give way increasingly to 'prosumer' processes of joint collaboration and integration."

One should note, furthermore, the enormous importance of research and development (R&D) in the contemporary technological enterprise. R&D is the basis of technological innovation: technological innovation is the motor of economic growth. According to some experts (e.g., Nobel Laureate Robert M. Solow of the Massachusetts Institute of Technology), as much as 85 per cent of US economic growth per capita as recorded in historical data is attributable to increases in productivity or technological innovation. Only about 15 per cent of the growth could be traced to the use of more inputs.

Research and development in high technology, however, is extremely costly, running into hundreds of billions of dollars in each one of the technologically leading countries. And not only is it costly, it is also extremely risky, especially in the early phases. The rate of failure has been estimated variously at between 7 and 20 to 1 or even 40 to 1. Thirdly, there is a long period of gestation, and it may be many years before there is a return on the capital invested. And lastly, the results of R&D may be useful not only for the company that undertook and paid for it, but for other projects. In other words, there may be considerable external effects that a private company may have no interest in promoting.

All this has triggered trends which have thoroughly transformed the R&D sector of the industrial enterprise, and we have seen the rise of R&D consortia to share and reduce the cost and spread the risk inherent in R&D in high technology during the early phase – the "pre-competitive" phase, as it is termed. On the other hand, we have seen an increasing involvement, first of the banks, and then of governments, in the financing of this R&D. Even in the United States, the staunchest defender of private enterprise, over 50 per cent of R&D is paid for by the Federal Government.

For most countries, however, even this public/private co-investment is not strong enough to make technology development competitive on an international scale. What has been emerging, therefore, has been a new form of international public/private cooperation, exemplified by systems like EUREKA and dozens of others. "The growth in international, inter-firm technical cooperation agreements represents one of the most important novel developments of the first half of the 1980s," as Margaret Sharp and Claire Shearman put it.[12] The sharing of risk and of cost in many cases serves to encourage firms to spend more on R&D than they would do otherwise.

EUREKA is a very simple model, flexile, decentralized, and cost-effective. Over a period of barely three initial years, it generated $5bn dollars of investments in R&D in high technologies. The formation of an R&D consortium of industrial giants such as Philips, Siemens, and SGS-Thomson generated an investment of over FF20 billion, divided among the three industries and the governments of the Netherlands, West Germany, France and Italy, within the EUREKA framework.

The institutional framework consists, basically, of four elements:
– a national coordinator in each participating country, whose task is to solicit projects in determined priority fields of high-tech R&D, with participants in at least two countries;
– the meeting of national coordinators, with the task of making a first selection among such projects;

– the meeting of Ministers of Science and Technology of the participating countries, who make the final project selection; and
– a small coordinating centre to service the two levels of meetings.

Projects selected as EUREKA projects are financed partly by the
industries (private sector) who made the proposal, partly by the governments, and partly by the European Union where this latter is a
partner to the project.

These new forms of public/private cooperation, at the national and
at the international level – not "privatization" – offers the possibility
of a synthesis between the necessarily more narrow financial, short-
range interests of the private sector, whose business is business, and
the wider social and environmental, long-term concerns and responsibilities of the state.

For developing countries, co-development of technology has a
number of special advantages: it has a built-in component of *training*.
Technicians from developing countries, selected for participation in
joint R&D, learn "on the job"; secondly, technologies developed
jointly need not be "adapted" subsequently for use in the developing
country, but are from the outset designed for such use; thirdly, there
is no problem with regard to "intellectual property rights." Technologies developed jointly are owned jointly, and there is already
a large literature on how such rights are managed. Technology co-
development will contribute to the broadening and opening of the
notion of "intellectual property" which is inevitable in any case.

Environment and development

In 1987 the International Ocean Institute published a proposal for the
establishment of a Mediterranean Centre for Research and Development in Marine Industrial Technology (MEDITECH).[13] The proposal was endorsed by the Government of Malta and supported
by UNEP and UNIDO. The International Ocean Institute was
requested to conduct a feasibility study, which was completed in
1988.[14] Subsequently, an expert meeting was organized by UNIDO
(Vienna, 1988). Several Mediterranean states offered to host the
centre, and as no agreement was reached on the eventual venue of
the centre's headquarters or secretariat, no further action ensued.

The proposal has been overtaken by a number of intergovernmental agreements on various forms of technology cooperation in
the Mediterranean and in other regions. Most important, it has been

overtaken by the United Nations Conference on Environment and Development (Rio, 1992), and the conventions, conferences and action plans that followed in its wake. All of these strongly reinforced the motives and principles underlying the proposal by stressing the absolute necessity of "technology transfer" to poor countries, if they are to do their part in the implementation of the new international instruments and attain "sustainable development." None of them exactly achieved what had been intended with the IOI proposal: i.e., on the one hand, to generate synergisms by mobilizing investments jointly from the public and the private sector at the international level; and, on the other, to create synergisms by utilizing various convention regimes in such a way that they reinforce each other. Perhaps the time has come to re-examine this project and adapt it to the needs of the next century.

A regional system for technology co-development within the framework of a revitalized Regional Seas Programme should be conceived as an implementation of:

- the Law of the Sea Convention (Part IX, Enclosed and Semi-enclosed Seas; Parts XIII, XIV, on regional cooperation; in marine science and technology, in particular, Articles 276, 277 – Regional Centres for the promotion of marine sciences and technologies);
- *Agenda 21*, chapter 17, Seas and Oceans; chapter 34, Technology);
- Biodiversity Convention (Article 4);
- Climate Convention (Article 5); and
- The Vienna Convention on the Protection of the Ozone Layer and the Montreal Protocol on Substances that Deplete the Ozone Layer.[15]

And, in addition, the recommendations of the Nordwijk Integrated Coastal Zone Management Conference (1994), the Global Plan of Action on land-based sources of pollution (Washington, 1995) and the implementation agreement of straddling stocks – all with regard to technology cooperation within a broad, culturally, socially and environmentally sustainable context.[16]

Pilot projects

Considering the great diversity among regions with regard to their needs, resource bases and institutional infrastructure, it is suggested that two pilot projects be initiated, one in the Mediterranean within the framework of the Regional Seas Programme under the revised Barcelona Convention; the other, in the Indian Ocean. While both should be based on the principles of (a) creating synergisms between public and private investments at the regional level, and (b) serving the needs of all the conventions, agreements, and programmes, the priorities of different regions will necessarily be very different. There will be greater emphasis on industrial technology in the Mediterranean; greater emphasis on village technologies in the Indian Ocean countries. This may also impact on the modes of financing, with greater private-sector participation in the Mediterranean than in the Indian Ocean.

- In the Mediterranean, the pilot project should be considered as a practical and cost-effective way of implementing the mandate of the Mediterranean Commission for Sustainable Development with regard to technology cooperation.
- A *network* or *system* should be built consisting of:
  (a) all contracting parties of the Barcelona Convention;
  (b) all regional scientific and technological centres and institutions as well as international scientific and technological institutions operating in the region;
- The network should be managed by four components:
  (a) national coordinators and representatives of regional and international scientific/technological institutions;
  (b) the meetings of the national coordinators and regional and international institutions;
  (c) the meeting of Ministers of Science and Technology;
  (d) the Coordinating Centre.
- Each contracting party should designate a national coordinator:
  (a) In the European member states, the EUROMAR coordinator might be designated for this purpose;[17]
  (b) In the other member states, a special coordinator would have to be designated and located in the most suitable national scientific/technological institution.
- The task of the national coordinators would be to solicit projects both from the public and private sector. To be eligible, projects must:
  (a) fall into one of the categories of technologies agreed upon by the contracting parties themselves. They would include aquaculture and genetic engineering technologies, the production of more selective fishing gear; waste recycling; water treatment technologies including sewage treatment; renewable energy from the sea such as OTEC or methane production by deep-sea microbes (methanococcus, which perhaps eventually could be cultivated in laboratories/factories on land); research on

hydrates, etc. Lists would have to be refined region by region, according to needs.

(b) have partners in at least two countries, including at least one developing country.

- National coordinators and representatives of regional and international institutions should meet twice a year to make a first selection among the proposed projects. The Ministers of Science and Technology (or equivalent) of the contracting parties should meet once a year to make the final project selection. These meetings should be held within the context of the Mediterranean Commission for Sustainable Development. They should constitute one of the "high-level segments" of the Commission, thus ensuring the proper linkage between joint technology development and the goals of sustainability and conservation aspired to by the various UNCED conventions, programmes and action plans.

- The projects selected would be financed half by the industries that initiated the proposal, half by governments and regional funding agencies. This would create the desired synergism between private and public investments at the regional level. The participation of developing countries should be (largely, but not necessarily wholly) financed through international funding institutions. By contributing to this financing, the industrialized contracting parties would fulfil their technology cooperation obligations under the Biodiversity and Climate Conventions while supporting their own industries.

The Coordinating Centre should consist of a core module and other modules which might be added or closed in accordance with needs and funding availabilities.

(a) the core module should service the meetings of the national coordinators and representatives of regional and international institutions. In cooperation with the Athens Coordinating Centre for the Mediterranean Action Plan, it should service the special high-level segments of the Mediterranean Commission for Sustainable Development making the final project selection.

(b) As soon as possible, there should be an additional model for the organization of training programmes. Training programmes should cover the sciences and technologies involved in the network's projects, and trainees should be directly involved in the projects as much as possible. Training programmes should also be of an interdisciplinary nature, cover management and project planning and give an introduction to regional cooperation and development and the emerging forms of ocean governance, as these provide the broader framework within which technology cooperation is to evolve. The training module should cooperate with existing training programmes and institutions.

(c) There should be a legal module, which should assist in the drawing-up of joint venture agreements, the sharing of intellectual property, and other legal questions arising from the projects.

(d) There should be a module for data handling and information and cooperation with technology cooperation systems as they may be established in other regional seas programmes.

The establishment of such systems of technology co-development within the scope of revitalized Regional Seas Programmes would be in full accord with the Programme for the Further Implementation of Agenda 21 adopted by the Special Session of the UN General Assembly, 23–27 June 1997.[18]

Regional Commissions on Sustainable Development

The establishment of Regional Commissions on Sustainable Development is desirable for a number of reasons.

The United Nations Commission on Sustainable Development is very limited in its means, while its tasks and responsibilities for the implementation of *Agenda 21* are very comprehensive. If it could decentralize its operations, relying on increased activities at the regional level, this would enhance its efficiency. Regional Commissions with appropriate linkages to the UN Commission would ensure coherence between regional and global policies as well as between regional and national sustainable development policies.

The Mediterranean countries, parties to the Barcelona Convention, have taken the first bold step in establishing such a Commission.

This Commission was established in 1995, in accordance with the recommendation of the Tunis Ministerial Conference, held in November 1994. The purpose of the Commission is:

to identify, evaluate and assess major economic, ecological and social problems set out in Agenda MED 21, make appropriate proposals thereon to the meetings of the Contracting Parties, evaluate the effectiveness of the follow-up to the decisions of the Contracting Parties and facilitate the exchange of information among the institutions implementing activities related to sustainable development in the Mediterranean;

to enhance regional cooperation and rationalize the intergovernmental decision-making capacity in the Mediterranean basin for the integration of environment and development issues.

The implementation of these terms of reference would obviously facilitate the work of the UN Commission on Sustainable Development.

The composition of this Commission is unusual, reflecting new trends that will take us into the next century. There are 36 members. Of these, 21 represent the Contracting Parties to the Barcelona Convention. The remaining 15 represent local authorities, socio-economic actors and non-governmental organizations working in the fields of environment and sustainable development.

Each Contracting Party to the Barcelona Convention shall be represented by one high-level representative (total 21), who may be accompanied by such alternates and advisers as may be required, in order to ensure interdisciplinary participation of relevant ministerial bodies of the Contracting Parties (e.g., ministries of environment, tourism, economy, development, industry, finance, energy, etc.).

Each of the three categories mentioned in section C.5 of the text of the Terms of Reference, i.e., local authorities, socio-economic actors and non-governmental organisations, shall be represented by five representatives (total 15) and an equal number of alternates, to be selected by the meeting of the Contracting Parties.

All 36 members shall participate in the Commission on an equal footing.[19]

The first of these three quoted paragraphs is particularly interesting because it departs from the UNEP tradition of having states represented by their Ministers for the Environment. The representative has to be "high-level" but he may be any "high-level" minister. The paragraph stresses the need for interdisciplinary participation of relevant ministerial bodies of the contracting parties.

The second paragraph is of special interest because, on the one hand, it provides the necessary linkage to local "grass-roots" constituencies, who obviously will make the nominations; the election of these representatives, however, is not made locally but by the meeting of contracting parties as a whole, which would ensure that candidates, though rooted in local constituencies and activities, must, nevertheless, be of a stature that is internationally recognized.[20]

The third paragraph is perhaps the most important one. It treats governments and non-governmental entities as equals. It recognizes the ongoing changing relationship between states and "civil society." It reflects the ongoing transformation of the concept of sovereignty.

The Mediterranean Commission on Sustainable Development (MCSD) initiated its activities in Rabat on 16–18 December 1996, with 30 members representing 17 Mediterranean governments and the EC, 3 local authorities, 3 socio-economic actors and 5 regional NGOs.

During that meeting, the MCSD decided to appoint task managers and constitute thematic working groups concentrating on a limited number of subjects over a specific period of time. Two of these groups were given priorities: the group working on sustainable management of coastal zones and the group on management of water demand. The first will be managed by Morocco, and the MEDCITIES network; the second, by Morocco and Tunisia. Tunisia had hosted the 1994 ministerial meeting, which took the decision for the establishment of the MCSD and also adopted the Agenda MED 21, adapting the important themes of the Rio *Agenda 21* to the Mediterranean.

After one year, Morocco and Tunisia will propose the first strategic and policy orientations. Other groups will deal with the no less urgent and great challenges posed to sustainable development by tourism, free trade and industry.

The establishment of the Mediterranean Commission on Sustainable Development is a bold step forward. Its structure and functions should be carefully studied by the contracting parties to all other Regional Seas Programmes, preferably first in the workshops already proposed by UNEP.

Regional security

This is the Year of the Ocean. The time has come to state it bluntly:

Sustainable development has three components which need to be integrated: socio-economic development; the conservation of the environment within which socio-economic development takes place; and peace and security, without which neither socio-economic development nor the conservation of the environment are possible.

Security has three components which need to be integrated: political/ military security, meaning security in the traditional sense; economic security, and environmental security. Without these latter two, political/military security is unattainable.

These two statements are universally recognized. Obviously they have institutional implications which have not been given sufficient attention. At the local and national level, there is no need for discussion. The state is basically responsible for all three components of security and has the institutional infrastructure to implement it.

At the global level, the UN Secretary General*'s Agenda for Peace* has begun to draw attention to the problem. The *Agenda* also stresses the importance of regional cooperation to enhance preventive diplomacy, peace-keeping, peacemaking and post-conflict peace-building. Regional organizations qualified to participate in this process:

could include treaty-based organizations, whether created before or after the founding of the United Nations, regional organizations for mutual security and defence, organizations for general regional development or for cooperation on a particular economic topic or function, and groups created to deal with a specific political, economic or social issue of current concern.

Obviously the organizations created by the Regional Seas Programmes and Conventions belong to these categories.

The *Agenda* further states:

Under the Charter, the Security Council has and will continue to have primary responsibility for maintaining international peace and security, but regional action as a matter of decentralization, delegation, and cooperation with the United Nations efforts could not only lighten the burden of the Council but also contribute to a deeper sense of participation, consensus and democratization in international affairs.

But Regional Seas Programmes have not yet taken up this challenge and opportunity. The Year of the Ocean, and the process, already initiated, of revitalizing the Regional Seas Programmes provide an excellent occasion for doing so.

A number of elements on which one could build are already in place. Joint surveillance and enforcement are already implemented in the South Pacific as well as in the Eastern Caribbean. This is one way of promoting economic and environmental security in the regional sea. Attention was drawn in chapter 4 to the way in which the Timor Gap Treaty on the establishment of a joint development zone between Indonesia and Australia has created an institutional framework to integrate resource management and security in the ocean. The structures evolving through the process of revitalizing the Regional Seas Programmes can be utilized in a similar way.

The broadly interdisciplinary, inter-ministerial approach already adopted by the Mediterranean states for the composition of the Mediterranean Commission on Sustainable Development should be extended also to the composition of the Bureau, that is, the Executive body of the Regional Seas System. At present, the Bureau is still composed of the Ministers of the Environment. This is out of phase with the ongoing development. The Bureau should be attended "by a high-level Minister" who, in each case, should be from the Ministry responsible for decisions on the issue under consideration. Thus, if a decision has to be taken on a fisheries problem, it should be the Ministers of Agriculture/Fisheries who should compose the Bureau and take the required decision. If an issue on science and technology is on the agenda, it should be the Ministers of Science and Technology, and if it is an issue of regional security or of naval cooperation for peaceful purposes, it should be the Ministers of Defence who should compose the Bureau. They could be accompanied by the Ministers of Foreign Affairs, or the other way round. They could serve the purpose of UN peace-keeping in cases of armed conflict requiring military responses, through the appropriate chain of command under the Secretary-General of the United Nations. They would function in this way as a virtual "Regional Security Council." This concept was proposed by the OAS for Africa. Its application to a regional sea, e.g., the Mediterranean, would be even more beneficial, considering the importance of this sea for the maintenance of peace on three continents. In the absence of armed conflict, naval regional cooperation could extend to joint surveillance and enforcement and to peaceful humanitarian activities such as search and rescue, disaster relief, or hydrological surveys, mapping, and other forms of oceanographic research. In institutional terms this is a simple extension and adaptation of a process already in course.

Not all Regional Seas Programmes will be able to move in this direction at the same pace. Power-political constellations may be impediments requiring less or more time to overcome. But the time has come to put the issue on the agenda for consideration for the next century.

Regional seas should be declared, wherever possible, as nuclear-free zones. This is another way of integrating environmental and political/military security and interpreting, developing, and implementing the new principle, enshrined in the Law of the Sea Convention (Article 88), reserving the high seas for peaceful purposes. This also includes the Exclusive Economic Zones.[21] Promising beginnings have been made already with the Declaration on the Indian Ocean as a Zone of Peace, the Antarctic Treaty, the Treaty of Tlatelolco establishing a Latin American Nuclear-Free Zone (LANFZ) – which should be extended to the Caribbean – and the Treaty of Rarotonga, with its Protocols. The Baltic, the Arctic, the Mediterranean, the Caribbean, the Indian Ocean, and the Asian seas might be good candidates for extending the application of this concept.[22]

Regional settlement of disputes, finally, could make another important contribution to regional security. The system for the peaceful settlement of disputes contained in Part XV and Annexes V-VIII could be utilized for this purpose. Regional Arbitration or Regional Special Arbitration Tribunals could be constituted under Annexes VII and VIII.

Regional seas may thus play a most interesting and complex role in the evolution of international law and organization in the next century. Physiologically, they approximate "large ecosystems" which form an ideal basis for ocean management. They generate an environment-driven communality of interests among coastal states. But environmental concerns must now be integrated into sustainable development concerns.

Regional seas are an essential element of linkage between national and global levels of ocean policy-making. They are of basic importance for the implementation of all UNCED and post-UNCED Conventions, Agreements and Programmes as well as of the UN Convention on the Law of the Sea.

Regional seas regimes overlap with the regimes of continental organizations. The Mediterranean Regional Sea regime thus overlaps with the European Union, the Organisation of African States,[23] the Regional Commissions of the United Nations for Europe, Africa, and West Asia together with their Development Banks. Regional seas are bridges facilitating intercontinental planning and policy-making.

The revitalization of the Regional Seas Programme is a priority issue. The establishment of technology cooperation systems, of regional commissions on sustainable development, and of institutional arrangements to integrate peaceful uses and regional security concerns would be essential components of this revitalization process.

Planet ocean

We now are moving to the widest of the oceanic circles, the global level, the level of the United Nations, which *will not wield power to crush the inner circle but will give strength to all within and will derive its own strength from it.*

Here, too, we can build on what is already on course. The building blocks are in place. What is needed is the vision of an architectural design, putting it all together. What is needed, of course, is political will. The building of an institutional framework for the global ocean regime may be a model for, and part of, the restructuring of the

United Nations for the next century. To this we shall return in the final chapter.

To bring together all the parts discussed in the previous sections of this chapter, four developments should be considered:

- The establishment of a forum where states and non-state entities can discuss the closely interrelated problems of ocean space as a whole (the "Ocean Assembly");
- the ocean policy-integration of all specialized agencies and programmes ("the competent international organizations" referred to throughout the Law of the Sea Convention);
- The restructuring of the Trusteeship Council for the new mandate of watching the evolution of the Common Heritage concept; and
- the revitalization of the International Sea-bed Authority.

Policy integration: The ocean assembly

When, with the adoption and opening for signature of the Law of the Sea Convention, UNCLOS III came to its end in 1982, it was clear that there no longer existed a body in the UN system capable of considering the closely interrelated problems of ocean space as a whole. During the decade and a half that has passed since then, the need for such a body has become ever more glaring.

This problem arises from a lacuna in the Convention itself. In this respect, as in some others, the Convention is unfinished business, a process rather than a product. Unlike other treaties, which provide for regular meetings of states parties to review and, eventually, to revise such treaties, the Law of the Sea Convention severely limits the mandate of the meetings of states parties restricting it, after the establishment phase, to the periodic election of judges to the International Tribunal for the Law of the Sea, the approval of the expenses of that institution, and amendments to the Statute thereof. The mandate of the Assembly of the International Sea-bed Authority, the only other body comprising all states parties, is obviously limited to sea-bed issues.

• Theoretically, there would be three ways of dealing with the problem:
  - One could, perhaps first informally and later by amendment, broaden the mandate of the meetings of states parties, enabling them to review the implementation of the convention and to formulate an integrated ocean policy.
  - One could broaden the mandate of the Assembly of the Inter-

161

national Sea-bed Authority, considering that, on the one hand, sea-bed mining is not going to require very much time for the foreseeable future, while, on the other, "the problems of ocean space are closely interrelated and need to be considered as a whole."

– The General Assembly of the United Nations could be given the responsibility for examining, periodically, all the interrelated problems of ocean space and generating an integrated ocean policy.

The first two alternatives would have the advantage of utilizing existing and otherwise under-utilized bodies for a function for which they would be well prepared. Both would have the disadvantage of a membership that is less than universal. It should also be noted that "closely interrelated problems of ocean space" arise also within other post-UNCED Convention regimes with a different membership. The first two alternatives would not be suitable for dealing with ocean-related interactions between various convention regimes, e.g., the overlaps between the Biodiversity and Climate Conventions and the Law of the Sea.

As emphasized in the Report of the Secretary-General of the United Nations,[24] it is only the General Assembly, with its universal membership, that has the capability of dealing with all the closely interrelated problems of ocean space, including those arising from the interactions of various convention regimes. The disadvantage of the General Assembly, however, is that it cannot possibly devote sufficient time to these problems, which would require several weeks at least every second year.

To solve this problem, the General Assembly should establish a Committee of the Whole to devote the time needed for the making of an integrated ocean policy. Representatives of the upgraded Regional Seas Programmes, the specialized agencies of the UN system with ocean-related mandates, as well as the non-governmental sector should participate in the sessions of this Committee of the Whole – a sort of "Ocean Assembly of the United Nations," meeting every second year. The integrated policy should be prepared by DOALOS in cooperation with the CSD.

Policy integration: Specialized agencies and programmes

Analogous to what happens in the national "circle," where almost all government ministries are involved in one way or another in ocean affairs, and ways have to found to harmonize and integrate their overlapping and often conflicting policies, almost all specialized agencies and programmes of the United Nations are involved in one way or another in ocean affairs. The International Maritime Organisation (IMO), the Intergovernmental Oceanographic Commission (IOC) and the International Sea-bed Authority (ISBA)[25] are exclusively devoted to ocean affairs (IMO for shipping; IOC for marine sciences, ISBA for sea-bed mining), while UNESCO, FAO, and UNEP have broader mandates including divisions for ocean affairs (UNESCO for marine sciences, culture and education; FAO for fisheries and aquaculture; UNEP for regional seas and marine environment) and others are otherwise involved with the oceans, such as the World Meterological Organization (WMO) with ocean-atmosphere interaction and its implications; the International Atomic Energy Agency (IAEA) for nuclear marine pollution; the United Nations Industrial Development Organization (UNIDO), with industrial marine technology; the International Labour Organization (ILO) for the protection of maritime workers; the World Health Organization (WHO) for ocean-related health problems, and so on.

Streamlining of the agencies and programmes for cost-effectiveness, elimination of overlaps and harmonization of policies has long been on the agenda of the United Nations and has been entrusted to the Administrative Committee on Coordination (ACC). In the wake of UNCED, the Secretary-General established a subcommittee of the ACC to deal specifically with the ocean-related policies and activities of the agencies and programmes, the ACC Subcommittee on Oceans and Coastal Areas, with its Secretariat within the IOC. Progress thus far has been disappointing. It is in fact doubtful whether policies can be integrated at the inter-Secretariat level. It is only at the level of the General Assembly that an integrated ocean policy can be framed, and this policy, then, should become the basis for the efforts of the ACC Subcommittee on Oceans and Coastal Areas.

If one wanted to compare intranational and international institutional arrangements, one could envisage the "Ocean Assembly" as the counterpart to a national parliament that determines policy. The specialized agencies and programmes would execute this policy like the ministries and departments of a national government. The ACC Subcommittee would act like an inter-ministerial committee or council responding to the interdisciplinary and trans-sectoral challenges of ocean and coastal management. Linkages between the upgraded Regional Seas Programmes and the decision-making process of the

163

"Ocean Assembly" must be as effective as the linkages between the government and the governments of states/provinces in a Federal State.

A new trusteeship council

In his address to the General Assembly, the Minister of Foreign Affairs of Malta proposed that the Trusteeship Council, which had practically completed its task of decolonialization, should be dedicated to a great new task: it should become the guardian of the principle of the Common Heritage of Mankind – not only in the international sea-bed, not only in the oceans, but as applicable to "the global commons" in general, including atmosphere, outer space, and the Antarctic. He elaborated his proposal further in his address to a workshop, "The United Nations: Second Generation," held in Malta in October 1994 under the auspices of the International Ocean Institute, the Foundation for International Studies, and the Ministry of Foreign Affairs of Malta. The concept was also adopted by the Commission on Global Governance in its report, *Our Global Neighbourhood.*

Meanwhile, a new need has emerged for trusteeship to be exercised over the global commons in the collective interest of humanity, including future generations. The global commons include the atmosphere, outer space, the ocean beyond national jurisdiction, and the related environment and life-support systems that contribute to the support of human life. The new global trusteeship also needs to encompass the responsibilities that each generation must accept towards future generations.[26]

During the same year, I tried to spell out the proposal in some more detail in my book *Ocean Governance and the United Nations.* I suggested that the Council should consist, as heretofore, of 53 members and that they should be elected by the General Assembly on the basis of equitable geographic representation. The present composition, established for the purpose of watching over the decolonialization process, is clearly not suitable for the new mandate.

The functions of the new Trusteeship Council would be:
– to consider reports submitted by Members of the United Nations, the specialized agencies and programmes as well as the International Sea-bed Authority and competent non-governmental organizations;

– to accept petitions and examine them in consultation with the agency or institution concerned; and

– to provide for periodic visits to locations where violations are suspected and take actions in conformity with the terms of its mandate.

The Trusteeship Council would hold in sacred trust the principle of the Common Heritage of Mankind. It would monitor compliance with this principle in accordance with international law, in ocean space, outer space, and the atmosphere as well as Antarctica, and report any infringement thereof to the General Assembly. It would deliberate on its wider application to matters of common concern affecting comprehensive security and sustainable development and the dignity of human life, and make its recommendations to the authorities and institutions concerned. The Trusteeship Council would act as the conscience of the United Nations and the guardian of future generations.

Between 1994 and 1997, the Maltese proposal was not given the attention it deserved – in spite of the endorsement of the Commission on Global Governance with its illustrious membership. The general objection was that it was not practical because it required Charter amendment on which there would be no agreement.

The relationship between the UN Commission on Sustainable Development and this new Trusteeship Council would be unclear and there might be overlaps of responsibilities.

Last but not least, the idea of expanding the application of the Common Heritage principle from the present limited scope of the deep sea-bed minerals to a wider sphere is still looked upon with dread and horror by the defenders of the status quo.

This situation changed rapidly when, to everyone's surprise, the Secretary-General of the United Nations, Kofi Annan, took up the proposal in his report (document A/51/950) dated 14 July 1997 to the 51st Session of the General Assembly, entitled "Renewing the United Nations: A Programme for Reform." Under the heading "A new concept of trusteeship," he wrote:

84. Although the United Nations was established primarily to serve Member States, it also expresses the highest aspirations of men, women and children around the world. Indeed, the Charter begins by declaring the determination of "We the peoples of the United Nations" to achieve a peaceful and just world order. *Relations between the United Nations and agencies of civil society are growing in salience in every major sector of the United Nations*

agenda. The global commons are the policy domain in which this inter-mingling of sectors and institutions is most advanced.

85. Member States appear to have decided to retain the Trusteeship Council. The Secretary-General proposes therefore *that it be reconstituted as the forum through which Member States exercise their collective trusteeship for the integrity of the global environment and common areas such as the oceans, atmosphere and outer space. At the same time, it should serve to link the United Nations and civil society in addressing these areas of global concern, which require the active contribution of public, private and voluntary sectors.* [Emphasis added]

Within three years, the proposal thus moved from the realm of Utopia, which could be conveniently ignored, to the realm of politics, and it may be there to stay. In the first paragraph, the Secretary-General rightly notes that "the global commons are the policy domain in which this intermingling of sectors and institutions is most advanced." By "global commons," in this context, he can only mean the oceans, because it is only in the emerging ocean and coastal regime that this development is taking place – thus confirming that this regime will be a model for and part of the new international order for the next century.

The Secretary-General studiously avoided the controversial term "Common Heritage of Mankind," and couched his proposal in more generic terms – less controversial because less defined – such as "common areas" and "areas of global concern," but what's in a name?

One could indeed imagine this new Trusteeship Council evolving into a sort of senate of wise persons watching over and deliberating on the evolving concept of the Common Heritage and its applications, and to advise the General Assembly, and in particular, its Committee of the Whole, dealing with the oceans, on emerging and evolving issues. Its relationship to that Committee of the Whole, or "ocean assembly," would be quite clear: They would not "overlap," with a consequent duplication of efforts. The General Assembly or its Committee of the Whole would be the only body composed of the full membership of the United Nations – therefore, the only body capable of generating a comprehensive integrated oceans policy. On the other hand, this Committee of the Whole or "Ocean Assembly" should be limited in its mandate to consideration of issues arising from the Law of the Sea, the ocean and coastal management-related parts of the UNCED conventions, agreements, and programmes and the ocean-related policies and activities of the specialized agencies and competent international organizations. This is indeed a wide enough mandate.

The Trusteeship Council, on the other hand, with its limited membership but a mandate far broader than the oceans, would consider issues arising from the Common Heritage concept in ocean policy in the broader context given by the UNCED process.

Its relationship to the UN Commission on Sustainable Development is a little harder to define because, as we tried to show in previous chapters, the concepts of common heritage and of sustainable development are inseparable. Thus it is not at the level of content, but on the level of process that the relationship must be defined. The Commission on Sustainable Development is an executive body, responsible for the implementation of *Agenda 21* and the other UNCED conventions, agreements, and programmes – a very broad, practical agenda. The attention it has been able to devote to the oceans has been inadequate. It would have no time to concern itself with the evolution of the Common Heritage principle.

The Trusteeship Council would be a deliberative and advisory body, and in its advisory function it could be as useful to the Commission on Sustainable Development as it would be to the "Ocean Assembly."

The international sea-bed authority

The last new piece in the institutional framework of the global "circle" is the International Sea-bed Authority, based on Part XI of the Law of the Sea Convention as modified – or contradicted – by the "Implementation Agreement" adopted by the General Assembly in July 1994.

The International Sea-bed Authority was established and inaugurated in Jamaica on 16 November 1994. Its governing bodies have held four plenary sessions (1995, 1996, 1997, 1998), each in two sections.[27]

The difficulties the authority has to face are of some magnitude. Partly they are due to defects in the provisions of the "Implementation Agreement,"[28] partly to historical changes affecting the future of seabed mining which would have made some changes inevitable in any case, whether through interpretation and development or through amendment in accordance with the provisions of the Convention.

167

Since manganese nodule mining is not likely to take place for the next 20 years, one might ask, who cares about the Sea-bed Authority? It might as well be closed down. I do not share this opinion. To my mind, the Sea-bed Authority is the only existing institutional embodiment of the fundamentally important principle of the Common Heritage of Mankind. If the Authority is allowed to fail and disappear, the Common Heritage of Mankind reverts to a status of disembodiedness. The new Trusteeship Council would be poorer if, in practical application, the Common Heritage principle were allowed to fail. If the Authority exists and succeeds, it is a pilot experiment for the management of the Common Heritage writ large.

The United Nations Conference on Environment and Development (UNCED) brought a new emphasis on "sustainable development" and "integrated coastal and ocean management." With its components of socio-economic development, environmental conservation, intra- and inter-generational equity, and peace, sustainable development must necessarily be based on the concept of the Common Heritage of Mankind, which has these very same components. The emphasis on integrated coastal and ocean management takes the Common Heritage concept out of the no-man's land of the deep seabed and broadens its scope to include the whole earth.

And there is yet another reason why the International Sea-bed Authority is important. Its disappearance would leave a gap among the existing "competent international organizations" dealing with the peaceful uses of ocean space and resources. The International Sea-bed Authority is the only existing global organization to deal with the non-living resources of the oceans, and it is needed to fulfil this function. To do this effectively, however, it will have to be reconceptualized, based on the experience of the last two decades and looking forward to the next.

The Implementation Agreement entered into force in July 1996, 30 days after ratification by the Netherlands. Provisional members – states not having ratified, or even signed, the Law of the Sea Convention – may continue to participate until 16 November 1998, but, after that date, there can be no more "provisional members."[29] Their possible exit may reopen the complex issues of the membership of the Council. Furthermore, funding by the United Nations ceased by "the end of the year following the year during which this Agreement enters into force," i.e., 31 December 1997.[30] Since then, the costs of the Authority have to be borne by the states parties. To put their money into it, the states parties will want to be sure that it is of some use to the international community. They are not likely to pay up. In fact, severe shortfalls were noted already during the Authority's spring 1998 session. If the problem is not resolved, the Finance Committee might declare meetings of the governing bodies "not cost-effective" and suspend them.[31] The Authority could go into a sleep or hibernation from which it might not awake. So the need for a re-conceptualization is urgent.

Two developments, however, should be noted: on the one hand, manganese nodule mining is not forthcoming, for a variety of economic, technological, environmental, and political reasons. On the other hand, new discoveries have changed interests in the deep-sea panorama. Taken together, these two developments have made large parts of Part XI of the Law of the Sea Convention as well as the Implementation Agreement obsolete. There is no way that we can ever return to Part XI as conceived in the 1970s. Here are some suggestions as to possible directions this reconceptualization might take.

Territoriality

Article 134 establishes that "This Part applies to the Area." The Area is defined by the limits to the outer continental shelf as given in Part VI of the convention. States have up to 10 years from the entry into force of the convention (16 November 1994) to decide on the limits of their outer continental shelf and to submit their data to the Commission on the Limits of the Continental Shelf (Article 4, Annex II). Add to this the time needed to reach an agreement between the Commission and the coastal states, and it becomes clear that the boundaries of the Area may remain undefined far into the next century. The boundaries between the Convention Area and the area of the Antarctic Treaty system, furthermore, are altogether undefined. These circumstances may make over-reliance on the territorial principle unrealistic.

Reliance on the territorial principle also makes, for instance, the implementation of Article 150(h) extremely difficult. This Article provides that activities in the Area should be carried out with a view to ensuring the protection of developing countries from adverse effects on their economies or on their export earnings resulting from a reduction in the price of an affected mineral, or in the volume of exports of that mineral, to the extent that such reduction is caused by activities in the Area, as provided in Article 151.[32]

Adverse effects on the economies of developing land-based producer states may be ascribed to a number of causes, such as production of the same minerals in areas under national jurisdiction, or cyclic or structural changes in demand and price structures, due to the introduction of new synthetics, recycling, or miniaturization of products making industrial processes less resource-intensive. As demonstrated by the long debates in the First Special Commission of the Preparatory Commission for the International Sea-bed and for the International Tribunal for the Law of the Sea,[33] it is extremely difficult, not to say impossible, to identify, separate, and quantify the "extent that such reduction is caused by activities in the Area."

Over-reliance on the territorial principle has also marred the effectiveness of the provisions on the management of living resources. The territorial boundary between the Exclusive Economic Zone and the adjacent high sea turned out to be an obstacle to rational management of the fisheries. If straddling stocks and highly migratory stocks are overfished in the high seas, they cannot be conserved in the EEZ. The 1995 Agreement for the Implementation of the Provisions of the United Nations Convention on the Law of the Sea of 10 December 1982 Relating to the Conservation and Management of Straddling Fish Stocks and Highly Migratory Fish Stocks (Straddling Stocks Agreement) mandates "compatibility" between conservation and management measures taken on the high seas and those taken in areas under national jurisdiction.[34]

Compatibility is equally needed between the rights and duties of the coastal state on the continental shelf and the rights and duties of the International Sea-bed Authority in the adjacent Area. Such compatibility does not exist between Parts VI (Continental Shelf) and XI (the Area) of the Convention, nor is it established by the Implementation Agreement. For example, there is a grey area with regard to certain living resources. Part VI, Article 77, provides that "the natural resources referred to in this Part consist of the mineral and other non-living resources of the sea-bed and subsoil *together with living organisms belonging to sedentary species, that is to say, organisms which, at the harvestable stage, either are immobile on or under the sea-bed or are unable to move except in constant physical contact with the sea-bed or the subsoil.*"

No reference to these living resources is to be found in Part XI, Article 133, which defines "resources" as "all solid, liquid, or gaseous mineral resources *in situ* in the Area at or beneath the sea-bed, including polymetallic nodules." This can easily be explained by the fact that in the 1970s very little was known about the living resources of the deep sea-bed.

The situation is further complicated by certain responsibilities of the Sea-bed Authority in the Area. Article 143 gives the Authority the right to coordinate marine scientific research in the Area as well as to carry out such research directly. Marine scientific research in the Area is not restricted to the "non-living resources" but will certainly include research on the fauna and flora of the sea-bed as well as "bio-prospecting."

Article 145 imposes on the Authority the duty to "adopt appropriate rules, regulations and procedures for ... *the protection and conservation of the natural resources of the Area and the prevention of damage to the flora and fauna of the marine environment.*" These are clearly *management responsibilities*. They are not touched on by the Implementation Agreement and thus remain valid. This provides a strong basis for extending the jurisdiction of the Authority to the living resources of the Area, including them in the Common Heritage of Mankind and providing "compatibility" between the regimes of the Continental Shelf and of the Area.

Article 142 of Part XI establishes that "Activities in the Area, with respect to resource deposits in the Area which lie across limits of national jurisdiction, shall be conducted with due regard to the rights and legitimate interests of any coastal state across whose jurisdiction such deposits lie." The Article requires consultation, notification, and cooperation between the Authority and the coastal state in such cases. The prior consent of the coastal state is required before the Authority may proceed with the exploitation of such resources.

The implementation of Article 142 presupposes that the territorial boundary between the Area and the continental shelf of the coastal state has been established which, as pointed out above, may not happen until sometime in the next century.

Article 83 of Part VI, referring to the delimitation of the continental shelf between states with opposite or adjacent coasts, provides that, where there is no agreement on the boundary, "the states concerned, in a spirit of understanding and co-operation, shall make every effort to enter into provisional arrangements of a practical nature and, during this transitional period, not to jeopardize or hamper the reaching of the final agreement. Such arrangements shall be without prejudice to the final delimitation."

In other words, states are encouraged to "freeze" their claims and establish "joint management zones" or "joint development zones" to enable them to proceed with resource exploration and exploitation. This practice has gained much currency during the past two decades, as pointed out in chapter 4.

There is no reason why the concept of joint management zones should be restricted to states with adjacent or opposite coasts. It might equally apply to relations between the coastal state and the International Sea-bed Authority. Instead of the extremely costly, cumbersome, and time-consuming procedure of establishing boundaries through the Commission on the Limits of the Continental Shelf, one could envisage this alternative procedure: beyond a 300-mile limit of the continental shelf, claims might be "frozen" in the case of resource discovery, and joint management zones might be established between the coastal state or states and the International Sea-bed Authority. Such an arrangement might be beneficial both for the coastal state and for the Authority. Nor is there any reason why the Authority could not enter into joint ventures with coastal states – especially developing coastal states, if they so wish – for the exploration and exploitation of sea-bed resources in the EEZ.

Such measures would serve to de-territorialize and functionalize the jurisdiction of the Authority in the next century and confirm its role as the UN institution in charge of dealing with the non-living resources of the oceans.

Overemphasis on manganese nodules

All the points raised here are more or less directly interrelated and overlapping. Thus the issues raised under the present heading relate directly to at least one of the issues raised under the previous heading as well as to those dealt with in the following section.

It is well known that UNCLOS III neglected to pay attention to deep-sea resources other than the manganese nodules. The official justification was that the nodules were the only resource with imminent prospects for commercial exploitation. Other deep-sea resources were music of the future. They still required long-term scientific research and exploration. The poor countries knew nothing about these developments. The industrialized countries kept their knowledge close to their chest. It was not until the late 1970s that some information about cobalt crusts and polymetallic sulphides began to percolate at the conference. By that time it was considered too late to incorporate this knowledge. True, the Convention defines the resources, which are the Common Heritage of Mankind, as "all solid, liquid or gaseous mineral resources *in situ* in the Area at or beneath the sea-bed, including polymetallic nodules"; and Article 151.9 endows the Authority with the power "to limit the level of production of minerals from the Area, other than minerals from polymetallic nodules, under such conditions and applying such methods as may be appropriate by adopting regulations in accordance with Article 151, paragraph 9."[35] True, also, Article 162.2.(o)(ii) provides that "Rules, regulations and procedures for the exploration for and exploitation of any resource other than polymetallic nodules shall be adopted within three years from the date of a request to the Authority by any of its members to adopt such rules, regulations and procedures in respect of such resources. All rules, regulations and procedures shall remain in effect on a provisional basis until approved by the Assembly or until amended by the Council in the light of any views expressed by the Assembly."[36]

Two reasons for this limitation concurred. One was the pervasive North-South confrontation in the First Committee responsible for Part XI. The South, throughout, advocated an Authority with comprehensive powers and a broadly inclusive interpretation of "activities in the Area." The North, throughout, attempted to restrict the powers of the Authority. "Activities in the Area" was to be interpreted as "nodule mining activities" – nothing else. To include other resources and activities relating to them would have broadened the power of the Authority, and the North resisted any such broadening.

At the same time, the South wanted a general framework for regulating and managing the exploration and exploitation of the Common Heritage of Mankind; the North insisted on a painstakingly detailed list of administrative and financial rules and regulations: so detailed, in fact, that they were applicable only to this one resource. Different sets of detailed rules and regulations would be needed for other resources in the future. This insistence on detail on the part, in particular, of the United States was due to its general distrust of the Authority, where decision-making would be in the hands of the majority of developing countries. Nothing should be left to the discretion of this Authority; every detail had to be settled in advance and carved in stone, subject to a complex amendment procedure. It was the overload of detail that excluded other resources from the scope of consideration in Part XI.

Science and exploration moved much faster than had been anticipated. The over-concentration on manganese nodules was obsolete at the time the Convention was adopted. It will be totally self-defeating in the next century. An International Sea-bed Authority restricted to the regulation of manganese nodule mining will be totally meaningless. All significant sea-bed activity would be carried out by the industrialized states outside of the Authority. No state would be willing to invest money in an obsolete bureaucratic structure. It is to be hoped that, as soon as possible, one or more delegations will invoke Article 162.2.(o)(ii) and request the consideration of rules and regulations for other deep-sea resources.

During the spring 1998 session, some delegations from developing countries began to ask questions about resources other than manganese nodules. They requested that the Secretary-General should prepare a report on these other resources. The International Ocean Institute, in cooperation with the Government of Jamaica, organized a seminar for the delegates, in August 1998, on these other resources, focusing, in particular, on the methane hydrates and the genetic resources of the deep sea-bed.

The decision-making system

Decision-making was not a big issue with regard to the Authority's Assembly, "the supreme organ of the Authority consisting of all the members" (Article 160). Following the pattern of all UN institutions based on the principle of sovereign equality of states, each member has one vote. The Implementation Agreement did not question this principle. Serious difficulties instead arose from the inter-related problems of the composition and the procedure of voting in the Council, the powerful executive organ of the Authority. The result of nine years of negotiations on this subject, embodied in Article 161 of the Convention,[37] reflects political compromise rather than the pursuit of executive efficiency. But the procedure is logical and implementable.

The Implementation Agreement maintains much of the language of Article 162, but basically changes the election and decision-making processes, complicating them almost beyond comprehension. The Authority's Assembly, which had two two-part sessions in 1995 and 1996, needed in fact six weeks within the two-year period, plus several days of intersessional consultations, to complete the process. Each day of work of the Assembly costs the United Nations about $10,000, to which the costs to governments, to send a delegate, have to be added – another $10,000 per delegate per half working session.

174

The Implementation Agreement provides (section 3, para. 9) that each of the interest groups mentioned under (a) to (c) shall be treated as a chamber. If, in the original text, four members representing each of these interest groups were to be elected into the Council as a whole, now we have three chambers of four members each. A fourth chamber consists of the six members to be elected under (d) together with all developing countries elected under (e). That makes a rather large chamber of developing countries, in the present case, the developing countries in Group (e) are 13, thus bringing the membership of the chamber of developing countries up to 19. The large membership of this "chamber," however, is not at all an advantage in decision-making. Quite the contrary. For the Agreement provides (section 3, para. 5 of the Annex) that "decisions by voting in the Council on questions of substance, except where the Convention provides for decisions by consensus in the Council, shall be taken by a two-thirds majority of members present and voting, provided that such decisions are not opposed by a majority in any one of the chambers referred to in paragraph 9." This effectively means that any two industrialized states represented in Chambers (a), (b), and (c) can veto any decision of the Council, whereas it takes 10 developing countries to exercise the same power.

Before electing the members of the Council, the Assembly has to establish lists of countries fulfilling the criteria for membership in the groups of states under (a) to (d). Each group of states under (a) to (d) will be represented in the Council by those members nominated by that group. Each group may nominate only as many candidates as the number of seats required to be filled by that group. When the number of potential candidates in each of the groups exceeds the number of seats available in each of these chambers, the principle of rotation will apply as a general rule. It is up to each group to determine how to apply this principle of rotation.

Thus the chambers are effectively elected, not by the Assembly, but by the nominating groups of states qualifying for each chamber. The Assembly has merely to rubber-stamp this self-election.

The whole procedure of composing the 36-member Council turned out to be a three-dimensional jigsaw puzzle. Extraordinarily difficult decisions had to be made, and matched, at three levels. At one level, each interest group had to produce its list of four, respectively six, members and agree, among its own members, on the process of rotation – that is, some members were effectively to be elected for only one or two years, after which they would have to yield their

175

place to another member of their group. At first, the rotation process was to extend over a 10-year period, to accommodate all candidates, but this period then was condensed to four years, with one exception, where a delegation has been assured re-election for four years in the year 2000 – a rather unusual procedure.

The whole process was stalled for about a year by the intransigence of the United States (not a party to the Convention, but a provisional member of the Authority) which did not want both India and China to be members of the chamber of highest investors, although they both qualified for membership. But to have them both in that chamber would have given them an equal vetoing power to that enjoyed, say, by France and Germany, the other two investors represented in the (b) chamber. India insisted as adamantly that it had a right to be there. In the end, and in an exemplary spirit of cooperation, India agreed to be in that chamber for a period of two years only, after which it will be replaced by the Netherlands, with the proviso that India will be re-elected for four years in the year 2000.

Then there was an interregional problem: How to divide the overall 36 seats among the traditional five regional groups (Africa, Asia, Latin America, Eastern European States, and Western Europe and others). After protracted negotiations, there was an agreement that Africa should have 10 seats, Asia 9, Latin America 7, Eastern Europe 3, and Western Europe and others 8. This, however, adds up to 37. The crafty solution to this problem of political arithmetic was a "floating seat." In a spirit of burden-sharing, each regional group would give up one seat during one of the first four years. This does not include the group of Eastern European States, which only gets three seats in any case. The Latin American and Caribbean group volunteered to be the first to give up one seat during the first year, followed by Western Europe and others in the second year, Africa in the third year, and Asia in the fourth.

So much for the interregional negotiations.

Within each regional group, the process of rotation had to be agreed, requiring time-consuming intraregional negotiations. Finally, the results of the regional consultations and the interest groups consultations had to be integrated and harmonized.

The result, reached on the second-to-last day of the third two-week working session of the Assembly, was unique in the annals of international negotiations. It took the inexhaustible patience and the jigsaw-puzzle-solving genius of the Assembly's President, Ambassador Djalal of Indonesia, to reach it. It contains, for instance, provisions like the following:

> In order to maintain the 9 seats allocated to the Asian Group when Poland occupies the seat relinquished by Indonesia in Group C after 2 years, Indonesia will occupy the seat relinquished by Poland in Group E so that Indonesia can complete its 4-year term unless it is able to secure a vacant seat in Group C.[38]

There was a sense of euphoria and victory when the ordeal of electing the Council was finally over. Ignoring the tormented history of the Council's election, one might indeed easily come to the conclusion that it is a good Council with a well-balanced membership. Could the same result not have been reached by simpler means? Was it necessary to impose this ordeal on the delegations and on the President? Should this ordeal be repeated? Looking at 1998 and the future of the Sea-bed Authority and its functions, it might seem advisable to review and revise the provisions on the composition and decision-making of the Council, if it is to be effective. In particular, one might keep in mind that, as the scope of the Authority's activities expands to include resources of the Common Heritage of Mankind other than manganese nodules, the "interest groups" represented in Chambers A through D may not be as meaningful as they appeared to be in the past decades.

Taking into account the tremendous changes which have taken place and the lessons learned, it would seem that, at present, the very objective of the Authority is somewhat nebulous. No one really knows if and when nodule mining is to begin. No one really knows what the Authority is to do during the indefinite period in which no nodule mining will take place.

To adjust and reconceptualize the Authority, and to make it useful to the international community, three steps might be undertaken.

First of all, a meaningful plan of work for the next five years should be prepared. Within the present framework, and in line with the present activities of states, this plan should concentrate on the development of human resources, on technology cooperation, and on studying long-term environmental impacts and the enhancement of biodiversity.

The Pioneer Investors' training programmes should be resumed and developed. They should be integrated into the other training activities within the UN system and outside of it.[39] The Division for Ocean Affairs and the Law of the Sea (DOALOS), in cooperation with the United Nations Development Programme (UNDP) and the

International Ocean Institute, are developing a series of programmes applying very advanced educational methodologies called "Train-Sea-Coast." The Sea-Bed Authority might join this undertaking to develop a curriculum for sea-bed mineral exploration and management.

Several states are engaged in technology testing and upgrading and in studying the environmental impact of these technologies. The Authority should take initiatives to associate itself with these activities. A cooperative venture in technology development, in conjunction with a four- or five-year environmental impact study, in association with the Authority and linked to a training programme, might form the backbone of the Authority's work plan for the next few years[40] and prepare the ground for the more sweeping, long-term changes which will be needed.

Secondly, when the housekeeping matters are left behind, ample time should be reserved for a general debate on the future of the Authority. This might be an essential contribution to a new vision of the Authority, to bring it into line with more recent developments such as the climate and biodiversity conventions to which deep sea-bed research could make important contributions. The delegations should also have the opportunity, during special hearings, to hear from the scientific community and the non-governmental sector. NGOs, especially those with competence on the environmental impact of sea-bed mining and on the interactions of the Authority's sea-bed mining regime and the regime established by the Biodiversity Convention, could make a useful contribution to the debate.

The third step that might be taken is for one or more delegations to take the initiative provided for in Article 162.2.(o)(ii) with regard to rules and regulations for the exploration and production of resources other than manganese nodules – after establishing whether, under the implementation agreement, such a request can be made. If the answer to this question were to be negative, the revision of paragraph 15 of the Annex to the Implementation Agreement becomes a matter of urgency – unless the Authority wants to permit that it be ruled out of the real utilization of the Area and its resources, which are the Common Heritage of Mankind.

Conclusions

The analysis of the present situation leads to the following recommendations:

A. Immediate short-term recommendations (five years)

1. Progressive interpretation and development of Implementation Agreement, Annex, section I, para. 5 (g), (h), and (i), formulating, adopting, and implementing cooperative plans for the scientific exploration of the deep sea-bed, joint technology development in conjunction with long-term environmental assessment and the development of human resources (training).

2. For this purpose:
   (a) to continue/develop the training programme adopted by the Preparatory Commission;
   (b) to resume the plan for joint exploration of a first mine site for the Enterprise adopted by the Preparatory Commission;
   (c) to consider the project for technology development and long-term environmental assessment proposed by the Delegation of the Federal Republic or Germany.

3. Decision to make rules and regulations for the exploration and exploitation of resources other than manganese nodules, under Article 162, para. 2 (o)(ii).

4. If requested, joint ventures with coastal developing states for the exploration of mineral resources on their continental shelves.

5. Decision to schedule ample time for a general debate on the future of the International Sea-bed Authority.

B. Long-term recommendations (2004 – 10 years after the entry into force of the convention and the establishment of the authority)

Review and Revision of Part XI and Implementation Agreement. A possible model for the long-term restructuring of the International Sea-Bed Authority is given in the Annex.

The Authority, though not a part of the United Nations system – a point that also might be reconsidered in the future – must nevertheless be closely linked with that system. Interactions with other convention regimes, e.g., the Biodiversity and Climate Convention regimes, must be properly articulated in cooperative arrangements. Thus the deep-sea fauna and flora, including the genetic resources, are common ground for cooperation between the Authority and the Biodiversity Convention organization. The methane hydrates, and their impact on climate change, are common ground for cooperation with the Climate Convention organization.

179

This has been a long chapter, following an emerging structure of ocean governance from the village to the planet as a whole. It is all there, for those who want to see, for those who want to go through the exercise described in the opening page of this book, of totally unfocusing and then refocusing to perceive a new dimension, to perceive the majesty of the oceanic circle.

Notes

1. See chapter 3 above.
2. Report by the World Commission on Environment and Development, 1987.
3. United Nations Conference on Environment and Development, Rio de Janeiro, 1992.
4. Hasler, 1998.
5. *Ibid.*
6. Fanning, 1997.
7. Bruce Gillies, 1999, "The Nunavut Final Agreement and Marine Management in the North," *Northern Perspectives* 23(1): 17–19. Canadian Arctic Resources Committee.
8. Jentoft and Mikalsen, 1994.
9. Welch, 1995.
10. Borgese, 1995.
11. UNEP, 1993.
12. *European Technological Collaboration,* 1987.
13. Malta: Foundation for International Studies, 1987.
14. Saigal, 1988.
15. The technology transfer programme of the Montreal Protocol, with its Multilateral Fund has been hailed as a success story. Anil Agarwal, Director of the Ministry of Environment and Forests of the Government of India, has some serious reservations: "Again, there is a growing feeling that new technologies will replace existing ones. This would take place largely in the North, and the South will have to bear the cost of subsequent conversions. The full implications are yet to be known, but the thought of technological dependence leaves a very uncomfortable feeling..." (UNEP, *Our Planet,* Vol.9, No. 2, 1997) Technology co-development or joint R&D, as proposed in these pages, would alleviate these concerns.
16. When the Law of the Sea Convention was adopted in 1982, it covered all uses of the oceans, directly or indirectly through reference to "the competent international organizations" and their conventions and programmes. The Convention could not take into account the developments of the 1990s, which, in their turn, are taking too little note of the Convention. Thus the ocean regime, again, is being splintered and sectoralized. Fundamentally, the problem cannot be solved until there is a forum where states and non-state actors can discuss the closely interrelated problems of ocean space as a whole, treating the Convention as a living and evolving organism incorporating and adjusting to new developments such as those of the 1990s. By a more liberal interpretation of the new legal instruments with regard to technology cooperation, however, one can, to some extent, anticipate and stimulate the new integration process.
17. Upon the publication of the IOI study, the Italian EUROMAR coordinator took the initiative of calling a meeting to discuss the possibility of opening EUROMAR to the participation of developing countries. The proposal at that time was defeated. The French delegation, in particular, insisted that EUREKA and EUROMAR had to remain European, as the principal purpose was to make European industry globally competitive. Today the situation is somewhat different. The European Union's emphasis on technical assistance to the

countries on the sourthern and eastern shores of the Mediterranean offers a far better chance of cooperation.

18. Paragraph 92 of this Programme reads: "Governments should create a legal and policy framework that is conducive to technology-related private sector investments and long-term sustainable development objectives. Governments and international development institutions should continue to play a key role in establishing public-private partnerships, within and between developed and developing countries and countries with economies in transition. Such partnerships are essential for linking the advantages of the private sector – access to finance and technology, managerial efficiency, entrepreneurial experience and engineering expertise – with the capacity of governments to create a policy environment that is conducive to technology-related private-sector investments and long-term sustainable development objectives." Paragraph 93 recommends the creation of centres for the transfer of technology at various levels, including the regional level. Paragraph 95 stresses the importance of taking appropriate measures to strengthen South-South cooperation for technology transfer and capacity-building.

19. UNEP(OCA)/MED IG > 8/CRP/9, paragraphs (a), 1–3.

20. A similar methodology, to attain the advantages mentioned above, was developed in the *Preliminary Draft of a World Constitution*, first published by the University of Chicago in 1948. Election by a universal body upon the nomination by local bodies was referred to as "exogenous representation." See *A Constitution for the World*, Santa Barbara, CA: Center for the Study of Democratic Institutions, 1965.

21. Jens Evenson, formerly Judge at the International Court of Justice, advocates this opinion. While he notes that the Law of the Sea Convention does not directly address the denuclearization of the oceans or related arms limitation issues, he concludes that "the Convention further codifies the principles which underlie the peaceful uses of ocean space. As such the Convention could serve as a legal basis for more directly addressing the issue of nuclear weapons at sea." Evenson, 1986.

22. See Lopez-Reyes, 1997.

23. "Economic Integration Organisations," which have a standing in all new convention regimes.

24. Doc.A/51/645.

25. ISBA is not a specialized agency but an independent intergovernmental treaty-created body with "observer status" at the UN and at the International Tribunal for the Law of the Sea.

26. Commission on Global Governance, 1995.

27. The first session, 1994–1995, was divided into three sections, including the Inaugural Session.

28. Agreement Relating to the Implementation of Part XI of the United Nations Convention on the Law of the Sea of 1982, 17 August 1994, A/RES/48/263.

29. Implementation Agreement, Annex, section I, para. 12(a).

30. *Ibid.*, para.14.

31. *Ibid.*, para.2.

32. The Implementation Agreement abandons the concept of "compensation" and replaces it with "economic assistance." However, the notion that such assistance is restricted to developing countries which suffer serious adverse effects on their export earnings ... resulting from a reduction in the price of an affected mineral ... *to the extent that such reduction is caused by activities in the Area*, is maintained (section 7, para.1).

33. See, for instance, Provisional Conclusions of the Deliberations of Special Commission 1 which can form the basis of its recommendations to the International Sea-bed Authority (Revised Suggestions by the Chairman, Provisional Conclusion 8): "The Authority should devise a methodology to determine the effects of sea-bed production on the price and volume of exports of the affected metals and to separate them from the effects caused by other factors. In devising such a methodology, the Authority shall take into account: world metal

market situation; change in consumption patterns; production from maritime zones under national jurisdiction; substitution; recycling; technological developments; other relevant factors, such as the general economic conditions, the government policies and the exhaustion of deposits within national jurisdiction of the developing land-based producer States concerned." In Renate Platzöder, ed. *The Law of the Sea Documents: 1983–1990*, Vol. XI. Dobbs Ferry, NY: Oceana Press, 1990.

34. Art.7, para.2. "Conservation and management taken on the high seas and those taken in areas under national jurisdiction shall be compatible in order to ensure conservation and management of the stocks overall. To this end, coastal states and states fishing on the high seas have a duty to cooperate for the purpose of achieving compatible measures in respect of straddling fish stocks and highly migratory fish stocks."

35. This power to limit, in future, the production of minerals derived from resources other than manganese nodules was cancelled by the Implementation Agreement in section 6, para.7.

36. The Implementation Agreement appears to limit the application of this provision to matters specified in sections 2 (The Enterprise), 5 (Transfer of Technology), 6 (Production Policy), 7 (Economic Assistance) and 8 (Financial Terms of Contract). This would not include resources other than manganese nodules. However, there is no statement to the effect that the provision regarding other resources "shall not apply."

37. The Council consists of 36 members who must be elected by the Assembly in the following order:

First, (a) four members from among states who are the largest consumers and/or importers of the metals produced from the nodules and have consumed and or imported more than 2 per cent of total world consumption or imports. Among these four there must be one state from the Eastern European (Socialist) region.

Second, (b) four members from among the eight states who have made the largest investments in nodule mining. Again, one state from the Eastern European region must be included.

Third, (c) four members from among states who are the largest producers and or exporters of the metals produced in the Area, and these four must include at least two developing countries whose exports of such minerals have a substantial bearing upon their economies;

Fourth, (d) six developing countries, representing special interests, including states with large populations, land-locked or geographically disadvantaged states, states who are large importers of these minerals, states who are potential producers, and least-developed states.

Fifth, and finally (e) 18 members are to be elected to ensure equitable geographic representation in the Council as a whole.

Members are elected for four years; during the first election, half of the members are elected for two years. To have staggered terms:

Each member has one vote.

Decision-making is based on a tier system. Procedural questions require a simple majority of members present and voting. Less controversial substantive questions require a two-thirds majority; more controversial questions require a three-fourths majority; the most controversial questions – concerning the protection of developing land-based producer states from adverse economic effects, or financial or other economic benefit sharing and some other matters as well as Amendments, are to be decided by consensus.

It is a cumbersome and complex process, but it could be implemented. How efficient it would have been remains an open question; how long the "interest groups" referred to under (a)–(b) might have changed – e.g., due to resources other than manganese nodules being exploited – remains another open question.

38. Document ISBA/A/L.8, 21 March 1996.

39. The Federal Republic of Germany, although under no obligation to do so, has offered a training programme which obviously should be utilized. The International Ocean Institute, in cooperation with China and India, and funded by the Nippon Foundation of Japan, is

conducting training programmes for managers and project planners in deep-sea activities. The intensive five-week programme takes place in India and China in alternate years. In 1997 it was conducted at the University of the West Indies in Kingston, Jamaica, to give the participants the opportunity for direct contacts with the International Sea-Bed Authority. The programme is directed by the Hon. Joseph Warioba of Tanzania, in cooperation with the Directors of IOI India and IOI China.

40. Such a programme was proposed in 1987 by the Federal Republic of Germany.

6

Recommendations and conclusions

In this chapter we shall try to summarize the recommendations made throughout this volume; and in conclusion we shall examine how the evolution of the system of ocean governance will affect the rest of the system and respond to the global *problématique* as a whole.

Natural and man-made causes converge to make this age, straddling two millennia:

– a transformation age,
– an information age, and
– an age of uncertainty.

Transformation affects our natural environment as well as our social, economic, and political environment. A climate change is altering the physical atlas of the globe. A reshuffling of the socio-political map is in process, with the end of the age of the nation state and the end of half a millennium of Eurocracy.

Information enhances our knowledge, our science, our technology; but the more we know, the better we know how little we know.

Transformation and information thus generate *uncertainty*, which must be acknowledged, with a feeling of awe for the ultimate mystery of existence, but can be kept at bay with the help of more and better information, risk management, and the precautionary principle.

Looking through the ocean darkly, we perceive nevertheless its interaction with the atmosphere that will largely determine climate change and the new physical atlas of the next millennium. We realize that, as the Secretary-General of the United Nations put it, "The global commons are the policy domain in which this intermingling of sectors and institutions is most advanced." Ocean policy and the emerging system of ocean governance are the lead sector in the reshuffling of the socio-political atlas. In physical terms, the ocean is the great moderator and equalizer of temperatures and climes. In socio-political terms, the ocean-born principle of the Common Heritage of Mankind may have the same function in the next century.

Following the order of the chapters in this volume, then, our recommendations would be the following.

Ocean perspectives: physical

– Major efforts and funding should be devoted to an enhancement of the marine sciences and technologies and to the exploration and monitoring of ocean processes through global services like GOOS. The financial contribution of the insurance industry in particular and the private sector in general should be encouraged and eventually systematized in the form of an ocean development tax.

Ocean perspectives: cultural

– The Year of the Ocean is generating a multitude of cultural, scientific, and educational manifestations and celebrations, revealing the ocean in the light of many civilizations and world views. These, however, may remain dispersed and unaccessible to most people.
– UNESCO should be requested to monitor, collect, and review this material and assemble it in a full-length feature film – "The Oceans and the Twenty-First Century." This film, utilizing the most advanced cinematographic technologies, such as wide or multiple screens with three-dimensional effect, should be shown in theatres world-wide, on television, and, in particular, in schools all over the world to increase popular awareness of the importance of the ocean in our lives and the lives of future generations.

Ocean perspectives: economic

– The impact of the ongoing process of transformation on our economic system is bound to be profound.
– The new system, emerging from the ocean, the great equalizer, and its principle of the Common Heritage of Mankind, would have to respond to the needs of the age of the information revolution and the end of Eurocentrism. It would have to embody, in one way or another, the following concepts:

(1) *Holistic approach*

Economics has social, political, environmental, cultural, and ethical dimensions. Its focus must be the human being. Its goal: the welfare of all.

(2) *Decentralization, community-based co-management*

The impact of high technology and the principles and methodologies of modern management converge with the ideas and ideals of the non-Western world views in their emphasis on communitarianism and a decentralized social economy, as espoused by Gandhiism. This implies:

· resource saving through greater discipline on the part of consumers, improving energy efficiency, and better organization of the production and distribution system;

· a reduction in consumption standards through "voluntary simplicity" and self-restraint;

· acceptance of substitutions between material and non-material consumption: fewer goods and more services or less time spent in market-oriented economic activities and more time allocated to non-economic activities and/or small-scale environmentally benign material production for self-consumption;

· reducing the demand for intra-urban transportation by redesigning cities;

· reducing long-distance transportation of materials and goods by better integration of local and regional economies.

(3) *Equity*

The goal of economics is not the greatest good for the greatest number – which might leave 51 per cent of the population free to exploit the remaining 49 – but the welfare of all. Implicit in the above is the basic presumption of equal dignity of and respect for the life and welfare of every individual. Translated into the sphere of economic policy, it entails top priority for meeting the most basic material needs (water, food, shelter, health, education) of everybody.

(4) *Intellectual property*

Intellectual property rights may have to be reviewed and revised in the context of the economics of the information age and sustainable development.

(5) *Uncertainty*

Decisions on socio-economic policy will have to be made in the light of uncertainty inherent in the system. Uncertainty can be reduced, not eliminated, through applying the precautionary principle and new concepts of risk management as developed by contemporary insurance economists. It can further be reduced by blending insights gained through improved scientific and technological methodologies with those gained through ancient wisdom and experience, in community-based co-management systems.

(6) *Work*

Work, as expression of self-development and fulfilment, is a basic human right. Theories of the post-industrial society, and the ideals of other cultures converge in distinguishing "work" from "paid employment" and stressing the importance of "service." This would imply:

- guaranteed minimum paid employment for everyone, sufficient to assure the basic necessities of life: shelter, food, health, and education;
- self-employment and "free enterprise" for the free time left by the part-time employment, to increase income and generate savings;
- a period of life to be devoted to unpaid service to the community, thus enhancing the common heritage and repaying what the community has provided at an earlier stage of life;
- such a scheme to be realized at the local community level, on the basis of co-management.

(7) *Wealth*

Wealth and welfare are a combination of natural or physical and biological, of man-made (cultural tools; goods and services) and of monetarized (capital) phenomena; this holistic view reflects our social, economic and environmental dimensions. Wealth is in stock not in flow. It is to be measured by human development indicators, including economic, social, cultural, ethical and environmental indicators:

- indicators are needed especially for non-marketed and non-marketable goods and services;
- non-remunerated work, i.e., work not exchanged and work exchanged, but not paid with money, must be included;
- deducted value, i.e., costs of man-made pollution and over-exploitation of resources, must be taken into consideration; and
- uncertainties inherent in complex systems have to be taken into account;

- indicators of vulnerability and indicators couched within frameworks of probability should systematically be developed.

(8) *Value*

The value of goods is not their "exchange value" ("market value") but their "utilization value." The longer their duration through inputs, paid or non-paid, of services such as training, maintenance, repairing, rebuilding, recycling and disposing services, the greater their value.

(9) *Ownership*

The seas and oceans and their resources are the Common Heritage of Mankind;

- "Resources" means non-living, living and genetic resources.
- Whether they are in areas under national jurisdiction or in the high seas or in or under the International Sea-bed Area, they must be managed sustainably, keeping in mind the needs of future generations; with special consideration for the needs of poor countries and poor people, aiming at the eradication of poverty. They are reserved for peaceful purposes, peace and security being basic for sustainable development.

- The principle of the Common Heritage of Mankind thus is the foundation of sustainable development, not only in the oceans, but globally. In accordance with the cultures of the vast majority of humankind, its application must be extended from the wealth of the oceans to wealth in general, not to be "owned" by humankind, whether individually or collectively, but to be held in trust, and to be administered on the basis of cooperation between civil society and the institutions of governance, at local, national, regional, and global levels.

(10) *Internal/international revenues*

taxation may be shared between municipal, national, regional, and global levels of governance, in accordance with the levels of services required.

- Gradually, a development tax might be levied on all commercial uses of the global commons, starting with the oceans.

(a) taxes might be levied on activities generating deducted value, converging with the ethical postulate of the prohibition of trade in weapons, drugs, etc.

(11) *Adaptive non-linear network*

The overall direction of the economy is determined by the interaction of many dispersed units (human beings). The

action of any one unit depends on the state and actions of an unlimited number of other units; leading, inevitably, to a system of multiple equilibria, thereby making impossible the prediction of unique future states:
- the units are not hierarchically arranged and all are free to follow their own way to the goal: the goal is one but the paths are many;

The following of this path should lead to an economy which is:
- flexible, adaptive and creative;
- non-exploitative, so that assets and income get equitably distributed;
- in harmony with the natural environment; and
- self-regulated, leading to restraint on unnecessary consumption; culturally determined.

(12) *Non-violence*

The socio-economic system for sustainable development is based on non-violence as applied to ownership, production, consumption, work, allocation, distribution, and in reforming economic systems:
- all disputes are to be settled peacefully through the appropriate mechanisms at all levels of governance.

Ocean perspectives: legal

- The point of break-through to the world of the next century is along the path of the evolving legal order. The United Nations Convention on the Law of the Sea, in its interaction with the Conventions, Agreements, and Programmes emanating from the United Nations Conference on Environment and Development, has set into motion a process of fundamental transformation.
- These new legal instruments should be seen as one single process generating one single dynamic system. Their overlaps should be utilized as common ground for common action, in such a way that they reinforce one another in the process of building a better world for the next century.
- To maintain the dynamism of the system, enabling it to keep adapting in a rapidly changing world, the mandate of the Meetings of States Parties to the Law of the Sea Convention should be broadened, and every second of these meetings (every six years)

should be constituted as a Review Conference of this Convention, including Part XI and the Implementation Agreement.

- The concept of sovereignty needs to be harmonized with the requirements of the age of information and sustainable development.
- To enhance peace and cooperation, territorial boundaries in the oceans, whether between states with adjacent or opposite coasts or between states and international areas, should be superseded by more functional joint development or joint management zones, integrating resource management and security management.
- Regional seas should eventually be reconceptualized as multi-functional joint management zones, with comprehensive mandates covering living and non-living resources, transport and communication, science and technology cooperation, coastal management, tourism, the conservation of the environment, and regional security.

Ocean perspectives: institutional

- Legal instruments need institutions for their implementation. Most needed institutions for the implementation of the new legal order for the seas and oceans are already in place. They need not be created *ex novo*. But they must be enabled to fulfil the new obligations accruing to them from the new laws and regulations. The following recommendations, based on the existing and emerging institutional framework, the guidelines provided by UNCED and the post-UNCED conventions, agreements and programmes, cast in the light of Gandhi's vision of the majesty of the oceanic circle, start at the village level, and follow through the widening circles of nation, region, and Planet Ocean as a whole.

The village

- The municipal council of a coastal village or town should elect a Marine Resources Council, composed of representatives of the port authority, ship-owners, fishing associations, maritime industries, the tourist board, research institutes, nongovernmental organizations, and consumer cooperatives.
- The Marine Resources Council should deliberate on all matters affecting the sustainable development of marine resources, the protection of the marine and coastal environment, research and

training in ocean affairs, and shall prepare legislation thereon for the Municipal Council.

- The Marine Resources Council should prepare short-term (one-year) and medium-term (five years) plans for sustainable resource development and the protection of the marine environment, and submit them, through the Municipal Council, to the Provincial Government.
- The Marine Resources Council should advise on the local implementation the Law of the Sea Convention, of Chapter 17 of the *Agenda*, of the marine-related parts of the Biodiversity and Climate Conventions, the Agreement on Straddling Stocks and Highly Migratory Stocks in the High Seas, the Global Programme of Action on the Prevention of Pollution from Land-based Activities, the Regional Seas Programme and other ocean-related agreements and programmes.
- The Marine Resources Council should meet as often as necessary.
- Municipalities, through their Marine Resources Councils, should cooperate, within their Province and with the municipalities of neighbouring provinces as well as with municipalities of neighbouring countries, on matters affecting their common ecosystem. Appropriate provincial, national or international conferences should be arranged for this purpose.

The nation

- Ocean governance in the circle of the state should provide for wide participation and an effective decision-making system linking government, research institutions, and interest groups.
- At the political level, there should be a Board of Ministers, preferably under the Chairmanship of the Prime Minister.
- The Board should be advised by a Parliamentary Commission on ocean affairs as well as by a Non-governmental Advisory Council comprising industry and science, and as well as the representatives of the Municipal Marine Resources Councils and NGOs.
- The work of these advisory bodies should be coordinated by the minister with the widest responsibility for ocean affairs.
- At the bureaucratic level there should be an Interdepartmental Commission, composed of senior officials of all the departments involved one way or another in ocean affairs. It might be chaired by a former Prime Minister. It would be the responsibility of this Commission to prepare the work for the Ministerial Board.

The region

– The updating and restructuring of Regional Seas Programmes is absolutely essential, not only to save that useful programme by itself, not only for the implementation of the Law of the Sea Convention, but of all the post-UNCED conventions and action programmes as well as for the strengthening of regional security, including economic and environmental security. All UNCLOS and UNCED created instruments call for and rely on regional cooperation and organization as an essential element.

– Four steps are recommended to enhance the revitalization of the Regional Seas Programme:

• *The establishment of regional "Ocean Assemblies"*
  The UNEP-initiated regional meetings for the implementation of the Global Programme of Action for the Prevention of Pollution from Land-based Activities should be institutionalized, and their mandate should be broadened to cover all the components of integrated ocean and coastal management in the circle of the region. They should take the place of the biennial meetings of the contracting parties to the Regional Seas Conventions, which thus should be attended also by competent regional and international organizations, including regional economic integration organizations, regional economic commissions of the United Nations, regional development banks, and non-governmental organizations.

• *The establishment of regional technology cooperation systems serving the needs of all post-UNCED conventions, agreements and programmes*
  The broadened mandate of regional seas conventions must include the establishment of regional systems for technology cooperation. The Law of the Sea Convention mandates, in Articles 276 and 277, the establishment of regional centres (which, in line with contemporary developments, might be regional systems) for technology development and transfer.

  (1) Such systems should be based on the most advanced concepts of technology development, generating a synergism of investments from the private and the public sector, at the regional level.

  (2) They should be conceived and structured in such a way that they can serve the needs of the Law of the Sea Con-

192

vention as well as all post-UNCED conventions and programmes.

(3) A list of priority technologies to be developed/transferred
(i.e., "co-developed") can be gleaned from the conventions
and plans of action themselves. They would include aquaculture and genetic engineering technologies, the production
of more selective fishing gear; waste recycling; water treatment technologies including sewage treatment; renewable
energy from the sea such as OTEC or methane hydrate
research and development. Lists would have to be refined
region by region, according to needs.

• *The establishment of regional commissions on sustainable development*
To enhance the effectiveness of the United Nations Commission
on Sustainable Development and link it more effectively to the
circles of regions, nations, and municipalities, regional commissions on sustainable development should be established within
Regional Seas Programmes.

Following the pioneering precedent set by the Parties to the
Barcelona Convention, the composition of these commissions
should be broadly interdisciplinary, including the governmental and the non-governmental sectors on an equal footing.

The governmental sector should be composed of ministers responsible for the subject on which a decision is to be made.
The non-governmental sector should be composed of local
authorities, socio-economic actors and non-governmental
organizations.

Compatibility between national and regional laws, regulations,
and management plans is essential for the functioning of the
whole systems. This requires appropriate linkages between
national and regional decision-making. Such linkages are
equally required between the regional level and the global
level of the United Nations (UN Commission for Sustainable
Development, General Assembly).

• *The establishment of regional systems for human security*
Sustainable development has three components which need to
be integrated: socio-economic development; the conservation
of the environment within which socio-economic development
takes place; and peace and security, without which neither socio-

economic development nor the conservation of the environment are possible.

Security has three components which need to be integrated: political security, meaning security in the traditional sense; economic security, and environmental security. Without these latter two, political security is unattainable.

These two statements are universally recognized. Obviously they have institutional implications which must be spelled out.

- The interdisciplinary approach pioneered by the Parties to the Barcelona Convention in the composition of the Mediterranean Commission on Sustainable Development should be extended to the composition of the bureaus or executive committees. These should be attended by ministers responsible for the subject on which a decision has to be taken. If the subject is one affecting regional security, it should be the Ministers of Defence and/or of Foreign Relations who should attend.
- They should serve the purpose of UN peace-keeping in cases of armed conflict requiring military responses, through the appropriate chain of command under the Secretary-General of the United Nations. In the absence of armed conflict, naval regional cooperation could extend to joint surveillance and enforcement and to peaceful humanitarian activities, such as search and rescue, disaster relief, or hydrological surveys, mapping, and other forms of oceanographic research. In institutional terms this is a simple extension and adaptation of a process already in course.

Planet ocean

Four steps are recommended in the global circle of the United Nations, to harmonize and integrate the whole structure from the village to the nation to the region to the planet, making it comprehensive, consistent, trans-sectoral and participational.

– *The "Ocean Assembly"*

The General Assembly should establish a Committee of the Whole to devote the time needed for the making of an integrated ocean policy. Representatives of the upgraded Regional Seas Programmes, the specialized agencies of the UN system with ocean-related mandates, as well as the non-governmental sector, should participate in the sessions of this Committee of the Whole – a sort of "Ocean Assembly of the United Nations," meeting every second year. The integrated policy should be prepared by DOALOS in cooperation with the CSD.

– *The competent international organizations: policy integration*

If one wanted to compare intranational and international institutional arrangements, one could envisage the "Ocean Assembly" as the counterpart to a national parliament that determines policy. The Specialized Agencies and Programmes would execute this policy like the Ministries and Departments of a national government. The ACC subcommittee would act like an inter-ministerial committee or council responding to the interdisciplinary and transsectoral challenges of ocean and coastal management. Linkages between the upgraded Regional Seas Programmes and the decision-making process of the "Ocean Assembly" must be as effective as the linkages between the government and the governments of states/provinces in a federal state.

– *A reconstituted Trusteeship Council*

Based on the Maltese initiative, and in accordance with the United Nations Secretary-General's report to the Fifty-first Session of the General Assembly (document A/51/950), the Trusteeship Council, having completed its mandate of decolonialization, should be dedicated to a new mission: the tutelage of the Common Heritage of Humankind and the Common Concerns of Humankind.

- The Council should consist, as heretofore, of 53 members. They should be elected by the General Assembly on the basis of equitable geographic representation.
- The functions of the new Trusteeship Council would be:
  - to consider reports submitted by Members of the United Nations, the specialized agencies and programmes, as well as the International Sea-bed Authority and competent non-governmental organizations;
  - to accept petitions and examine them in consultation with the agency or institution concerned; and
  - to provide for periodic visits to locations where violations are suspected and take actions in conformity with the terms of its mandate.
- The Trusteeship Council should hold in sacred trust the principle of the Common Heritage of Mankind. It shall monitor compliance with this principle in accordance with international law, in ocean space, outer space, and the atmosphere as well as

Antarctica and report any infringement thereof to the General Assembly. It shall deliberate on its wider application to matters of common concern affecting comprehensive security and sustainable development and the dignity of human life, and make its recommendations to the authorities and institutions concerned. The Trusteeship Council should act as the conscience of the United Nations and the guardian of future generations.

– *The International Sea-Bed Authority*
Short-term initiatives are needed to make the Authority useful to the international community. Such initiatives should include:

(1) Progressive interpretation and development of Implementation Agreement, Annex, section I, para. 5 (g), (h), and (i), formulating, adopting, and implementing cooperative plans for the scientific exploration of the deep sea-bed, joint technology development in conjunction with long-term environmental assessment and the development of human resources (training).

(2) Decision to make rules and regulations for the exploration and exploitation of resources other than manganese nodules, under Article 162, para. 2 (o)(ii).

(3) If requested, joint ventures with coastal developing states for the exploration of mineral resources on their continental shelves.

(4) Decision to schedule ample time for a general debate on the future of the International Sea-bed Authority.

Long-term concerns should be considered at a Review Conference constituted by the Meeting of States Parties in 2003. Points to be considered might include:

• Composition and voting in the Authority's Council;
• Status of the living resources, including the genetic resources of the deep sea-bed and below it; and
• Boundaries between the Area and coastal states and between the Area and the Antarctic Treaty System and the option of replacing them with Joint Development Zones.

Epilogue

This is the system we see emerging from the deep sea-bed, where the principle of the Common Heritage of Mankind was introduced first to the oceans, then to the coastal areas, to the world at large – in widening circles reflecting the majesty of the oceanic circle.

Ocean governance, during the past 30 years, has certainly undergone a systems change, which is still evolving: a process which will go on and never be completed.

Changes affecting a part of a system will affect the system as a whole. Since ocean governance and terrestrial governance are parts of one system, the evolution of ocean governance will necessarily impact on the system as a whole, in a dialectic process, in which terrestrial governance tends to *slow down* ocean governance, and ocean governance, which, in spite of this, has evolved at an amazing rate, will tend to *accelerate* change in terrestrial governance, at local, national, regional, and global levels – "levels" as seen from land, "circles" as seen from the sea.

All "circles" or "levels" are, in a way, mirror images of one another. If national governments move from a "sectoral" to a "transsectoral" and interdisciplinary approach, so will the United Nations. If national governments tend to decentralize, building on the principle of subsidiarity, so will the United Nations. If a new relationship is evolving between governments and "civil society," this will be reflected in the "circle" of the United Nations – or the other way round. At a certain point in time, one "circle" will be ahead or fall behind a bit, but the difference will even out in the longer term.

At this time, movement at the *local* level appears to be accelerating, while the nation state has its rigidities. Its "perceived interests" often reflect bygone times. The "circle" of the United Nations is clearly in motion, albeit slowed down by the rigidities of the nation state.

The greatest movement, during the coming decade, will be seen at the "circle" of the region, where rigidities are least developed and there is, at this moment, the greatest need for, and openness to, the introduction of new concepts and approaches. Here, I think, new breakthroughs are possible, with "ripple effects" on all other circles.

The emerging systems envisaged in this book respond to the needs not only of the ocean but of the whole earth. Greater autonomy to cultural, linguistic, and religious communities; stronger supranational and regional bonds constitute developments that should get us beyond the present crisis of sovereignty – on land as at sea. Sustainable development, in its complex interaction with human security, will generate new structures for ocean as for global governance. Integrating sustainable development and security at the regional level will eventually feed back to the structure and function of the Security Council, still based on the political map of half a century ago, a world that is no more. It is not only the membership of the Security Council that is obsolete: it is its underlying concept of security. The new concept of security, comprising economic and environmental security together with political security, will have to be reflected in the structure and functions of a Security Council for the next century, and what will happen in ocean governance, the lead sector, will have its effects on it.

If nations can accept the obligation of peaceful settlement of disputes in the oceans, as they have done with the entry into force of the Law of the Sea Convention, they will be able to do it in the emerging framework of global governance in the United Nations system.

Last but not least, the emergence of an "ecological world view," stimulated by the converging impacts of economic/ecological crises and the end of Eurocentrism, and most advanced in our relations to the sea, is intrinsically of a universal nature. The Darwinian paradigm, which comprises the competitive market as well as the class struggle, the tragedy of the commons and the life-boat mind set, will go down with Eurocentrism.

"Ecology" was born, a hundred years ago, in the steppes of Siberia, linking Europe and Asia. It was there that Kropotkin discovered cooperation among the beasts of the wild and mutual aid as a factor of evolution. Whether this led him to a more optimistic view of humankind and an emerging social order based on voluntary cooperation and mutual aid, or whether it was his social theory and value system that he projected onto nature, seeing what he wanted to see, is of no consequence. Cause and effect are a feedback loop.

The emerging ecological world view, our new respect for nature and the value of all species in biodiversity will lead us to build a social, economic, and political order that reflects this world view and its values, or maybe we choose this world view because we have realized that no other can save our human universe. The respect we will have for each other we will have for all living things. Respect for life encompasses both. Peace and harmony with nature will enhance peace and harmony among the people of the earth.

Annex

An International Sea-Bed Authority For the Twenty-First Century

PART XI
THE AREA

SECTION 1. GENERAL PROVISIONS

Article 133
Use of terms

For the purposes of this Part:
(a) "resources" means all solid, liquid or gaseous mineral resources *in situ* in the Area at or beneath the sea-bed, including polymetallic nodules and sulphides, cobalt crusts, hydrates and hydrocarbons;
(b) living organisms belonging to the sedentary species, that is to say, organisms which, at the harvestable stage, either are immobile on or under the sea-bed or are unable to move except in constant physical contact with the sea-bed or the subsoil;
(c) genetic resources including the thermophile bacteria of the deep sea-bed.

Article 134
Scope of this Part

1. This Part applies to the management and development of the mineral resources of the seas and oceans, including the Area and its resources.
2. Nothing in this Article affects the establishment of the outer limits of the continental shelf in accordance with part VI or the validity of agreements relating to delimitation between States with opposite or adjacent coasts.

Article 135
Legal status of the superjacent waters and air space

Neither this Part nor any rights granted or exercised pursuant thereto shall affect the legal status of the waters superjacent to the Area and that of the air space above these waters.

SECTION 2. PRINCIPLES GOVERNING THE AREA

Article 136
Common Heritage of Mankind

The Area and its resources are the common heritage of mankind.

Article 137
Non-appropriability of the Common Heritage of Mankind

1.   No State shall claim or exercise sovereignty or sovereign rights over any part of the Area or its resources, nor shall any State or natural or juridical person appropriate any part thereof. No such claim or exercise of sovereignty or sovereign rights nor such appropriation shall be recognized.
2.   All rights in the resources of the Area are vested in mankind as a whole on whose behalf the Authority shall act.
3.   No State or natural or juridical person shall claim, acquire or exercise rights with respect to the resources recovered from the Area except in accordance with this Part. Otherwise, no such claim, acquisition or exercise of such rights shall be recognized.

Article 138
Benefit of mankind

1.   Activities in the Area shall, as specifically provided for in this Part, be carried out for the benefit of mankind as a whole, irrespective of the geographical location of States, whether coastal or land-locked, and taking into particular consideration the interests and needs of developing States and of people who have not attained full independence or other self-governing status recognized by the United Nations in accordance with General Assembly resolution 1514 and other relevant General Assembly resolutions.
2.   The Authority shall provide for the equitable sharing of financial and other benefits derived from deep sea-bed mining activities through any appropriate mechanism, on a non-discriminatory basis.

Article 139
Use of the Area exclusively for peaceful purposes

The Area shall be open to use exclusively for peaceful purpose by all States, whether coastal or land-locked, without discrimination and without prejudice to the other provisions of this Part.

Article 140
Protection of the marine environment

Necessary measures shall be taken in accordance with this Convention and with other Conventions such as the Framework Convention on Climate Change and the Biodiversity Convention as well as the Regional Seas Convention, with respect to activities in the Area, to ensure effective protection for the marine environment and biodiversity, from harmful effects which may arise from such activities. To this end the Authority shall adopt appropriate rules, regulations and procedures for *inter alia:*
(a) the prevention, reduction and control of pollution and other hazards to the marine environment, including the coastline, and of interference with the ecological balance of the marine environment, particular attention being paid to the need for protection from harmful effects of such activities as drilling, dredging, excavation, disposal of waste, construction and operation or maintenance of installations, pipelines and other devices related to such activities;
(b) the protection and conservation of the natural resources of the Area for future generations, the prevention of damage to the flora and fauna of the marine environment and the conservation of biodiversity.

Article 141
Marine scientific research

1.   Marine scientific research in the Area shall be carried out exclusively for peaceful purposes and for the benefit of mankind as a whole, in accordance with Part XIII.
2.   The Authority may carry out marine scientific research concerning the Area and its resources and make the appropriate institutional arrangements to enable it to do so. It may also enter into contracts for that purpose and cooperate with the competent international organisations such as the Intergovernmental Oceanographic Commission of UNESCO or the Regional Centres for the advancement of marine science and technology established in accordance with Articles 276 and 277 of this Convention.
3.   The Authority shall promote, encourage and coordinate the conduct of marine scientific research in the Area and shall disseminate the results of such research and analysis, especially among developing countries.
4.   States Parties may carry out marine scientific research in the Area. States Parties shall promote international co-operation in marine scientific research in the Area by
(a) participating in international programmes and encouraging co-operation in marine scientific research by personnel of different countries and of the Authority;
(b) ensuring that programmes are developed through the Authority or other international organisations as appropriate for the benefit of developing States and technologically less-developed States with a view to
   (i)   strengthening their research capabilities
   (ii) training their personnel and the personnel of the Authority in the techniques and applications of research
   (iii) fostering the employment of their qualified personnel in research in the Area,
(c) effectively disseminating the results of research and analysis through the Authority or other international channels when appropriate.

Article 142
Transfer of technology

1. The Authority shall take measures in accordance with this Convention
   (a) to acquire scientific knowledge and environmentally sustainable technology relating to activities in deep sea exploration and exploitation; and
   (b) to promote and encourage the transfer to developing States of such technology and scientific knowledge so that all States Parties benefit therefrom.

Article 143
General conduct of States in relation to the Area

The general conduct of States in relation to the Area shall be in accordance with the provisions of this Part, the principles embodied in the Charter of the United Nations and other rules of international law in the interests of maintaining peace and security and promoting international co-operation and mutual understanding.

Article 144
Responsibility to ensure compliance and liability for damage

1. States Parties shall have the responsibility to ensure that activities in the Area, whether carried out by States Parties, or State enterprises or natural or juridical persons which possess the nationality of States Parties or are effectively controlled by them or their nationals, shall be carried out in conformity with this Part. The same responsibility applies to international organizations for activities in the Area carried out by such organizations.

2. Without prejudice to the rules of international law, damage caused by the failure of a State Party or international organization to carry out its responsibilities under this Part shall entail liability; States Parties or international organizations acting together shall bear joint and several liability. A State Party shall not however be liable for damage caused by any failure to comply with this Part by a person whom it has sponsored, if the State Party has taken all necessary and appropriate measures to secure effective compliance.

3. States Parties that are members of international organizations shall take appropriate measures to ensure the implementation of this article with respect to such organizations.

Article 145
Rights and legitimate interests of coastal States

1. Activities in the Area, with respect to resource deposits in the Area which lie across limits of national jurisdiction, shall be conducted with due regard to the rights and legitimate interests of any coastal State across whose jurisdiction such deposits lie.

2. Consultations, including a system of prior notification, shall be maintained with the State concerned, with a view to avoiding infringements of such rights and interests. In cases where activities in the Area may result in the exploitation of resources lying within national jurisdiction the prior consent of the coastal State concerned shall be required.

3.   As a general rule the establishment of joint development zones or joint management zones shall be encouraged with respect to such resource deposit within areas between 300 and 400 nautical miles measured from the base lines from which the territorial sea of the coastal State is measured.

4.   Neither this Part nor any rights granted or exercised pursuant thereto shall affect the rights of coastal States to take such measures consistent with the relevant provisions of Part XII as may be necessary to prevent, mitigate or eliminate grave and imminent danger to their coastline, or related interests from pollution or threat thereof or from other hazardous occurrences resulting from or caused by any activities in the Area.

Article 146
Joint Ventures between the Authority and the Coastal State

Upon request by a coastal State, the Authority may enter into a contract or joint venture with that State for the exploration and exploitation of the mineral resources within its Exclusive Economic Zone.

Article 147
Protection of human life

With respect to activities in the Area, necessary measures shall be taken to ensure effective protection of human life. To this end the Authority shall adopt appropriate rules, regulations and procedures to supplement existing international law as embodied in relevant treaties.

Article 148
Accommodation of activities in the Area and in the marine environment

1.   Activities in the Area shall be carried out with reasonable regard for other activities in the marine environment.

2.   Installations used for carrying out activities in the Area shall be subject to the following conditions:

(a) such installations shall be erected, emplaced and removed solely in accordance with this Part and subject to the rules, regulations and procedures of the Authority. Due notice must be given of the erection, emplacement and removal of such installations, and permanent means for giving warning of their presence must be maintained;

(b) such installations may not be established where interference may be caused to the use of recognized sea lanes essential to international navigation or in areas of intense fishing activity;

(c) safety zones shall be established around such installations with appropriate markings to ensure the safety of both navigation and the installations. The configuration and location of such safety zones shall not be such as to form a belt impeding the lawful access of shipping to particular maritime zones or navigation along international sea lanes;

(d) such installations shall be used exclusively for peaceful purposes;

(e) such installations do not possess the status of islands. They have no territorial sea of their own, and their presence does not affect the definition of the territorial sea, the exclusive economic zone or the continental shelf.

3.   Other activities in the marine environment shall be conducted with reasonable regard for activities in the Area.

Article 149
Participation of developing States in activities in the Area

The effective participation of developing States in activities in the Area shall be promoted as specifically provided for in this Part, having due regard to their special interests and needs, and in particular to the special need for the land-locked and geographically disadvantaged and small island developing States among them, to overcome obstacles arising from their disadvantaged position.

Article 150
Archaeological and historical objects

All objects of an archaeological and historical nature found in the Area shall be preserved or disposed of for the benefit of mankind as a whole, particular regard being paid to the preferential rights of the State or country of origin, or the State of cultural origin, or the State of historical and archaeological origin.

SECTION 3. DEVELOPMENT OF RESOURCES OF THE AREA

Article 151
Policies relating to activities in deep sea-bed mining

1.   Production policies on deep sea-bed mining shall be based on the principle of the Common Heritage as defined in Articles 137–140 above.

2.   Production policies shall aim at sustainable development and shall include environmental impact assessment, the use of environment-friendly technology, and the conservation of biodiversity.

3.   Production policies shall be in accordance with international trade law and the pertinent rules and regulations adopted by the International Trade Organisation.

4.   Production policies shall enhance co-operation, not competition, in ocean space and maximize internationalization of environmentally sustainable technology development. The Authority shall seek the assistance of the Global Environment Facility and of industrialized countries who shall act in accordance with their obligations under the Climate Convention (Article 4) and the Biodiversity Convention (Article 25).

5.   Based on the principle of equity inherent in the concept of the Common Heritage of Mankind, and striving to contribute to the eradication of poverty essential for the attainment of sustainable development, the Authority shall seek the support of international funding agencies and industrialized countries to assist developing countries in the diversification of their industries and the lessening of their dependence on the export of commodities the prices of which may decline or collapse, whether due to activities in the Area or in areas under the jurisdiction of other States or to structural changes in demand for such commodities that may be caused by

developments of synthetics, recycling, miniaturization or other aspects of the new phase of the industrial revolution of which sea-bed mining will be a part.

Article 152
Exercise of powers and functions by the Authority

1. The Authority shall avoid discrimination in the exercise of its powers and functions, including the granting of opportunities for activities related to sea-bed exploration and exploitation.
2. Nevertheless, special consideration for developing States, including particular consideration for the land-locked, geographically disadvantaged and small island developing States among them, as specially provided for in this Part, shall be permitted.

Article 153
System of research and development, exploration and exploitation

1. Activities in the Area and related sea-bed activities shall be carried out in cooperation with the Authority on behalf of mankind as a whole and in accordance with this article as well as other relevant provisions of this Part and the relevant Annexes, and the rules, regulations and procedures of the Authority.
2. Scientific cooperation, research and development, exploration, and exploitation of resources shall be carried out through the Enterprise System, which is the operational arm of the Authority, in accordance with Section 4 of this Part.

Article 154
Periodic Review Conferences

1. Part XI of the Convention shall be reviewed and revised by the States Parties as part of the review process of the Convention as a whole.
2. The mandate of the meetings of States Parties shall be broadened accordingly.
3. Amendments adopted by a Review Conference shall not affect rights acquired under existing contracts and agreements.

SECTION 4. THE AUTHORITY
SUBSECTION A. GENERAL PROVISIONS

Article 155
Establishment of the Authority

1. There is hereby established the International Sea-Bed Authority, which shall function in accordance with this Part.
2. All States Parties are *ipso facto* members of the Authority.
3. Observers at the Third United Nations Conference on the Law of the Sea who have signed the Final Act and who are not referred to in article 305, paragraph 1 (c), (d), (e) or (f), shall have the right to participate in the Authority as observers, in accordance with its rules, regulations and procedures.
4. The seat of the Authority shall be in Jamaica.

5.   The Authority may establish such regional centres or offices as it deems necessary for the exercise of its functions.

Article 156
Nature and fundamental principles of the Authority

1.   The Authority is the organization through which States parties shall, in accordance with this Part, organize and regulate activities in the Area, with a view to enhancing scientific research in the deep sea, promoting international cooperation in research and development of deep-sea technologies, developing the resources of the Area, and protecting the environment and biodiversity in the deep sea.
2.   The powers and functions of the Authority shall be those expressly conferred upon it by this Convention. The Authority shall have such incidental powers, consistent with this Convention, as are implicit in and necessary for the exercise of those powers and functions with respect to activities in the Area and in cooperation with States Parties.
3.   The Authority is based on the principle of the Common Heritage, on the principle of sustainable development, and on the principle of the sovereign equality of all its members.
4.   All members of the Authority shall fulfil in good faith the obligations assumed by them in accordance with this Part in order to ensure to all of them the rights and benefits resulting from membership.

Article 157
Organs of the Authority

1.   There are hereby established, as the principal organs of the Authority, an Assembly, a Council and a Secretariat.
2.   There is hereby established the Enterprise System as the operational part of the Authority.
3.   Such subsidiary organs as may be found necessary may be established in accordance with this Part.
4.   Each principal organ of the Authority and the Enterprise System shall be responsible for exercising those powers and functions which are conferred upon it. In exercising such powers and functions each organ shall avoid taking any action which may derogate from or impede the exercise of specific powers and functions conferred upon another organ.

SUBSECTION B. THE ASSEMBLY

Article 158
Composition, procedure and voting

1.   The Assembly shall consist of all the members of the Authority. Each member shall have one representative in the Assembly, who may be accompanied by alternates and advisers.
2.   The Assembly shall meet in regular annual sessions and in such special sessions as may be decided by the Assembly, or convened by the Secretary-General at the request of the Council or of a majority of the members of the Authority.

3.   Sessions shall take place at the seat of the Authority unless otherwise decided by the Assembly.

4.   The Assembly shall adopt its rules of procedure. At the beginning of each regular session, it shall elect its President and such other officers as may be required. They shall hold office until a new President and other officers are elected at the next regular session.

5.   A majority of the members of the Assembly shall constitute a quorum.

6.   Each member of the Assembly shall have one vote.

7.   Decisions on questions of procedure, including decisions to convene special sessions of the Assembly, shall be taken by a majority of the members present and voting.

8.   Decisions on questions of substance shall be taken by a two-thirds majority of the members present and voting, provided that such a majority includes a majority of the members participating in the session. When the issue arises as to whether a question is one of substance or not, that question shall be treated as one of substance unless otherwise decided by the Assembly by the majority required for decisions on questions of substance.

9.   When a question of substance comes up for voting for the first time, the President may, and shall, if requested by at least one-fifth of the members of the Assembly, defer the issue of taking a vote on that question for a period not exceeding five calendar days. This rule may be applied only once to any question, and shall not be applied so as to defer the question beyond the end of the session.

10.   Upon a written request addressed to the President and sponsored by at least one-fourth of the members of the Authority for an advisory opinion on the conformity with the Convention of a proposal before the Assembly on any matter, the Assembly shall request the Sea-Bed Disputes Chamber of the International Tribunal for the Law of the Sea to give an advisory opinion thereon and shall defer voting on that proposal pending receipt of the advisory opinion by the Chamber. If the advisory opinion is not received before the final week of the session in which it is requested, the Assembly shall decide when it will meet to vote upon the deferred proposal.

Article 159
Powers and functions

1.   The Assembly, as the sole organ of the Authority consisting of all the members, shall be considered the supreme organ of the Authority to which the other principal organs shall be accountable as specifically provided for in this Convention. The Assembly shall have the power to establish general policies in conformity with the relevant provisions of the Convention on any question or matter within the competence of the Authority.

2.   In addition, the powers and functions of the Assembly shall be:

   (a)   to elect the members of the Council in accordance with article 160;

   (b)   to elect the Secretary-General from among the candidates proposed by the Council;

   (c)   to elect, upon the recommendation of the Council, half of the members of the Governing Board of each Enterprise; the same Board Members may serve on the Boards of several Enterprises.

(d) to establish such subsidiary organs as it finds necessary for the exercise of its functions in accordance with this Part. In the composition of these subsidiary organs due account shall be taken of the principle of equitable geographical distribution.

(e) to adopt the financial rules, regulations and procedures submitted by the Council;

(f) to assess the contribution of members to the administrative budget of the Authority in accordance with an agreed scale of assessment based upon the scale used for the regular budget of the United Nations until the Authority shall have sufficient income from other sources to meet its administrative expenses;

(g) to determine the limits of the borrowing power of the Authority;

(h) to decide upon the equitable sharing of financial and other economic benefits derived from the activities in the Area, consistent with this Convention and the rules, regulations and procedures of the Authority;

(i) to consider and approve the proposed annual budget of the Authority submitted by the Council;

(j) to examine periodic reports from the Council and from the Enterprise system and special reports requested from the Council or any other organ of the Authority;

(k) to initiate studies and make recommendations for the purpose of promoting international co-operation concerning activities in the Area and related activities in relation to the deep sea-bed and encouraging the progressive development of international law relating thereto and its codification;

(l) to consider problems of a general nature in connection with activities in the area and related activities arising in particular for developing States, particularly for land-based producers, land-locked and geographically disadvantaged and small island developing States as well as the least developed States, and to formulate recommendations thereon;

(m) to suspend the exercise of rights and privileges of membership pursuant to article 185;

(n) to discuss any question or matter within the competence of the Authority and to decide as to which organ of the Authority shall deal with any such question or matter not specifically entrusted to a particular organ, consistent with the distribution of powers and functions among the organs of the Authority.

SUBSECTION C. THE COUNCIL

Article 160
Composition, procedure and voting

1. The Council shall consist of 36 members of the Authority elected by the Assembly according to the principle of ensuring an equitable geographic distribution of seats.

2. In electing the members of the Council the Assembly shall assure that
(a) land-locked, geographically disadvantaged small island developing and least

developed States are represented to a degree which is reasonably proportionate to their representation in the Assembly;

    (b) each regional group (Africa, Asia, Eastern Europe, Latin America & Caribbean, Western Europe and Others) shall prepare a list containing twice the number of candidates to which each regional group is entitled. The Assembly as a whole shall elect 36 members from these lists.

3. Elections shall take place at regular sessions of the Assembly. Each member of the Council shall be elected for four years, on staggered terms.

4. Members of the Council shall be eligible for re-election, but due regard should be paid to the desirability for rotation of membership.

5. The Council shall function at the seat of the Authority, and shall meet as often as the business of the Authority may require, but not less than three times a year.

6. A majority of the members of the Council shall constitute a quorum.

7. Each member of the Council shall have one vote.

8. (a) Decisions on questions of substance shall be taken by a majority of the members present and voting.

    (b) Decisions on questions of substance shall be taken by a two-thirds majority of the members present and voting, provided that such majority includes a majority of the members of the Council.

    (c) As a general rule, decisions shall be taken by consensus, and voting shall be resorted to only after all means to reach consensus have been exhausted.

    (d) For the purpose of subparagraph (c), "consensus" means the absence of any formal objection. Within 14 days of the submission of a proposal to the Council, the President of the Council shall determine whether there would be a formal objection to the adoption of the proposal. If the President determines that there would be such an objection, the President shall establish and convene, within three days following such determination, a conciliation committee consisting of not more than nine members of the Council, with the President as chairman, for the purpose of reconciling the differences and producing a proposal which can be adopted by consensus. The committee shall work expeditiously and report to the Council within 14 days following its establishment. If the committee is unable to recommend a proposal which can be adopted by consensus, it shall set out in its report the grounds on which the proposal is being opposed.

9. The Council shall establish a procedure whereby a member of the Authority not represented on the Council may send a representative to attend a meeting of the Council when a request is made by such member, or a matter particularly affecting it is under consideration. Such a representative shall be entitled to participate in the deliberations but not to vote.

Article 161
Power and functions

1. The Council is the executive organ of the Authority. The Council shall have the power to establish, in conformity with this Convention and the general policies established by the Assembly, the specific policies to be pursued by the Authority on any question or matter within the competence of the Authority.

2. In addition, the Council shall

(a) supervise and co-ordinate the implementation of the provisions of this Part on all questions and matters within the competence of the Authority and invite the attention of the Assembly to cases of non-compliance;

(b) propose to the Assembly a list of candidates for the election of the Secretary-General;

(c) recommend to the Assembly candidates for the election of members of the Joint-Venture Boards of the Enterprise system;

(d) establish, as appropriate, and with due regard to economy and efficiency, such subsidiary organs as it finds necessary for the exercise of its functions in accordance with this Part.

(e) adopt its rules of procedure including the method of selecting its President;

(f) enter into agreements with the United Nations or other international organizations on behalf of the Authority and within its competence, subject to approval by the Assembly;

(g) consider the reports of the Enterprise System and transmit them to the Assembly with its recommendations;

(h) present to the Assembly annual reports and such special reports as the Assembly may request;

(i) issue guidelines and directives to the Enterprise System in accordance with Article 170;

(j) approve plans of work. The Council shall act upon each plan of work within 60 days of its submission;

(k) make recommendations to the Assembly with regard to assistance to land-based producer developing States affected by a reduction of revenues of ocean-related commodities;

(l) (i) recommend to the Assembly rules, regulations and procedures on the equitable sharing of financial and other benefits derived from the utilisation of deep-sea resources as well as from the payments and contributions made to the Authority pursuant to Article 82 of the Convention;

    (ii) propose to the Assembly rules, regulations and procedures for the exploration for and exploitation of any resource other than polymetallic nodules. Such rules, regulations and procedures shall be adopted within three years from the date of a request to the Authority by any of its members to adopt such rules, regulations and procedures in respect of such resource. All rules, regulations and procedures shall remain in effect on a provisional basis until approved by the Assembly or until amended by the Council in the light of any views expressed by the Assembly;

(p) submit the proposed annual budget of the Authority to the Assembly for its approval;

(q) make recommendations to the Assembly concerning suspension of the exercise of the rights and privileges of membership pursuant to article 185;

(r) institute proceedings on behalf of the Authority before the Sea-Bed Disputes Chamber in cases of non-compliance;

(s) notify the Assembly upon a decision by the Sea-Bed Disputes Chamber in proceedings instituted under subparagraph (r), and make any recommendations which it may find appropriate with respect to measures to be taken;

(t) issue emergency orders, which may include orders for the suspension or adjustment of operations, to prevent serious harm to the marine environment and its living resources arising out of activities in the Area;

(u) disapprove areas for exploitation in cases where substantial evidence indicates the risk of serious harm to the marine environment and its biodiversity;

(v) establish appropriate mechanisms for directing and supervising a staff of inspectors who shall inspect activities in the area to determine whether this Part, the rules, regulations and procedures of the Authority, as well as the reservation of the Area for exclusively peaceful purposes, are being complied with;

(w) make recommendations to the Assembly concerning policies on any question or matter within the competence of the Authority.

Article 162
Organs of the Council

1. There are hereby established the following organs of the Council
   (a) a Scientific and Technological Commission;
   (b) a Legal and Economic Planning Commission;
   (c) a Finance Commission;

2. Each Commission shall be composed of 15 members, elected by the Council from among the candidates nominated by the States Parties. However, if necessary, the Council may decide to increase the size of a Commission having due regard to economy and efficiency;

3. States Parties shall nominate candidates of the highest standards of competence and integrity with qualifications in relevant fields so as to ensure the effective exercise of the functions of the Commissions.

4. In the election of members of the Commissions, due account shall be taken of the need for equitable geographical distribution.

5. No State Party may nominate more than one candidate for the same Commission. No person shall be elected to serve on more than one Commission.

6. Members of the Commissions shall hold office for a term of five years. They shall be eligible for re-election for a further term.

7. In the event of death, incapacity or resignation of a member of a Commission prior to the expiration of the term of office, the Council shall elect for the remainder of the term, a member from the same geographical region.

8. Members of Commissions shall have no financial interest in any activity relating to exploration and exploitation in the deep sea-bed. Subject to their responsibilities to the Commissions upon which they serve, they shall not disclose, even after the termination of their functions, any industrial secret, proprietary data which are transferred to the Authority, or any other confidential information coming to their knowledge by reason of their duties for the Authority.

9. Each Commission shall exercise its functions in accordance with such guidelines and directives as the Council may adopt.

10. Each Commission shall formulate and submit to the Council for approval such rules and regulations as may be necessary for the efficient conduct of the Commission's functions.

11. The decision-making procedures of the Commissions shall be established by the

rules, regulations and procedures of the Authority. Recommendations to the Council shall, where necessary, be accompanied by a summary of the divergencies of opinion in the Commission.

12.   Each Commission shall normally function at the seat of the Authority and shall meet as often as is required for the efficient exercise of its functions.

13.   In the exercise of its functions, each Commission may, where appropriate, consult another commission, any competent organ of the United Nations or of its specialized agencies or any international organizations with competence in the subject-matter of such consultation.

Article 163
The Scientific and Technological Commission

1.   A Commission for the provision of scientific, technical and technological advice is hereby established to provide the Assembly and the Council and, as appropriate, other bodies with timely advice relating to the implementation of this Part. The Commission shall be multidisciplinary. It shall comprise government representatives competent in the relevant field of expertise. It shall report regularly to the Council and, through the Council, to the Assembly on all aspects of its work.

2.   Under the authority of and in accordance with guidelines laid down by the Council, and upon its request, this body shall:

(a) Provide scientific and technical assessments of the status of biological diversity as it may be affected by activities in the Area;

(b) Prepare scientific and technical assessments of the effects of types of measures taken in accordance with the provisions of this Convention;

(c) Identify innovative, efficient and state-of-the-art technologies and know-how relating to the sustainable use of the resources of the Area and the conservation of biological diversity and advise on the ways and means of promoting development and/or transferring such technologies;

(d) Provide advice on scientific programmes and international cooperation in research and development related to the sustainable use of the resources of the area and the conservation of biological diversity; and

(e) Respond to scientific, technical, technological and methodological questions that the Council or the Assembly and its subsidiary bodies may put to it.

Article 164
The Legal and Economic Planning Commission

1.   Members of the Legal and Economic Planning Commission shall be experts in economic and legal matters relating to ocean mining and related fields of expertise.

2.   The Commission shall:

(a) draft rules, regulations and procedures for the consideration of the Council;

(b) propose, upon the request of the Council, measures to implement decisions relating to activities in the Area taken in accordance with this Convention;

(c) review the trends and the factors affecting supply, demand and prices of materials which may be derived from sea-bed mining, bearing in mind the interests of both importing and exporting countries, and in particular of the developing States among them;

(d) review plans of work for activities in the Area and submit appropriate recommendations to the Council;

(e) supervise, upon the request of the Council, activities in the Area, where appropriate, in consultation and collaboration with any Enterprise carrying out such activities and report to the Council;

(f) recommend to the Council that proceedings be instituted on behalf of the Authority before the Sea-Bed Disputes Chamber, in accordance with this Part;

(g) make recommendations to the Council with respect to measures to be taken, upon a decision by the Sea-Bed Disputes Chamber in proceedings instituted in accordance with subparagraph (e);

(h) in consultation with the Scientific and Technological Commission, make recommendations to the Council to disapprove areas for exploitation in cases where substantial evidence indicates the risk of serious harm to the marine environment;

(i) make recommendations to the Council regarding the direction and supervision of a staff of inspectors who shall inspect activities in the Area to determine whether the provisions of this Part, the rules, regulations and procedures of the Authority, as well as the reservation of the Area for exclusively peaceful purposes, are being complied with;

3. The members of the Commission shall, upon request by any State Party or other party concerned, be accompanied by a representative of such State or other party concerned when carrying out their function of supervision and inspection.

Article 165
The Finance Commission

1. The members of the Finance Commission shall be elected with due consideration of the need for equitable geographical distribution. They shall include the 5 largest contributors to the budget of the Authority.

2. The Finance Commission shall make recommendations on the following matters:

(a) draft financial rules, regulations and procedures of the organs of the Authority and the financial management and internal financial administration of the Authority;

(b) assessment of contributions of members to the administrative budget of the Authority in accordance with Article 159.2 (e) of the Convention;

(c) all relevant financial matters, including the proposed annual budget prepared by the Secretary-General of the Authority in accordance with article 173 of the Convention and the financial aspects of the implementation of the programmes of work of the Secretariat;

(d) the administrative budget;

(e) financial obligations of States Parties arising from the implementation of his Part as well as the administrative and budgetary implications of proposals and recommendations involving expenditure from the funds of the Authority;

(f) rules, regulations and procedures on the equitable sharing of financial benefits derived from activities in the Area and the decisions to be made thereon.

3. Decisions in the Finance Commission on questions of procedure shall be taken by a majority of members present and voting. Decisions on questions of substance shall be taken by consensus.

4. Decisions by the Assembly and the Council on the matters enumerated in paragraph 2 above shall take into account the recommendations of the Finance Commission.

SUBSECTION D. THE SECRETARIAT

Article 166
The Secretariat

1. The Secretariat of the Authority shall comprise a Secretary-General and such staff as the Authority may require.

2. The Secretary-General shall be elected for four years by the Assembly from among the candidates proposed by the Council and may be re-elected.

3. The Secretary-General shall be the chief administrative officer of the Authority, and shall act in that capacity in all meetings of the Assembly, of the Council and of any subsidiary organ, and shall perform such other administrative functions as are entrusted to the Secretary-General by these organs.

4. The Secretary-General shall make an annual report to the Assembly on the work of the Authority.

Article 167
The staff of the Authority

1. The staff of the Authority shall consist of such qualified scientific and technical and other personnel as may be required to fulfil the administrative functions of the Authority.

2. The paramount consideration in the recruitment and employment of the staff and in the determination of their conditions of service shall be the necessity of securing the highest standards of efficiency, competence and integrity. Subject to this consideration, due regard shall be paid to the importance of recruiting the staff on as wide a geographical basis as possible.

3. The staff shall be appointed by the Secretary-General. The terms and conditions on which they shall be appointed, remunerated and dismissed shall be in accordance with the rules, regulations and procedures of the Authority.

Article 168
International character of the Secretariat

1. In the performance of their duties the Secretary-General and the staff shall not seek or receive instructions from any government or from any other source external to the Authority. They shall refrain from any action which might reflect on their position as international officials responsible only to the Authority. Each State Party undertakes to respect the exclusively international character of the responsibilities of the Secretary-General and the staff and not to seek to influence them in the discharge of their responsibilities. Any violation of responsibilities by a staff member

shall be submitted to the appropriate administrative tribunal as provided in the rules, regulations and procedures of the Authority.

2.   The Secretary-General and the staff shall have no financial interest in any activity relating to the exploration and exploitation of the deep sea-bed. Subject to their responsibilities to the Authority, they shall not disclose, even after the termination of their functions, any industrial secret, proprietary data which are transferred to the Authority, or any other confidential information coming to their knowledge by reason of their employment with the Authority.

3.   Violations of the obligations of a staff member of the Authority set forth in paragraph 2 shall, on the request of a State Party affected by such violation, or a natural or juridical person, sponsored by a State Party, and affected by such violation, be submitted by the Authority against the staff member concerned to a tribunal designated by the rules, regulations and procedures of the Authority. The Party affected shall have the right to take part in the proceedings. If the tribunal so recommends, the Secretary-General shall dismiss the staff member concerned.

4.   The rules, regulations and procedures of the Authority shall contain such provisions as are necessary to implement this article.

Article 169
Consultation and co-operation with international and non-governmental organizations

1.   The Secretary-General shall, on matters within the competence of the Authority, make suitable arrangements, with the approval of the Council, for consultation and co-operation with international and non-governmental organizations recognized by the Economic and Social Council of the United Nations.

2.   Any organization with which the Secretary-General has entered into an arrangement under paragraph 1 may designate representatives to attend meetings of the organs of the Authority as observers in accordance with the rules of procedure of these organs. Procedures shall be established for obtaining the views of such organizations in appropriate cases.

3.   The Secretary-General may distribute to States Parties written reports submitted by the non-governmental organizations referred to in paragraph 1 on subjects in which they have special competence and which are related to the work of the Authority.

SUBSECTION E. THE ENTERPRISE SYSTEM

Article 170
The Enterprise System

1.   The Enterprise System shall be the operational part of the Authority.

2.   Each Enterprise shall, within the framework of the international legal personality of the Authority, have such legal capacity as is provided for in the joint-venture agreement establishing each Enterprise. The Enterprise system shall act in accordance with this Convention and the rules, regulations and procedures of the Authority, as well as the general policies established by the Assembly and shall be subject to the directives and control of the Council.

3. Each State Party, desirous to participate in the Enterprise System, shall designate an entity as a Signatory to the Enterprise System. Signatories may be State enterprises or persons natural or juridical which possess the nationality of States Parties or are effectively controlled by them or their nationals, when designated by such States, or any group of the foregoing, in accordance with the provisions of this Convention.

4. Any State Party, or group of States Parties, having designated a Signatory, has the right to establish an Enterprise as a joint venture with the Authority to carry out an approved project covering research and development and/or exploration and/or production.

5. Each Enterprise should have at least one developing country as a partner in the joint venture.

6. Each Enterprise is financed by the Authority and by the Signatories in proportions to be determined by each Joint Venture Agreement.

   (a) As a general rule, this proportion should approximate 50–50.

   (b) For its part of the financing of an Enterprise, the Authority shall initially seek the support of international funding and bilateral aid agencies in accordance with their obligations under international law to assist in the development and transfer of environmentally sustainable technology and the conservation of biodiversity.

   (c) Profits shall be shared between the Authority and the Signatories in proportion to their investment.

6. Each Enterprise is governed by its own Joint-Venture Board.

   (a) The Joint-Venture Board of an Enterprise shall consist of 16 members.

   (b) Eight of the members shall be designated by the Signatories, and 8 shall be designated by the Council of the Authority, taking into account the principle of equitable geographical representation, with due regard to the interests of developing countries.

   (c) The eight members designated by the Council of the Authority may be designated to serve on more than one Joint-Venture Board.

   (d) Each member of the Governing Board shall have one vote. Each Signatory shall have a voting participation proportionate to his investment; each member designated by the Council shall have a voting participation equivalent to one-eighth of the Authority's investment.

7. Activities in the Area shall be carried out in accordance with a plan of work and approved by the Council.

8. The Authority shall exercise such control over its Enterprises as is necessary for the purpose of securing compliance with the relevant provisions of this Part and the Annexes relating thereto, and the rules, regulations and procedures of the Authority, and the plans of work approved in accordance with paragraph 7. States Parties shall assist the Authority by taking all measures necessary to ensure such compliance.

9. The Authority shall have the right to take at any time any measures provided for under this Part to ensure compliance with its provisions and the exercise of the functions of control and regulation assigned to it thereunder or under any Joint-Venture agreement. The Authority shall have the right to inspect all installations in the Area to ascertain compliance with rules and regulations as well as reservation for exclusively peaceful purposes.

10. Joint-Venture agreements establishing an Enterprise for Exploration and/or

exploitation shall provide for security of tenure. Accordingly, such agreements shall not be revised, suspended or terminated without the consent of the Signatory or Signatories involved.

Article 171
Inventions and technical information

1.   The Authority, in connection with any work performed by it or on its behalf and in joint venture with it, shall acquire in inventions and technical information those rights, but no more than those rights, which are necessary in the common interests of the Authority and of the Signatories in their capacity as such. In the case of work done under a joint-venture agreement, any such rights obtained shall be on a non-exclusive basis.

2.   For the purpose of paragraph 1. the Authority, taking into account its principles and objectives and generally accepted industrial practices, shall, in connection with such work involving a significant element of study, research or development, ensure for itself:

   (a) the right to have disclosed to it without payment all inventions and technical information generated by such work;

   (b) the right to disclose and to have disclosed to Parties and Signatories and others within the jurisdiction of any Party such inventions and technical information, and to use and to authorize and to have authorized Parties and Signatories and such others to use such inventions and technical information without payment.

3.   The Authority shall also ensure for itself the right, on fair and reasonable terms and conditions, to use and to have used inventions and technical information directly utilized in the execution of work performed on its behalf but not included in paragraph 2, to the extent that such use is necessary for the reconstruction or modification of any product actually delivered under an agreement co-financed by the Authority, and to the extent that the person who has performed such work is entitled to grant such right.

4.   The Council may in individual cases approve a deviation from the policies described in 2(b) and (3), where in the course of negotiation it is demonstrated to the Council that failure to deviate would be detrimental to the interests of the Authority.

5.   With respect to inventions and technical information in which rights are acquired by the Authority otherwise than pursuant to paragraph 2, the Authority, to the extent that it has the right to do so, shall upon request:

   (a) disclose or have disclosed such inventions and technical information to any Party or Signatory subject to reimbursement of any payment made by or required of the Authority in respect of the exercise of this right of disclosure;

   (b) make available to any Party or Signatory the right to disclose or have disclosed to others within the jurisdiction of any Party and to use and to authorize and have authorized such others to use such inventions and technical information;

   (i) without payment in connection with any sea-bed mining operation in conjunction therewith;

   (ii) for any other purpose, on fair and reasonable terms and conditions to be settled between Signatories or others within the jurisdiction of any Party and the Authority or the owner of the inventions and technical information or any other authorized entity or person having a property interest therein, and subject to reimbursement of any payment made by or required of the Authority in respect of the exercise of these rights.

6. The disclosure and use, and the terms and conditions of disclosure and use, of all inventions and technical information in which the Authority has acquired any rights shall be on a non-discriminatory basis with respect to all Signatories and others within the jurisdiction of Parties.

7. Nothing in this article shall preclude the Authority, if desirable, from entering into contracts with persons subject to domestic laws and regulations relating to the disclosure of technical information.

SUBSECTION F. FINANCIAL ARRANGEMENTS OF THE AUTHORITY

Article 172
Funds of the Authority

The funds of the Authority shall include:
(a) assessed contributions made by members of the Authority in accordance with article 159.2(f);
(b) funds transferred from the Enterprise System;
(c) funds received pursuant to article 82;
(d) funds borrowed pursuant to article 175;
(e) voluntary contributions made by members or other entities.

Article 173
Annual budget of the Authority

The Secretary-General shall draft the proposed annual budget of the Authority and submit it to the Council. The Council shall consider the proposed annual budget, request the comments of the Finance Commission, and submit the budget, together with the comments and any recommendations thereon, to the Assembly, in accordance with article 161.2.(p).

Article 174
Expenses of the Authority

1. The contributions referred to in article 172, subparagraph (a), shall be paid into a special account to meet the administrative expenses of the Authority until the Authority has sufficient funds from other sources to meet these expenses.

2. The administrative expenses of the Authority shall be a first call upon the funds of the Authority. Except for the assessed contributions referred to in article 172, subparagraph (a), the funds which remain after payment of administrative expenses may, *inter alia:*
   (a) be shared in accordance with article 138 and article 159.2(h);
   (b) be used to invest in the Enterprise System in accordance with article 170 paragraph 6.

Article 175
Borrowing power of the Authority

1.   The Authority shall have the power to borrow funds.
2.   The Assembly, on the advice of the Finance Commission, shall prescribe the limits on the borrowing power of the Authority in the financial regulations adopted pursuant to article 159.2(g).
3.   The Council shall exercise the borrowing power of the Authority.
4.   States Parties shall not be liable for the debts of the Authority.

Article 176
Annual audit

The records, books and accounts of the Authority, including its annual financial statements, shall be audited by an independent auditor appointed by the Assembly.

SUBSECTION G. LEGAL STATUS, PRIVILEGES AND IMMUNITIES

Article 177
Legal status

The Authority shall have international legal personality and such legal capacity as may be necessary for the exercise of its functions and the fulfilment of its purposes.

Article 178
Privileges and immunities

To enable the Authority to exercise its functions, it shall enjoy in the territory of each State Party the privileges and immunities set forth in this subsection. The privileges and immunities relating to the Enterprise System shall be determined in each joint-venture agreement.

Article 179
Immunity from legal process

The Authority, its property and assets, shall enjoy immunity from legal process except to the extent that the Authority expressly waives this immunity in a particular case.

Article 180
Immunity from search and any form of seizure

The property and assets of the Authority, wherever located and by whomsoever held, shall be immune from search, requisition, confiscation, expropriation or any other form of seizure by executive or legislative action.

Article 181
Exemption from restrictions, regulations, controls and moratoria

The property and assets of the Authority shall be exempt from restrictions, regulations, controls and moratoria of any nature.

Article 182
Archives and official communications of the Authority

1. The archives of the Authority, wherever located, shall be inviolable.
2. Proprietary data, industrial secrets or similar information and personnel records shall not be placed in archives which are open to public inspection.
3. With regard to its official communications, the Authority shall be accorded by each State Party treatment no less favourable than that accorded by the State to other international organizations.

Article 183
Privileges and immunities of certain persons connected with the Authority

Representatives of States Parties attending meetings of the Assembly, the Council or organs of the Assembly or the Council, and the Secretary-General and staff of the Authority, shall enjoy in the territory of each State Party:
(a) immunity from legal process with respect to acts performed by them in the exercise of their functions, except to the extent that the State which they represent or the Authority, as appropriate, expressly waives this immunity in a particular case;
(b) if they are not nationals of that State Party, the same exemptions from immigration restrictions, alien registration requirements and national service obligations, the same facilities as regards exchange restrictions and the same treatment in respect of travelling facilities as are accorded by that State to the representatives, officials and employees of comparable rank of other States Parties.

Article 184
Exemptions from taxes and customs duties

1. Within the scope of its official activities, the Authority, its assets and property, its income, and its operations and transactions, authorized by this Convention, shall be exempt from all direct taxation and goods imported or exported for its official use shall be exempt from all customs duties. The Authority shall not claim exemption from taxes which are no more than charges for services rendered.
2. When purchases of goods or services of substantial value necessary for the official activities of the Authority are made by or on behalf of the Authority, and when the price of such goods or services includes taxes or duties, appropriate measures shall, to the extent practicable, be taken by States Parties to grant exemption from such taxes or duties or provide for their reimbursement. Goods imported or purchased under an exemption provided for in this article shall not be sold or otherwise disposed of in the territory of the State Party which granted the exemption, except under conditions agreed with that State Party.

3. No tax shall be levied by States Parties on or in respect of salaries and emoluments paid or any other form of payment made by the Authority to the Secretary-General and staff of the Authority, as well as experts performing missions for the Authority, who are not their nationals.

SUBSECTION H. SUSPENSION OF THE EXERCISE OF RIGHTS AND PRIVILEGES OF MEMBERS

Article 185
Suspension of the exercise of voting rights

A State Party which is in arrears in the payment of its financial contributions to the Authority shall have no vote if the amount of its arrears equals or exceeds the amount of the contributions due from it for the preceding two full years. The Assembly may, nevertheless, permit such a member to vote if it is satisfied that the failure to pay is due to conditions beyond the control of the member.

Article 186
Suspension of exercise of rights and privileges of membership

1. A State Party which has grossly and persistently violated the provisions of this Part may be suspended from the exercise of the rights and privileges of membership by the Assembly upon recommendation of the Council.
2. No action may be taken under paragraph 1 until the Sea-Bed Disputes Chamber has found that a State Party has grossly and persistently violated the provisions of this Part.

SECTION 5. SETTLEMENT OF DISPUTES AND ADVISORY OPINION

Article 187
Sea-Bed Disputes Chamber of the International Tribunal for the Law of the Sea

The establishment of the Sea-Bed Disputes Chamber and the manner in which it shall exercise its jurisdiction shall be governed by the provisions of this section, of Part XV and of Annex VI.

Article 188
Jurisdiction of the Sea-Bed Disputes Chamber

1. The Sea-Bed Disputes Chamber shall have jurisdiction under this Part in disputes with respect to activities in the Area falling within the following categories;
   (a) disputes between States Parties concerning the interpretation or application of this Part of the Convention;
   (b) disputes between a State party and the Authority concerning:
      (i) acts or omissions of the Authority or of a State Party alleged to be in violation of this Part or of rules, regulations and procedures of the Authority adopted in accordance therewith; or
      (ii) acts of the Authority alleged to be in excess of jurisdiction or a misuse of power;

    (c) disputes between parties to a joint-venture agreement or other contract, being States Parties, Signatories, or the Authority or any of its Enterprises, concerning
        (i) the interpretation or application of a relevant agreement, contract or plan of work; or
        (ii) acts or omissions of a party to the agreement or contract relating to activities in the Area and directed to either party or directly affecting its legitimate interests;
    (d) any other disputes for which the jurisdiction of the Chamber is specifically provided in this Convention.

2. Disputes arising from the interpretation or application of joint-venture agreements between the Authority and States Parties or Signatories covering areas under national jurisdiction shall be settled in accordance with the terms of the joint-venture agreement and with Part XV of the Convention.

Article 189
Submission of disputes to a special chamber of the International Tribunal for the Law of the Sea or an ad hoc chamber of the Sea-Bed Dispute Chamber or to binding commercial arbitration

1. Disputes between States Parties referred to in article 188, subparagraph (a), may be submitted:
    (a) at the request of the parties to the dispute, to a special chamber of the International Tribunal for the Law of the Sea to be formed in accordance with Annex VI, articles 15 and 17, or
    (b) at the request of any party to the dispute, to an *ad hoc* chamber of the Sea-Bed Disputes Chamber to be formed in accordance with Annex VI, article 36.

2. (a) Disputes concerning the interpretation or application of a joint-venture agreement referred to in article 188 paragraph 1(c) or paragraph 2 shall be submitted, at the request of any party to the dispute, to binding commercial arbitration, unless the parties otherwise agree. A commercial arbitral tribunal to which the dispute is submitted shall have no jurisdiction to decide any question of interpretation of this Convention. When the dispute also involves a question of the interpretation of Part XI with regard to activities in the Area, that question shall be referred to the Sea-Bed Disputes Chamber for a ruling.
    (b) If, at the commencement of or in the course of such arbitration, the arbitral tribunal determines, either at the request of any party to the dispute or *proprio motu*, that its decision depends upon a ruling of the Sea-Bed Disputes Chamber, the arbitral tribunal shall refer such question to the Sea-Bed Disputes Chamber for such ruling. The arbitral tribunal shall then proceed to render its award in conformity with the ruling of the Sea-Bed Disputes Chamber.
    (c) In the absence of a provision in the agreement or contract on the arbitration procedure to be applied in the dispute, the arbitration shall be conducted in accordance with the UNCITRAL Arbitration Rules or such other arbitration rules as may be prescribed in the rules, regulations and procedures of the Authority, unless the parties to the dispute otherwise agree.

Article 190
Limitation on jurisdiction with regard to decisions of the Authority

The Sea-Bed Disputes Chamber shall have no jurisdiction with regard to the exercise by the Authority of its discretionary powers in accordance with this Part; in no case shall it substitute its discretion for that of the Authority. Without prejudice to Article 192, in exercising its jurisdiction pursuant to Article 188, the Sea-Bed Disputes Chamber shall not pronounce itself on the question of whether any rules, regulations and procedures of the Authority are in conformity with this Convention, nor declare invalid any such rules, regulations and procedures. Its jurisdiction in this regard shall be confined to deciding claims that the application of any rules, regulations and procedures of the Authority in individual cases would be in conflict with the contractual obligations of the parties to the dispute or their obligations under this Convention, claims concerning excess of jurisdiction or misuse of power, and to claims for damages to be paid or other remedy to be given to the party concerned for the failure of the other party to comply with its contractual obligations or its obligations under this Convention.

Article 191
Participation and appearance of sponsoring States Parties in proceedings

1.   If a Signatory is a party to a dispute referred to in article 188, the sponsoring State shall be given notice thereof and shall have the right to participate in the proceedings by submitting written or oral statements.
2.   If an action is brought against a State Party by a Signatory sponsored by another State Party in a dispute referred to in article 188, subparagraph (c), the respondent State may request the State sponsoring that Signatory to appear in the proceedings on behalf of that Signatory. Failing such appearance, the respondent State may arrange to be represented by a juridical person of its nationality.

Article 192
Advisory opinions

The Sea-Bed Disputes Chamber shall give advisory opinions at the request of the Assembly or the Council on legal questions arising within the scope of their activities. Such opinions shall be given as a matter of urgency.

EXPLANATORY NOTES TO ANNEX

Article 133
Subparagraph (b) is introduced to enhance compatibility between Part XI and VI. The wording is taken over from Article 77.4 of the Convention.
   Subparagraph (c) is to keep the Convention in line with the latest development in deep sea-bed research and exploration.

Article 134
By simplifying this Article, an attempt has been made to de-emphasize the territorial aspect of the Authority's mandate and emphasize the functional aspect.

Articles 137–140

In these Articles, Articles 137, 140, 141 and 145 of the Convention have been regrouped as these Articles, somewhat dispersed in the Convention, define the principle of the Common Heritage: non-appropriability; management for the benefit of humankind as a whole; reservation for peaceful purposes; and conservation of resources and environment for future generations.

Also, a reference to the more recent Conventions on Climate and Biodiversity, as well as the evolving Regional Seas Conventions, has been introduced, since the sea-bed mining regime created by this Part will have to interact with the regimes created by these other Conventions.

Articles 141 and 142

A few minor changes are suggested in what in the Convention was Article 143, on Marine Scientific Research.

Part XI does not provide for any institutional mechanism through which the Authority could conduct marine scientific research in the Area. The idea evidently was that research should be contracted for. But given the fundamental importance of scientific research, applied research, and research and development, for the Authority and for the Enterprise, in whatever form it shall survive, it is suggested that the Authority should make "the appropriate institutional arrangements to enable it to do so." This phrasing is broad enough to cover institutional arrangements both with other institutions or within the Authority itself.

Cooperation with the Intergovernmental Oceanographic Commission of UNESCO in marine scientific research in the deep ocean appears natural. This would include the role of the deep sea-bed and its volcanic activities in the carbon dioxide cycle and its impact on the climate.

There is no UN forum that has paid any attention to the implementation of Articles 276 and 277 of the Convention, mandating the establishment of these centres. Obviously they would be extremely useful, particularly in regional seas bordered by developing countries, for human resource development and technology cooperation and development. If, in the next century, such a centre were to be established in the Caribbean, its close cooperation with the Jamaica Authority would be mutually beneficial. The Authority should have organic links with all regional centres that should be established next century for the development of environmentally and socially sustainable development.

It is not so much the "dissemination" of research results that needs to be coordinated: It is the conduct of scientific research that needs to be coordinated. The sentence has been recast in that sense.

In the present situation and the foreseeable future, the Authority should give priority to the enhancement and the internationalization of marine scientific research and technology development for deep-sea research and exploration, as these are the activities carried out today by the most technologically advanced countries. International cooperation in the development of the high technologies required will have a confidence-building effect and facilitate industrial cooperation at a later stage.

Article 142 is a simplified version of Article 144 in the Convention which is somewhat redundant, the essence being that, through international cooperation, technology should be "transferred" to the Authority, and, through the Authority, to developing countries.

Article 144
This is Article 139 of the Convention. References to Annex 3 have been omitted. Annex 3 is almost totally obsolete and should be omitted.

Article 145
The new feature in this Article is the encouragement to establish joint management zones or joint development zones in an area between 300 and 400 miles off the coast of a coastal state where the exact limit of the continental shelf may be very difficult, costly and time-consuming to determine. If, instead, broad-shelf states were ready to "freeze" their claims (without renouncing them) and to establish such joint zones, the Convention could dispense with the Commission on the Limits of the Continental Shelf, which would constitute a considerable financial savings.

Article 146
Article 146 is new, inspired by the desire to make the Authority as useful, especially to developing countries, as soon as possible.

Article 149
In accordance with more recent developments, in particular the Barbados Conference (1994) on Small Island Developing states, these states have been added, throughout, to the other disadvantaged states needing special consideration.

Articles 150–155
Section 3 of Part XI, entitled "Development of Resources of the Area," and comprising Articles 150–155, has been radically reconceptualized. In the Convention, the Articles covering policies relating to activities in the Area (Article 150), including Production policies (Article 151), are narrowly geared to the exploration and exploitation of manganese nodules in a precisely limited geographical Area. This concept is obsolete. An International Sea-Bed Authority for the twenty-first century must have a vastly broadened scope. Policies must cover international cooperation in scientific research in the deep sea; research and development of the necessary technologies; exploration and production, not restricted to manganese nodules but including all deep-sea resources. The policy framework must be such as to make the Authority relevant, in step with the most advanced scientific and technological developments, and immediately useful to the international community, and especially to poor countries. The policy framework must be in accordance with the new concepts generated by UNCED and post-UNCED developments (sustainable development, biodiversity, climate, eradication of poverty) which are in fact fully compatible with the principle of the Common Heritage of Mankind. The Common Heritage of Mankind principle, furthermore, must not remain restricted to a few preambulary articles, but it must permeate the policy framework.

Article 153 departs from the Parallel System, which was an unfortunate political compromise: the least practical and cost-effective system that could have been devised. Now that the parallel system has, for all practical purposes, been abolished by the Implementation Agreement – leaving, for the foreseeable future, states and their companies as the only operators in the Area – the time has come to think of a better system for the next century. There is now a general agreement, included also in the Implementation Agreement (section 2, paragraph 2), that the Enterprise, if and when it becomes operational, should operate through joint ventures. UNCLOS III, as well as the Prepcom, has produced quite a literature on joint ventures between companies as well as between states, and there are precedents where inter-governmental organizations have quite successfully built the private sector into a joint-venture relationship with the intergovernmental structure. In the following section, the INMARSAT statute has been used as a model. This model was brought to the attention of UNCLOS III by the Delegation of Austria back in 1977, during an intersessional meeting in Geneva under the chairmanship of Ambassador Jens Evensen of Norway, who included it in his report to the First Committee. Many Delegations expressed interest in this approach – but the decision had already been taken in favour of the parallel system, and there was a resistance to change.

The concept of review conferences, abolished by the Implementation Agreement, has been reinstated (Article 154). Most modern conventions contain provisions for review conferences at regular intervals, to keep the convention relevant and in step with ongoing changes. This Report (chapter 4, 6) recommends the broadening of the functions of the Meeting of States Parties, to enable it to sit as a Review Conference for the whole Convention, including Part XI and the Implementation Agreement, every six years.

Article 156

The nature and principles of the Authority have been modified. The principle of the Common Heritage, underlying that of sustainable development, is as basic to the Authority as the principle of the sovereign equality of all its members.

Article 159

The composition, powers, and functions of the Assembly remain basically unchanged. Reference to "interests" to be represented in subsidiary organs [(d)] has been omitted. The Authority is a political, intergovernmental institution with broad responsibilities which it must meet in an independent and objective fashion. Of course it will be aware of "interests," but these must not be built into its organs. Reference to the "competence" of members of subsidiary bodies has also been omitted. It is self-understood that the members of subsidiary bodies must be competent in the area with which they are to deal. This special requirement seems somewhat demeaning and patronising towards developing countries.

The two budgetary specifications in (f)(i) and (ii) in the Convention have been omitted. They are subsumed in the new (g) which is comprehensive. This was done in response to the general need to streamline the text and unburden it from excessive detail.

The new subparagraph (j) has been made more comprehensive and comprises, in a more general form, the functions described under (k) and (l) in the Convention.

Article 160

Article 161 of the Convention, establishing the composition, procedure, and voting in the Council, has been greatly streamlined. Recalling the ordeal of the election of the first Council in 1995–6, and based on the desire not to repeat this demeaning experience, the "chamber system," as well as the representation of interest groups, has been abandoned. Financial interest groups are represented, in proportion to their investment, on the joint-venture boards of the Enterprise system. The Authority – let it be repeated – is an intergovernmental political institution with broad responsibilities of a scientific, technological, economic, environmental nature. Interest groups have no place in its organs. One should add to this that a Convention should retain its basic validity for as long as possible whereas interest groups may change very quickly. For example, extending the functions of the Authority from nodule mining to a broader range of activities, which is essential if the Authority is to remain relevant, will necessarily change the "interest groups."

The Enterprise System will make a lot of detailed investment and related financial decisions. The decision-making of the Council will be of a broader and more political nature. The decision-making process has been streamlined accordingly.

Article 161

The powers and functions of the Council have been streamlined as much as possible. Most of the provisions of the Convention remain relevant. Subparagraph (u) includes among the responsibilities of the Inspectorate verification of compliance with the reservation for peaceful purposes of the Area. Since this is a fundamental principle of the Convention, whose implementation is to be reviewed by the periodic review conferences, compliance must be monitored.

Article 162

Considering the fundamental importance of science and technology for the activities of the Authority, the establishment of a Scientific and Technological Commission has been suggested here. This is in line with more recent conventions, such as the Climate and Biodiversity Conventions.

In accordance with the Implementation Agreement, a Finance Committee is already being established. It is here called a "commission" rather than a "committee," just as a matter of editorial consistency.

Article 163

This article has been adapted from the Biodiversity Convention.

Article 164

In accordance with section 1, paragraph 4, of the Annex to the Implementation Agreement, the functions of the Economic Planning Commission and the Legal and Technical Commission have been merged and adapted to the broader scope of the Convention.

Article 165

This article is taken over and adapted from the Implementation Agreement.

Article 170

The structure of the Enterprise System is adapted from the Statutes of the International Maritime Satellite Organization, INMARSAT, which has successfully integrated the private sector into the structure of a public international organization. The difference is that INMARSAT is a single-purpose organization, so that the Signatories are structured into the Council of the Organization. The whole organization functions as an Enterprise.

The Sea-Bed Authority is a multi-purpose system, with an operational subsystem.

The Council has many responsibilities which are beyond the scope of the operational subsystem. It is therefore at the level of the subsystem that the Signatories must be integrated into the structure. It is this level that is the commercial level, at which financial and other commercial interests must be safeguarded and reflected in the decision-making system.

This system, which transcends the illusory parallel system, already abolished, for all practical purposes, by the Implementation agreement, should be acceptable both to the friends of the Enterprise, since there is now a consensus that a joint-venture approach is the only solution to the problems of the Enterprise; it should be equally acceptable to the friends of the private sector; for, if the private sector functions well within the two-tier (states parties/ signatories) joint-venture system of INMARSAT, there is no reason why it should not function equally well in an analogous system applied to the Enterprise.

The Enterprise system is decentralized and flexible, reflecting the multi-purpose nature of the International Sea-Bed Authority. Each joint-venture agreement will be tailored to the specific needs of each Enterprise, the mode of its financing and its activities.

Article 171
This article is adapted from the Statutes of INMARSAT.

Remaining Articles
In the remaining articles only minor editorial adaptations have been made.

Bibliography

Ahmad, Sheikh Mahmud. 1974. *Economics of Islam*. Lahore: Muhammad Ashraf.

Annan, Kofi, Secretary-General to the United Nations, Press Conference, 1 May, 1997, *The New York Times*, 2 May, 1997.

Barde, J.-P. and D.W. Pearce, (eds.). 1991. *Valuing the Environment: Six Case Studies*. OECD, London: Earthscan.

Bates, M. 1960. *The Forest and the Sea: A Look at the Economy of Nature and the Ecology of Man*. New York: Random House.

Baudelaire, Charles Pierre. 1857. *Les fleurs du mal*.

—— 1996. *Ocean Governance and the United Nations*. Halifax: Centre for Foreign Policy Studies, Dalhousie University.

Borgese, Elisabeth Mann. 1975. *The Drama of the Oceans*. New York: Abrams.

—— 1986. *The Future of the Oceans: A Report to the Club of Rome*. Montreal: Harvest House.

Borgese, Elisabeth Mann. 1987. *Mediterranean Centre for Research and Development in Marine Industrial Technology*. Malta: Foundation for International Studies.

—— (ed.). 1965. *A Constitution for the World*. Santa Barbara, CA: Center for the Study of Democratic Institutions.

—— (ed.). 1997. *Peace in the Oceans: Ocean Governance and the Agenda for Peace*. The Proceedings of Pacem in Maribus XXIII, Costa Rica, 1995. Paris: UNESCO. Intergovernmental Oceanographic Commission, Technical Series No. 47.

Borgese, G.A. 1943. *Common Cause*. New York: Duell, Sloan and Pierce.

Boutros-Ghali, Boutros. 1995. *An Agenda for Peace, 1995: With the new supplement and related UN Documents*. Report by the Secretary-General to the United Nations General Assembly. 2nd ed. New York: United Nations.

Briguglio, L. 1995. *Small Island Developing States and Their Economic Vulnerabilities*. Malta: Foundation for International Studies.

Buchanan, James. 1994. *The Greening of Technology Transfer: Protection of the Environment and of Intellectual Property*. Franklin Pierce Law Center, 9 April 1994, Afternoon Session, On website http://www.fplc.edu/green/after.htm.

Cleveland, Harlan. 1996. *Hail and Farewell*. Speech to the Hubert H. Humphrey Institute of Public Affairs, University of Minnesota.

Commission on Global Governance. 1995. *Our Global Neighbourhood*. Oxford: Oxford University Press.

Court of Justice of the European Communities, 1963 Decision, *American Journal of International Law* 58: 1.

Cronan, David. 1992. *Marine Minerals in Exclusive Economic Zones*. London: Chapman and Hall.

De Groot, R.S. 1992. *Functions of Nature: Evaluation of Nature in Environmental Planning, Management and Decision Making*. Groningen: Wolters-Noordhoff.

229

Dillon, William. 1992. U.S. Geological Survey, Marine and Coastal Geology Program, Washington, D.C., September.

Dror, Yehezkel. 1995. *The Capacity to Govern: A Report to the Club of Rome.*

Drucker, Peter. 1992. *Managing the Future: The 1990s and Beyond.* New York: Dutton.

Earney, Fillmore C.F. 1990. *Marine Mineral Resources.* London: Routledge.

Englezos, P. 1993. "Clathrate Hydrates," *Industrial and Engineering Chemistry Research* 32(7).

Evenson, Jens. 1986. "The Law of the Sea Regime." In: R.B. Byers, ed. *The Denuclearisation of the Oceans.* New York: St. Martin's Press.

Fanning, Lucia M. 1997. The Co-Management Paradigm: Criteria for Sustainable Marine-Resource Management. Master's thesis, Halifax, Dalhousie University.

Gandhi, M.K. 1947. *India of My Dreams.* R.K. Prabhu, ed. Bombay.

GESAMP. 1997. *State of the Marine Environment Report.* (in prep).

—— 1998. *Review of Land-based Activities Affecting the Marine Environment.* (in prep).

Giarini, Orio. 1980. *Dialogue on Wealth and Welfare: An Alternative View of World Capital Formation.* New York: Pergamon Press.

—— 1987. Working Paper prepared for the International Centre for Ocean Development (ICOD). Halifax, unpublished.

—— 1988. *The Emerging Service Economy.*

Giarini, Orio and Patrick M. Liedtke. 1997. *Wie wir arbeiten werden. Der neue Bericht an den Club of Rome mit einem Vorwort von Ernst Ulrich von Weizsaecker.* Hamburg: Hoffmann und Campe.

Giarini, Orio and Max Börlin. 1991. "Toward Estimating the Contribution of Oceans to Wealth and Welfare." In: J. Vandermeulen and S. Walker, eds. *Ocean Technology, Development, Training and Transfer.* Proceedings of Pacem in Maribus XVI, August 1988. Oxford: Pergamon Press.

Giarini, Orio and Walter Stahel. 1989. *The Limits of Certainty.* Dordrecht: Kluwer Academic Publishers.

Gillies, Bruce. 1995. "The Nunavut Final Agreement and Marine Management in the North." *Northern Perspectives* 23(1): 17–19. Canadian Arctic Resources Committee.

Glowka, Lgle. 1996. "The Deepest of Ironies: Genetic Resources, Marine Scientific Research, and the Area," *Ocean Yearbook* 12. Chicago: Chicago University Press.

Graham, Darid M. 1997. "Editorial," *Sea Technology*, March.

Gray, K. 1993. "The Ambivalence of Property." In: G. Prins, ed. *Threats Without Enemies: Facing Environmental Insecurity*, London: Earthscan Publications.

Hammond, A.L. 1995. *Environmental Indicators: A Systematic Approach to Measuring and Reporting on Environmental Policy Performance in the Context of Sustainable Development.* Washington, DC: World Resources Institute.

Hardy, A. 1965. *The Living Stream.* New York; Harper & Row.

Hasler, Richard. 1998. "Towards Political Ecologies of Scale: Conceptualizing Community-based Coastal and Fisheries Co-Management on the West Coast of South Africa." *Ocean Yearbook 14.* Chicago: University of Chicago Press (forthcoming).

Hegel, G.W. Friedrich. 1821. *Grundlinien der Philosophie des Rechts.*

Hempel, Gotthilf. 1992. "The Alfred Wegener Institute, Bremerhaven." In: E.M. Borgese, ed. *Ocean Frontiers: Explorations by Oceanographers on Five Continents.* New York: Abrams.

Heywood, V.H. and R.T. Watson. 1995. *Global Biodiversity Assessment.* UNEP, Cambridge: Cambridge University Press.

Holland, John H. 1990. "The Global Economy as an Adaptive Process." In: P.W. Anderson *et al.*, eds. *The Economy as an Evolving Complex System.* Redwood City, Calif: Addison Wesley Pub. Co.

Huq, A.M. 1985. "Welfare Criteria in Gandhian Economics." In: Romesh Diwan and Mark Lutz, eds. *Essays on Gandhian Economics.* Delhi: Gandhi Peace Foundation.

IMO/FAO/UNESCO/WMO/WHO/IAEA/UN/UNEP Joint Group of Experts on the Scientific Aspects of Marine Pollution. 1990. *State of the Marine Environment,* Reports and Studies No. 39. Nairobi: UNEP.

International Sea-bed Authority, Kingston, Jamaica: Document ISBA/A/L.8, 21 March 1996.

Jagota, S.P. 1992. "Joint Development Zones," *Ocean Yearbook 10.* Chicago: University of Chicago Press.

Jentoft, Svein and Knut H. Mikalsen. 1994. "Regulating Fjord Fisheries: Folk Management or Interest Group Politics?" In: Christopher L. Dyer and James R. McGoodwin, eds. *Folk Management in the World's Fisheries: Lessons for Modern Fisheries Management.* Niwot: University Press of Colorado.

Jones, O.A. and R. Endean (eds.). 1973. *Biology and Geology of Coral Reefs,* Vol. 1. London: Academic Press.

Judson, W. Irwin. 1996. Marine Pharmaceuticals: A Special Case of the Common Heritage of Mankind. Unpublished manuscript.

Kerr, Richard A. 1997. "Did a Blast of Sea-Floor Gas Usher in a New Age?" *Science* 275, 28 February.

Khalid, Fazlun and Joanne O'Brien (eds.). 1992. *Islam and Ecology.* New York: Cassel.

King, Alexander and Bertrand Schneider. 1991. *The First Global Revolution: A Report by the Council of the Club of Rome.* London: Simon and Schuster.

Lockspeiser, E. 1962. *Debussy, His Life and Mind.* London: Cassell.

Lopez-Reyes, Ramon. 1997. "Maritime Zones of Peace: A Regime of Peace on the Seas." In: E.M. Borgese, ed. *Peace in the Oceans: Ocean Governance and the Agenda for Peace.* The Proceedings of Pacem in Maribus XXIII, Costa Rica, 1995. Paris: UNESCO. Intergovernmental Oceanographic Commission, Technical Series No. 47.

Lovelock, J.E. 1979. *Gaia: A New Look at Life on Earth.* New York: Oxford University Press.

Mann, Thomas. 1960. "Lübeck als geistige Lebensform." *Collected Works.* Vol. XI. Frankfurt am Main: S. Fischer Verlag.

—— 1934. "Meerfahrt mit Don Quijote," *Collected Works.* Vol. IX. Frankfurt am Main: S. Fischer Verlag.

Manolis, Mikis. 1996. Functional Sovereignty and the Political Organization of Ocean Space: Creeping Jurisdiction or Multilateral Cooperation? Master's thesis. Halifax: Dalhousie University.

Miller, Robert C. 1966. *The Sea.* 2nd ed. New York: Random House.

Morven, M. 1980. *Legends from the Sea.* New York: Crescent Books.

Naqvi, Syed Nawab Haider. 1995. *Islam, Economics and Society*. New York: Kegan Paul.

Natural Resources Canada. 1995. *Canadian Minerals Yearbook*.

Needham, Joseph. 1965, 1971. *Science and Civilisation in China*, Vol. 4, Parts 2 and 3. Cambridge: Cambridge University Press.

Newman, E. 1967. *Wagner as Man and Artist*. New York: Dover Publications.

—— 1994. *Environmental Indicators: A Core Set*. Paris.

—— 1994a. *Natural Resource Accounts: Taking Stock in OECD Countries*. Paris.

—— 1995. *OECD Environmental Data Compendium*. Paris.

OECD. 1996. *Maritime Transport, 1993*. Paris.

Panos Institute. 1997. *Insurance Day*, 31 July. Geneva.

Prus, Gwyn. 1998. "Oceanguard: The Need, Possibility, and the Concept." *Ocean Yearbook* 14. Chicago: University of Chicago Press.

Revelle, Roger. 1992. "The Scripps Institution of Oceanography, California." In: E.M. Borgese, ed. *Ocean Frontiers: Explorations by Oceanographers on Five Continents*. New York: Abrams.

Rosensohn, Nicole and Schneider, Bertrand. 1993. *For a Better World Order: The Message from Kuala Lumpur*. Bilbao: Fundacion BBV.

Roush, Wade. 1997. "Putting a Price Tag on Nature's Bounty." *Science* 276, 16 May.

Ruggie, John Gerard. 1993. "Territoriality and Beyond: Problematizing Modernity in International Relations." *International Organization* 47(1).

Saigal, Krishan. 1988. *Mediterranean Centre for Research and Development in Marine Industrial Technology: Feasibility Study*. Malta: International Ocean Institute.

—— *Sustainable Development: The Spiritual Dimension*. (forthcoming).

Sachs, I. 1992. "Transition Strategies for the 21st Century." Nature and Resources 28(1).

Scheingold, Stuart A. 1972. "Lessons of the European Community for an Ocean Regime." In: E.M. Borgese, ed. *Pacem in Maribus*. New York: Dodd, Mead and Co.

Schneider, Bertrand. 1988. *The Barefoot Revolution: A Report to the Club of Rome*. London: IT Publications.

Sharp, Margaret and Claire Shearman. 1987. *European Technological Collaboration*. London: Royal Institute of International Affairs, Routledge and Kegan Paul.

Sheng, F. 1995. *Real Value for Nature: An Overview of Global Efforts to Achieve True Measures of Economic Progress*. Gland, Switzerland: WWF International.

Sri Aurobindo Ghose. 1972. *Sri Aurobindo*, Vol. XII. Pondicherry: Sri Aurobindo Birth Centenary Library.

Stanners, D.A. and P. Bourdeau (eds.). 1995. *Europe's Environment: The Dobris Assessment*. European Copenhagen: Environment Agency.

Sustainable Strategies for Oceans: A Co-Management Guide. 1998. The National Round Table on the Environment and the Economy, Ottawa.

The Dhammapada. 1987. Translated by Juan Mascaro, Penguin Books edn.

Timor Gap Cooperation Treaty of 1989, ILM 29(3), May 1990.

Tinbergen, Jan. (ed.) 1976. *Reshaping the International Order (RIO): A Report to the Club of Rome*. London: Pergamon.

United Nations Conference on Environment and Development (UNCED). 1992. *Agenda 21*. Rio de Janeiro.

—— 1992. Framework Convention on Climate Change. United Nations.

—— 1992. Convention on Biological Diversity. United Nations.

UNDP. 1997. *Human Development Report 1995*. New York: Oxford University Press.

UNEP/DEIA. 1996. *Report of the Meeting on Integrated Environmental Assessment/ Global Environmental Outlook (IEA/GEO) Core Data Working Group*, DPCSD Office, New York, January 1996. Nairobi.

UNEP. 1991. *Island Directory*. UNEP Regional Seas Directories and Bibliographies, No. 35.

—— 1993. *Environmental Data Report, 1993–1994*. Prepared by the GEMS Monitoring and Assessment Research Centre, London, UK, in co-operation with World Resources Institute, Washington, D.C., and the UK Department of the Environment. Oxford: Blackwell.

—— 1995. *The UNEP Biodiversity Programme and Implementation Strategy: A Framework for Supporting Global Conservation and Sustainable Use of Biodiversity*. Nairobi.

—— 1996. Draft Proposal Submitted by the United Nations Environment Programme on Institutional Arrangements for Implementation of the Global Programme of Action for the Protection of the Marine Environment from Land-Based Activities (28 October 1996).

—— 1997. *Global Environment Outlook 1997* (GEO-1). Nairobi.

UNESCO. 1983. *The Impact of Science on Society*, No. 3/4.

United Nations. 1994. Report of the Secretary-General of the United Nations, Doc. A/51/645.

United Nations. 1993. *Satellite System of Integrated Environmental and Economic Accounting SEEA*, Handbook of National Accounting, Studies in Methods, Series F, No. 61. New York.

—— 1993. *United Nations Convention on the Law of the Sea, 1982*, New York: United Nations.

—— 1994. *System of National Accounts*, Studies in Methods, Series F, No. 2, Rev. 4. New York.

—— 1994. *Agreement Relating to the Implementation of Part XI of the United Nations Convention on the Law of the Sea of 1982*, 17 August 1994, A/RES/48/263.

—— 1995. UN System-wide Earthwatch Programme Document. UNEP/EWWP2/WP2/rev.1.

—— 1996. *Indicators of Sustainable Development: Framework and Methodologies*. New York: United Nations.

—— 1996. *Agreement for the Implementation of the Provisions of the United Nations Convention on the Law of the Sea of 10 December 1982 Relating to the Conservation and Management of Straddling Fish Stocks and Highly Migratory Fish Stocks*, Doc. A/51/383, 4 October 1996.

US Bureau of Mines. 1995. *Minerals Yearbook*.

Vallas, L. 1967. *The Theories of Claude Debussy*. New York: Dover Publications.

van Dieren, W. (ed.). 1995. *Taking Nature into Account: A Report to the Club of Rome: Toward a Sustainable National Income*. New York: Copernicus.

Venezia, William A. and John Holt. 1995. "Turbine Under Gulf Stream: Potential Energy Source." *Sea Technology*. Arlington, VA: Compass Publications, September.

Wapner, Paul. 1997. "Environmental Ethics and Global Governance: Engaging the International Liberal Tradition." In: *Global Governance: A Review of Multilateralism and International Organisations* 3(2) May–August. Boulder, CO: Lynne Rienner Publishers, Inc.

Welch, Harold E. 1995. "Marine Conservation in the Canadian Arctic: Regional Overview." *Northern Perspectives* 23(1): 5–17. Canadian Arctic Resources Committee.

World Bank. 1995. *Monitoring Environmental Progress: A Report on Work in Progress*, Washington, DC: Environmentally Sustainable Development.

—— 1997. *World Development Indicators*. Washington, DC: The World Bank.

World Commission on Environment and Development. 1987. *Our Common Future*. Oxford: Oxford University Press.

World Resources Institute. 1997. *World Resources 1996–97: A Guide to the Global Environment*, Report by the WRI and the International Institute for Environment and Development. New York: Basic Books.

Index